ONCE A POMMIE SWAGMAN

NICK THOMAS

JoJo
PUBLISHING

Once a Pommie Swagman
Nick Thomas

Published by Classic Author and Publishing Services Pty Ltd
First published 2014

'Yarra's Edge'
2203/80 Lorimer Street
Docklands VIC 3008
Australia

Email: jo-media@bigpond.net.au or visit www.classic-jojo.com

© Nick Thomas

JoJo Publishing Imprint

Editor: Anne van Alkemade
Designer / typesetter: Chameleon Print Design
Printed in China by Inkasia

National Library of Australia Cataloguing-in-Publication entry

Author:	Thomas, Nick, author.
Title:	Once a pommie swagman / Nick Thomas ; editor, Anne van Alkemade.
ISBN:	9780987607683 (paperback)
Subjects:	Thomas, Nick.
	Men--Australia--Biography.
	Hitchhiking--Australia--Biography.
	Swagmen--Australia--Biography.
	British--Australia--Biography.
	Australia--Social life and customs--1945-1965--Biography.
Other Authors/Contributors:	Van Alkemade, Anne, editor.
Dewey Number:	920.710994

CONTENTS

As it was 1

(1) Uncle Alf, Mr Archer and mad bastards 5

(2) Sugar babies 15

(3) Meanderings, memories and mateship 25

(4) Molinari's Cafe 37

(5) Milk bar days and wayward ways 51

(6) Jerky Joe and Kangaroo Point 61

(7) Grandfather, mountain retreats, Mr Willard
    and bloody Gympie 81

(8) Auntie Marge and Constable Waring 99

(9) Mrs Hayes 115

(10) The Proserpine show: Jimmy Sharman and Carol 129

(11) Dunny carters, public bars and Mr Personality. 149

(12) Magnetic Island 161

(13) The Flinders Highway 183

(14) Julia Creek 199

(15) J & J Bourke & Co. 215

(16) William Forsyth Remington Fellows 229

(17) God Save the Queen! Davey Crockett, and John and
     Emma Richards 243

(18) The Golambino Bros. 251

(19) The cherry orchard, and Danny and Ronnie 267

(20) Sons and mothers 285

*This book is dedicated to the memory of Reg Hillier;
the only man from the Northern Territory to be killed in
combat during the Vietnam war. I was there the day he died.
While not claiming to be a personal mate, to us younger soldiers
in the small community of an infantry company at War,
Reg was a reassuring mentor; composed, courageous,
and much respected by officers and men alike.
We all lost much more than a mate that day. Lest we forget.*
—Nick Thomas

AS IT WAS

*F*ew countries can have changed as dramatically as Australia since 1961. The population was only just over ten million; steam trains plied the major routes; agriculture was the major industry and in many outer suburbs of Sydney the dunny cart came once a week to take away your unmentionables. Businessmen were highly affronted if they couldn't park their cars right outside their Pitt Street offices; the Opera House was a hole in the ground; Brisbane International Airport was a collection of unsightly tin huts — much like Brisbane itself in fact — Perth was a sleepy country town and Cairns a mangrove swamp.

Socially, too, the country was unrecognisable. Aborigines were not allowed to vote. *God Save the Queen* was sung with gusto in picture theatres. Obesity was a rare genetic disorder; drugs were something you got from the chemist; people addressed each other as Mr and Mrs, and women were not allowed into the public bars of hotels. Eating out was a special treat and churches were the only places allowed to open on Sundays, when even mowing the lawn was frowned upon by some.

But since the mid-fifties these and many other seemingly entrenched conventions had been increasingly challenged.

Not haunted by the traumas of war and Depression — or so readily influenced by the church — the young were rebelling. The pillars of social behaviour from previous generations — sexual probity, obedient acquiescence to authority and parental control — all came under siege. It was not a planned or organised rebellion, more a subconscious one stoked by Elvis, the novelty of take-away food, Col Joy, stovepipe pants, Marilyn Monroe and James Dean. However, this rebellion was confined mainly to the cities. In the country, attitudes remained very much as they had always been: hard-working, conservative and religious. In 1961 the city/country divide was a chasm, the outback truly was 'outback' and few city people ventured there. Many country children had never seen the sea, there was no television and the goings-on in 'the big smoke' were as remote and irrelevant as events in China.

Vast stretches of the major highways were little more than tracks, often devoid of traffic for hours; sometimes days at a time; even the great east coast highways — the Pacific and the Bruce — hard as that might be to imagine. Bridges were washed away and towns cut off when it rained, and if you broke down you could be stuck for weeks. Outside cities public transport was virtually non-existent and overtaking lanes and dual carriage ways were called 'the other side of the road'. Hitchhiking was recognised and encouraged as a legitimate form of transport and the original backpackers the 'swagmen' were a common sight west of the ranges, although overseas tourists were like wombats in Tunisia; rarely seen.

Today swagmen, even hitchhikers, have become endangered species, hounded to the brink of extinction by the three bastions of progress: laws, rules and regulations. In 1961 there were no speed cameras, no breathalysers and most cars weren't even fitted with seat belts, never mind it being a punishable offence not to wear them. Farmers would stop to pick up even the drunkest or most rancid swagman, knowing they could chuck him in the back of the ute with the dogs. Interstate truck drivers would screech to a halt the moment they saw a hitchhiker, glad of the company to help keep them awake. You could travel in the back of a semi-trailer without the police batting an eye, you could ride pillion on a motorcycle without wearing a helmet, and, outside cities, people could drive as fast as they wanted with little or no fear of being stopped. Driving at one hundred *miles* an hour and more was not uncommon on country roads, despite their terrible condition and very few people were pulled up because their tyres were worn, their vehicle not registered or their insurance lapsed.

Day-to-day living was also more relaxed in the country. People were more trusting and more welcoming and strangers were viewed with curiosity rather than suspicion. Few people locked their cars on the high street when they went shopping, hotel residence doors were left unlocked all night, guards were not too bothered if you jumped on a freight train, and shoplifting and graffiti were virtually unheard of. Above all there was not the myriad by-laws and council policies dictating where we can and cannot smoke, swim, eat, sleep, play ball games, park cars, pitch tents, light fires, hose gardens or ride push-bikes. All this, coupled with a relatively benign climate, no man-eating animals, a fertile, vast, fantastic countryside and a welfare system that ensured nobody starved, meant that in 1961, good or bad, right or wrong, no country in the world — not even the much touted USA — was more attractive, more hospitable or better suited to life on the open road than Australia.

In essence there were three types who took to the roads. The first group was the original fair-dinkum swagmen, homeless vagabonds who not only carried all their worldly possessions on their backs but, for some, the psychological baggage of war, disaster or personal tragedy that so often derails life. In the main, the swaggies were unsociable loners who kept themselves to themselves. Sometimes they might find employment on a farm or cattle station, and sometimes they might get drunk for weeks on end. Some were real characters, others complete bums, but almost all of them were scornful, occasionally resentful of the two other upstart groups that were increasingly invading their patch.

Itinerant workers, who may or may not have their own transport but still lived fairly rough for most of the year, followed the seasonal work up and down the country as they had done since the Depression. Many were married with families to feed; paying the mortgage was their holy grail no matter the cost to family life caused by long separations.

The third group was the newly emancipated young from the cities. Whether idle surfers intent only on catching the next wave, or wayward youths looking for excitement or just something to do, few in this group had particular goals or aims other than not being prepared to enslave themselves to the soulless nine-to-five grind their fathers had been forced to endure all their lives. Life had to be better than that! The problem was most of them were spectacularly ill-prepared for the nomadic, transient lifestyle they set out on; meaning they were rarely comfortable, frequently hungry, often delinquent and occasionally stupid. Only one thing was common to these three groups; they were almost exclusively male; some no more than boys.

ONE

Uncle Alf, Mr Archer and mad bastards

As it happened, Glen had been born a Pom too and both of us were sixteen when we first set off in 1961, although I could have passed for fourteen physically and mentally. Glen, being a little taller, at least looked more or less his age, even if he didn't act it. He also sounded like a Pom; his family had emigrated to Australia when he was ten and Lancashire accents are firmly embedded by that age. I was only two when we arrived, so could say "Hooroo," "Strewth" and " Ow ya goin' mate," as unselfconsciously as Chips Rafferty.

My father died three months previously; a lengthy and unpleasant death. Glen's father was still alive but it should have been him that was dead, so unpleasant was his life. My dad had been a really lovely bloke, whereas Glen's was a violent alcoholic and many a day Glen had come to school bearing the marks of his father's anger the night before. The "six o'clock swill" was the main culprit. His dad worked in the city and went straight to the pub when he got off the train every evening. Dinner time became trauma time and if Glen could absent himself from that meal, he did.

The decision to hitchhike north was taken with all the meticulous consideration and planning that rudderless teenagers are noted for; three minutes probably … might have been five. A few of us were on my back veranda in Epping; Lloyd Price blaring out *"Cause you got … personality; walk and personality; smile and personality; charm and …"*. It was a cool, mid-May afternoon. Winter was in the air and we'd been grappling with the eternal dilemmas of youth: boredom and lack of money; neither of which we'd been remotely successful at solving.

Then Jimmy Mickleton suddenly announced that Ray Harvey's uncle had made a fortune cutting sugar cane in Ballina the year before.

"… went up there in June, came back in September and bought a house."

"Bullshit!"

"It's not bullshit! Eight quid a ton they pay, and if you're any good you can cut five ton a day!" Jimmy claimed defiantly.

"Forty quid a day!" Glen whispered in awe. Amazing what we believe when we want to, but they did reckon it was warmer up that way.

Glen's mum was not too happy when he called to say he was "going away for a bit", but he hung up before she could talk him out of it. I was much luckier. My stepmother had returned to England for a few months after my dad died, and my sister had moved into a flat so I had no such problems. Mind you, we were a bit organised; we both had a swag, canvas kit bags stuffed with a few extra pairs of undies, shirts and trousers, a beach towel, and of course our duffle jackets; couldn't have a shower without them on in the winter. We also had a tin opener, two packets of Marlboro each, four tins of sausages and beans, a bag of broken biscuits *and* a packet of Marella Jubes. To top it off, Glen had ninepence and I had one and six, enough to buy a bag of chips and a milkshake. What more could we possibly need? We'd be in Ballina by the morning and quids in the next day.

*

"Where youse off to?" the truck driver yelled.

"Ballina!" we yelled back, clambering up and into the cab, the engine rearing up between the driver's and the only slightly larger passenger's seat like a big heater. We squeezed in and the driver gave us a reassuring grin. There was something uncle-like about him, warm and cosy, like the truck. "You're in luck," he bellowed. "Got to be in Brisbane for breakfast or I'll miss out on me bonus." We roared off up Pennant Hills Road, gears crunching.

The truck was a Bedford Commer, or Commer knocker as they were known. "Reliable as my bowels," the driver yelled, noticing our concern as the engine shrieked in protest at being asked to climb the first of the steep, winding hills of the Gosford road. The descent down to the Hawkesbury River Bridge was a relief to the ears, if not the nervous system; miles meant money, and when he could, he let the old truck have her head. We just hung on and enjoyed the thrill.

His name was Alf, and although conversation was limited to the moments when the engine was quieter, we chatted away like long-lost buddies. He wanted to know all about us, and when we'd exhausted our short lives he told us a bit about his. He owned the truck himself, it transpired, was married with two kids and lived in Albury-Wodonga, a handy base for the Melbourne-Sydney-Brisbane run he did several times a month. "Hitchhiked about the country meself for a while just after the war; got back and couldn't settle, so I just took off, did a bit of this and a bit of that, a bit like you two are planning I guess, although I never cut sugar cane," and saying this, he glanced at us with a slightly quizzical look. "How old are you?"

By now I was used to being asked this question, not that it bothered me particularly; in fact, looking younger than my age had its advantages. When I was fourteen I played half the season for the under-twelve cricket team until someone discovered. It caused a bit of a ruckus and the teacher was severely reprimanded. I had a great time, though, and scored buckets of runs. Alf didn't comment when we told him, just smiled again and shook his head with wonder.

"What!" we chimed in sensitive chorus.

"Oh, nothing, nothing. I was just picturing two sixteen-year-old Poms cutting sugar cane, that's all."

It was gone midnight when we pulled up outside a roadside café near Karuah and, despite the dexy tablets we'd taken, Glen and I were entering that soporific state where your head keeps flopping to one side, waking you up with a start. Soon after we'd crossed the Hawkesbury River Alf reached around behind his seat and pulled out a large jar of little white pills. "Want one?" he grinned. "Help keep you awake." We thought they were sweets and took the proffered pill without giving it a thought. "Don't suck it, swallow it," he advised. For the next three hours we were like hyperactive ten-year-olds on Tartrazine, singing at the tops of our voices, jumping up and down in our seats and laughing uproariously at things that didn't deserve a frown.

He bought us a huge meal, a chocolate milkshake and a packet of cigarettes each, and Glen and I grinned at each other with boyish delight; good stuff, this hitchhiking. It was half way up the steep hill out of Bulahdelah that the Commer's engine first began to sound anything but reliable. "Bloody fuel pump," Alf cursed with a resigned air. Somehow or other he managed to coax another hour or so out of her before the old girl finally coughed and spluttered and came to a standstill a few miles from Kempsey. It didn't take long for our big heater to lose its effectiveness, but, like the good uncle he was, Alf looked after us; he built a fire and gave us two thick blankets and a canvas sheet to lay on the ground. We slept like little boys. When we woke in the morning he had already made a billy of tea. During the night he'd apparently waved down another truck and help was on its way. We sat about, warming our hands on our enamel mugs — Alf's mugs, that was.

Suddenly he almost spat his tea out. "For Christ's sake! How long has that been there?" and he flicked the tin of beans off the fire, spitting on his fingertips. Who would have thought putting a hole in a can would have been so important! Almost as important as having a spoon, we discovered. Good old Alf. It was amazing what he seemed to have in that cab. "Bloody Poms!" He shook his head in wonder and although it was said light-heartedly, with no hint of malice, there was an element of the mockery, the disdain, even the outright contempt with which the English were viewed by many Australians, especially old soldiers. Of course at school and by other kids on the streets I was used to being taunted occasionally about being a Pom, but there were three people in particular in my childhood whose fervent depth of feeling on the subject left a lasting impression on me. I was nine when I first encountered Mr Archer.

"What in tarnation are you doing, Pommie boy!" he'd thunder from across the playground. "Nothing, sir."

"Well, cut it out! Hear me! And if I catch you at it again, you'll swing! Get my drift, Pommie boy!"

Getting Mr Archer's 'drift' was not difficult. He was the deputy head of Epping Primary School, chief disciplinarian, sixth form teacher and sports master. A garrulous man who brooked no nonsense, he had served in Tobruk and New Guinea and wore his medals with pride even when he didn't have them on. His prejudices and opinions were also unashamed and in your face, as they were across the nation in those days. If truth is the first casualty of war, civility is surely the second.

Japs, dagos, chinks, wogs and squareheads — all were abused and insulted with equal vigour by Mr Archer. As for Poms, well, the evidence of their dithering military incompetence and treachery was damning. The sudden arrival of thousands of the lily-white whinging bastards shortly after the war merely compounded it. Quite apart from being weak-chinned and pathetic, Poms didn't like the heat, didn't like the flies, didn't like hard work and didn't like washing. They came out for a tenner, thought the world owed them a living and then half of them went crawling back after a year because they couldn't cope! In short, according to Mr Archer, the English were self-opinionated, arrogant, class conscious, dirty, lazy, gutless snobs. And as for Winston Churchill! "Don't get me bloody well started on that bastard!"

My sister had passed through his class several years before, but because she was a female and he, at heart, was a gentleman, she was spared the full weight of his opinions. Those he saved for me, knowing I was progressing inexorably up through the school and would eventually end up under his control. "Ah!" he bellowed the first day I walked into his class, having been in Australia by then for eight years, most of them at his school. "The little Pom! Right, you sit here in front of me, where I can keep an eye on you. Don't trust you lot, never have!"

Fortunately for me, Mr Archer had an interest to which he was fanatically addicted. In the centre of the playground was a hard, rough, extremely dangerous concrete cricket pitch, and on his instructions every boy in the school had to meet him there after school, on or near the day of their ninth birthday. Standing at one end, a box of old cricket balls at his feet, Mr Archer would direct the boy to stand at the other end, no bat, no pads, nothing. The boy was also left under no illusion as to what would happen if he dared back away or put so much as a toe outside the crease.

We stood there, alone, rooted to the spot, desperately trying not to wet ourselves. "Do you like cricket, boy!" He'd glare down the pitch once you were in position. When you whispered timidly that you loved the game, he would snort contemptuously, snarl: "Well let's see if you're any good at it!" and proceed to hurl ball after ball at you, most of them aimed directly at your head. "Don't duck, boy! Don't duck! Catch the confounded thing. Catch it!" By some miraculous fluke I passed this initiation with flying colours, catching the first three balls he threw at me, one of them one-handed. That was it; I was in the junior eleven. As far as Mr Archer was concerned, if a boy could catch a cricket ball he could do no wrong, even a Pommie boy, although he was at pains to point out that the only things Poms usually caught with any regularity were colds and buses.

Despite his oft-stated dislike of foreigners, and by association all things foreign, he didn't seem to think it ironic that his pride and joy was his black 1937 Citroen 11B, one of those two-door coupé things with a long bonnet and spare wheel housed in a mould in the lid of the dickie seat. Not a large vehicle, but somehow, every sports day, he managed to get the entire cricket team and our gear into it and drive us to the match. We used to sit squashed together, three or four in the front bucket seat, the rest of the team crammed into the back and the dickie seat, legs round our ears.

In my last year at the school we won our last match, won it easily as it happened, and by so doing won the league for the second year running. As we packed up after the game, excited and full of ourselves, Mr Archer didn't say a word; he just wedged us into the car as usual and set off back to school. Going up Epping High Street, he suddenly veered off the road and into the paddock behind the Epping Hotel. "Get out and stretch your legs for a minute," he instructed us, and disappeared into the bar. We didn't really think anything of it and were standing about congratulating ourselves when he suddenly reappeared carrying a tray with twelve schooners of beer on it. Without a word, he solemnly handed each boy a glass and, taking his own, glared at us. "If one parent gets to hear about this you're all bloody dead! Congratulations, you were men out there today!" and as he downed his beer so we downed ours, and giggled all the way back to school.

Mr Archer was a kind and conscientious man hiding behind a loud bark and ingrained prejudices. He introduced me to Aussie sporting competitiveness, racism, beer and how many a 1950s 'true blue' viewed the world. I remember him with some affection. He had the conflicting characteristics common to many post-war Australians: intolerance, bitterness, insecurity and anger tempered by decency, honesty, courage and humour. I just wonder sometimes how I might have felt if I hadn't so fortuitously caught those cricket balls.

As the hours passed and the promised help failed to materialise, it

11

was obvious the financial cost of the breakdown was weighing heavily on Alf. Yet, when his supposed arrival time in Brisbane came and went, he said no more than a murmured, "There goes me bonus". If anything he was more concerned about us and by midday when Glen and I were beginning to get a bit fidgety he suggested we try to get another lift. "You're welcome to stay, but I think I'm going to be here awhile. If you're on the road somewhere up ahead I'll pick you up again."

Then he disappeared behind the cab for a few moments, rummaged in the large toolbox bolted to the chassis and emerged with two pieces of canvas rolled up and tied with a piece of rope so we could sling the roll over our shoulders. "If you're going to be sleeping rough you'll need these … catch your death otherwise." He also gave us two spoons and two mugs, and finally he pressed a couple of bob into each of our hands. "Buy yourselves a decent feed tonight, and don't go putting anymore cans on the fire without opening them first!"

We almost changed our minds; it would have been great to stay with him longer, and although we parted with warm handshakes and wishes of good luck, it was with some sadness. We couldn't begin to imagine how much money he was losing because of the breakdown, but whatever it was, we knew for sure 'Uncle' Alf didn't deserve his bad luck. We never saw him again.

The truck had come to rest on a bend. It was not the ideal place to wait for a lift so we wandered up the road a hundred yards or so. There hadn't been much traffic all morning, and it was some time before a battered 1947 Dodge pick-up came hurtling around the corner, virtually on two wheels. If that wasn't alarming enough, then the sight of the young driver literally standing on the brakes and screeching to a halt a few yards beyond us, tyres smoking, should have warned us off. He did turn the radio down a fraction so he could hear us, but didn't seem too bothered where we were going. The seat next to him was full of clothes and other stuff, so he jerked his thumb at the back. "Jump in."

Dented and rusty with an old coat hanger serving as an aerial, to say the ute had seen better days was a compliment. Whole sections of the floor in the back had simply rusted away and the drive shaft, axle and, even more disconcerting, the road, were clearly visible, seemingly only inches below us. Finding somewhere to sit so our legs didn't fall through was a challenge and we ended up cramped, one on either side, hard up against the back of the cab. There was no glass in the little rear window which made conversation easier, or would have done if we could have heard each other. The second we were settled he shot off with Bobby Darren at full volume: "Goodbye cruel world, I'm off to join the circus, gonna be a broken-hearted clown …"

Objectionable as it may be to everybody else, it is necessary for the young that they don't have fully-developed moral and social consciences, simply because common sense and responsibility are incompatible with being rash and having a good time. Nothing more effectively stifles childish recklessness than sensible behaviour.

Despite this handicap, even Glen and I could tell instantly that the driver was a complete dickhead. Not that we were any smarter; we had the chance to escape when he stopped briefly in Grafton for fuel, but in our defence I think we were so traumatised we dared not let go of our grip. That there wasn't much traffic about was truly fortunate; had there been more, I am sure we would not have lived to tell the tale. He overtook every vehicle in front of us as soon as he came up behind it regardless of its size or the road situation; and the drivers of the vehicles coming towards us must have been amazed as we flashed past. I will never know how we didn't clip them or smash head on into a few of them as we careened around corners. The tarmac flashing by so close beneath was truly mesmerising, and stones and gravel constantly flicked up and shot around the back of the ute like ricocheting bullets. We clung on for dear life, certain that at each bend and bump we would fall through.

Rarely did he drop below fifty miles an hour; wind, stones, screaming tyres, unbelievably loud music; all that was missing was thunder and lightning. When he finally dropped us off in Ballina we felt like we'd been in Luna Park for a fortnight with unlimited funds. Stirling Dickhead, however, was completely unruffled as though he did that sort of thing every day, which he probably did. He just gave us a cheery wave and screamed off like a drag racer, Ray Charles entertaining the neighbourhood. *"Hit the road, Jack, and don't you come back no more, no more, no more, no more. Hit the road, Jack, and don't you come back no more. WHAT YOU SAY!"*

We treated ourselves to a dinner Alf would have approved of, before walking out to the surf club where we had to wash under a tap as the shower was broken. We slept the night on the beach, the roar of the surf a perfect soundtrack to our dreams of mad bastards in fast cars.

TWO

Sugar babies

First thing in the morning we presented ourselves at the police station. Alf had told us that in country towns, if you wanted work you went to the police, because they knew everybody in their area and what jobs, if any, were going.

The police were also the dispensers of 'the susso', more officially known as sustenance payments, introduced in the 1930s to help feed the hundreds of thousands of unemployed who took to the roads in search of work. When I was only five or six there was a boy in my class who used to sing a little song about it. At the time I didn't understand what it meant, but it was one of those silly little ditties that stay with you forever:

> *"Oh we're on the susso now,*
> *We can't afford a cow.*
> *We live in a tent,*
> *We pay no rent*
> *Oh we're on the susso now."*

The payments were in the form of food vouchers, and to qualify for one you had to satisfy the police you were a certain distance away from your home and a genuine unemployed 'bona-fide' traveller. Officially the allocation was one voucher per person per fortnight from any one town, but it was a very haphazard process and in many towns the police would only give out one a month. Only basic items such as bread, potatoes, eggs, tinned food and a prescribed quantity of biscuits, flour, tea and sugar — all of which were still sold by weight in country stores could be obtained with the vouchers, no alcohol or cigarettes. It was only enough food to last a man three or four days, five if he eked it out, but it very neatly solved two problems. Firstly, that nobody starved to death; and secondly, that bums, vagrants and the unemployed were moved on, saving the police an onerous task.

Keep travelling from town to town and itinerants could eat quite well; stop for more than a week and they either had to find work or go hungry. It was quite clever really.

Sergeant Pearce wasn't particularly enamoured to see us. Looking after the domestic problems of vagrants was not why he'd become a policeman. After grilling us as to why I wasn't at kindergarten and did our parents know where we were, he eventually parted with a voucher for each of us as if the cost of it was coming straight out of his wages. When we asked about employment he sighed impatiently and called out to somebody in the back room. "Hey, Norm, anybody you know employing nappy soilers at the moment?" The head of a young constable, presumably Norm's, appeared round a doorway. "Reg Butt has been burning off all week. He might have started hiring."

Sergeant Pearce's tolerance finally cracked when, after he'd shown us how to get to Butt's farm, which was about ten miles out of town, we asked if there was any chance of a lift. "Jesus Christ!" he exploded. "Next you'll be wanting me to do the bloody work for you!" Then his face softened slightly and he looked at his watch, gave a resigned shrug and grabbed his hat. "Come on, then. Going out for a bit, Norm. Be back in half an hour," he called over his shoulder. Ah, the benefits of a cherubic face.

*

Butt's farm house wasn't really a house as such, more a patchwork of rusty corrugated iron sheets held together by rough wooden posts. It looked just like the house in "There was a crooked man" — complete with a crooked dog that roused itself lazily from its similarly constructed kennel to come and sniff our feet.

Then the door opened and we were confronted by a creature from another fable — the ogre in *Billy Goat Gruff*. His face had obviously been re-organised in a boxing ring and he had massive arms, hairy shoulders, huge boots, thick grey trousers held up with braces and a blue singlet he hadn't taken off since the depression.

"Hello, Mr Butt," I greeted him with cocky assurance. "Nick, Glen. The police said you were looking for …"

"Ever cut cane before?"

"Well … not exactly, but we've seen …"

"Right! Go down the shed and see Charlie. Team pay, four quid a ton, meals in," and he slammed the door in our faces.

The shed in question was about half a mile away across the plantation, one mile via the dirt track. Halfway there a man in a tractor swept past us with no intention of offering us a lift, and covering us with dust. He stopped outside the shed and left the engine running as he went inside to await our arrival. It chugged away, sounding impatient. The shed was a long, rough, weatherboard building with a corrugated iron roof. There was no ceiling, and a maze of pinpricks of sunlight shone through. The walls were unlined and the floor was nothing but hard packed mud. Thick grass grew under the double metal bunks, two dozen or more of which lined either side, with straw mattresses, stained pillows and thin blankets piled on them. Off one end of the shed was a small office and store room, and off the other end was a water tank, beside which were several tables with wash bowls on them. Thirty yards away was an equally rundown and flyblown dunny.

Charlie was, in stature, almost the exact opposite to Mr Butt and his singlet, in which he'd obviously been born, more or less held him together. The few teeth he had were stained dark brown from years of smoking the ridiculously thin cigarettes he rolled himself, so thin the paper stuck to his lips and the thing went out almost as soon as he'd lit it so he was constantly re-lighting. "Grab yerselves a bunk," he muttered, cursing his battered flint lighter which only seemed to work every tenth go. "Machetes and boots are in the store. Be down at field nine at five thirty in the mornin'. Dinna's at six thirty in the mess hut behind the house."

"Where's field nine?" we asked as he climbed back onto the tractor.

"Yer've got the rest of the day to find it, ain't ya!" and, struggling once more with his lighter, he roared off.

Hand harvested cane farms were made up of relatively small, two or three hundred yard, roughly square, individual fields, separated by tractor access roads that also acted as fire breaks. On large plantations there could be up to fifty of these fields, and a few days before each one was due to be harvested it was set alight, which meant a pall of thick, black, sweet-smelling smoke hung over the area every day during harvest time. The burn off was done principally to get rid of the mountains of dead leaves that accumulated over the time it took the cane to grow to maturity, and which made cutting virtually impossible if they remained. It was also done to flush out the nightmare-inducing numbers of snakes and cane toads, huge, revolting creatures the size of rugby balls. The cane stalks themselves didn't burn; they did, however, become covered with a clinging black soot that got everywhere. You only had to walk past a sugar field at harvest time to look like a coal miner.

There were eight in our team, the leader being a squat, leathery little man whom we discovered was a Hungarian refugee. He barely spoke any English, which didn't seem to matter as many of the other men were migrants and couldn't speak English either. Or if they did, they only seemed to know about five words, none of them very flattering. Each team was allocated a field that only they cut down, stacked in bundles and loaded onto trailers, which were marked with the team number and towed away at intervals by Charlie to be weighed. Occasionally the ogre himself would appear to check progress, but most of the time he left us to it.

We were paid as a team, with bonuses for each ton above our quota, a figure Glen and I were never told. The head cutter got the most, the rest, supposedly, being paid equal amounts, swapping jobs around as the day went on. That first morning there were no introductions, no welcomes, we were just handed half a dozen battered enamel mugs. "You look, you learn," said the Hungarian. He'd split the team into four pairs: two cutting, one stacking and one making tea, copious quantities of which, black and sweet, was drunk all day long. Each team had its own drum of water on a brazier beside its field, and for the first three hours we were constantly running back and forth tending it and distributing tea. The following three hours we stacked the lengths of cane onto trailers as we'd seen the others doing. Finally our turn came to cut, and we gripped our machetes with boyish glee and set off as fast as we could down our row, following the Hungarian who was the only one of the team to cut all day.

There was an art to cutting cane, a sort of figure of eight rhythm you got into. Stooping down to grasp the stalk at its base, you'd slash through it with the razor-sharp machete; known as a billhook; preferably in one cut. Then, standing up, you'd swivel the stalk round and lop off the top, tossing the five-foot length of cane to the side where it was gathered by your stacker. Ideally it was all done in one continuous, smooth movement.

Stoop, slash, stand, swivel, lop, drop. Stoop, slash, stand, swivel, lop, drop.

Good teams could cut between five and ten ton a day. I don't think Glen and I cut a ton between us in three.

No more than four members of the team were cutting at any one time, mainly because the stackers following couldn't keep up and everybody would eventually get in each other's way. Working in staggered rows — the second cutter not beginning his row until the first was a few yards into his — the quickest cutters went first and at the end of their row they rested, sharpened their machetes and had a mug of tea until the last cutter arrived. Then they would set off back up the field in a similar way. If you were the last cutter in a fast cutting team, it was relentless torture. The quicker men raced ahead, getting a much longer break and setting off as soon as you arrived, often not leaving enough time even for a swig of tea.

It was indescribably hard work, and within minutes we were covered head to foot in black soot that became sticky and glue-like when mixed with sweat. Blisters the size of marbles appeared on our palms, and even more painfully in the crevices of our thumbs. Each time we looked up the Hungarian seemed to be another twenty yards in front of us, and he didn't stop once going down his row. By the time we reached him for our first gulp of tea, we felt like we'd been working for a week. By the afternoon break on the second day, both of us, and worse, the Hungarian and the rest of the team, knew we were hopelessly out of our depth.

Each day started at six and finished at six, with only three forty-minute breaks, sometimes less, breaks during which we dared not let go of our machetes for fear of not being able to grasp them again. At each break we were fed massive chunks of bread covered in fresh honey, brought out to the fields by the ogre's wife and their three daughters, all of whom, much to the amusement of the men, looked like they'd spent time in the same boxing ring as the ogre, although we didn't see if they had hairy shoulders. By the last break of the day, we could barely pick the bread up. The only light relief came on our second morning, when Glen trod on a dozing carpet snake and came running out of the field, face ashen despite the soot. Even the ogre was amused. The blisters on our hands throbbed continuously, despite urinating on them several times a day as recommended by the others in the team. Not that we ever saw any of them doing it, and despite the grins it wasn't until the third day that we got the joke.

Dinner was served in a shed behind the main house, and each team of cutters not only had its own rough hewn wooden table and benches, but team members sat in the same position every night. Promptly at six thirty Mrs Ogre and her daughters would appear carrying plates of food and these they would plonk down, one in front of each position, senior cutters first, along with a knife and fork, returning to the kitchens and repeating the process until everyone had been served. If anybody was late their food would just sit there getting cold, and if they hadn't turned up by seven o'clock, when the four women emerged to clean up, the plate was simply picked up and the food dumped into the pig swill bucket along with the other scraps. The meals were always the same, meat of some sort with gravy, cabbage, carrots and potatoes and a chunk of bread, and for pudding there was jelly and custard. Breakfast was at five thirty sharp, two fried eggs, bacon, sausage, tomato and toast, similarly dispensed.

At the time there were five teams working on the farm, and every night the main focus of interest was the notice board at the end of the mess shed. Pinned there was a list of the tonnage cut that day by each team and their position in the 'Team Bonus Scheme'. Glen and I were in team three, and while we were there team three remained firmly in fifth and last position. That this was a situation he and I were entirely responsible for was all too obvious. Nobody said anything outright, and being sent to Coventry by men who barely said a word anyway may not sound much of a punishment, but the dark glares were more frightening than any curse.

Back in the bunkhouse at night, this silent treatment turned to real abuse from a few of the men when they came stumbling back from the hotel bars that we were too young to enter. For three nights we barely slept, in fear not only of the men but of snakes; on the first night a man calmly removed a huge king brown snake that had curled up in his dirty clothes under his bunk. On the third night it poured with rain, the noise was deafening and within minutes it was almost as wet inside the shed as it was out.

The men were taken to and from the pub sitting on one of the trailers towed by Charlie so, on their return this night, they were drenched which didn't help their mood. One of them came staggering over to our bunk and started shaking it violently, shouting his head off. We couldn't hear a word he said, never mind understand him, but that wasn't necessary; we knew what he was on about. Glen was in the top bunk and, not getting the response he wanted from either of us, the man suddenly grabbed Glen by the throat and started shaking his head. Fortunately the Hungarian was close by and came running over, dragging the enraged man away.

Back-breaking work, violent, surly and resentful co-workers, lumpy straw mattresses, pillows that smelt of other men's sweat and a leaking shed full of angry drunks, farting and snoring their heads off in unison with the croaking toads — so, we only lasted four days. The Hungarian spared us the ignominy of having to quit when he came to us at the end of the fourth day and said bluntly, "Tomorrow you go, here you money," and he gave us each two pounds. Small fortune as it was to us, it was probably much less than we should have received but we were too exhausted and too scared to complain. We couldn't get away quickly enough and left Butt's farm immediately, despite the descending gloom. We settled for the night under the bridge on the banks of the Richmond River and in the dark we ate the baked beans and sausages we'd got with our food voucher, spilling less of it down our shirts than we might have had it not been for Alf's spoons. It was cold, the ground was damp and smelt of urine and we got covered in ants, but it still beat the cutter's shed.

The next morning, it was time to assess the situation. Going home wasn't an option; Glen's dad would be on the warpath. Besides, how could we face the others if we went back now? There was only one thing for it; keep heading north.

One of the older men in our team who'd been slightly more hospitable towards us, in that he at least spoke to us occasionally, told us about a place Glen and I had never heard of called Magnetic Island. "Spent a few months up there a couple of years ago, paradise on earth," he assured us. The nights were always warm and balmy, so sleeping on the beaches was no problem. There were plenty of fish to be caught in the coral lagoons, and easy money could be made scaling palm trees and picking coconuts for the holidaymakers, a task for which my smaller frame was ideally suited, apparently. If not, there were several smallholdings on the island that always wanted casual labour. It sounded a magical place, the name alone being enough to draw us to it. Magnetic Island, here we come! This settled, and being flush with funds, we decided to kit ourselves out a bit better. We bought a frying pan and a billy, tin plates and knives and forks; eating cold beans out of the tin in the dark was for amateurs!

Morale restored for having so brilliantly sorted out our domestic situation and formulating a plan of action, we walked back out to the surf club again, washed our filthy clothes under the tap and spent the day drying them. The next morning, after demolishing a huge breakfast at a cafe in Ballina, we also tried to wangle another food voucher, but despite our protestations that we'd been sacked from Butt's Farm and were therefore entitled, Sergeant Pearce was having none of it. It was move on or go hungry time, not that we were too bothered; we still had several tins of food, plenty of tea, sugar and biscuits, and a few bob in our pockets — enough to get to Magnetic Island and back probably so who needed a hand out? With the confidence of the well organised and the contentment of the well fed, we strolled a mile or so out of town and stuck out our thumbs. It did cross my mind to ask Sergeant Pearce for a lift out there, but I thought better of it.

THREE

Meanderings, memories and mateship

*O*nly when you begin to travel do you start to understand ignorance and insularity. Growing up in 1950s Sydney, I had no real idea of the size of Australia, or of Sydney itself. This was despite the fact that up until the age of eight I had travelled quite a bit. When aged two I'd sailed to Australia from England, and when I was four my mother had taken us to live with her parents in Queensland for a year. For a few years in the early fifties my sister and I had gone to New Guinea during the school holidays to visit our mother.

Of New Guinea I have many memories, but as with all young childhood holidays and travel they are fleeting and were mostly disjointed. From the age of eight until Glen and I set off, my entire world had centred around Epping; the creek at the bottom of our garden, school, trains to Circular Quay and ferries to Manly at the weekends. Epping in those days was virtually out in the country, twelve miles from the centre of Sydney. We were surrounded by bush. On hot days in the summer my stepmother would take a few of us to Balmoral for a swim, and a couple of times a year we might go shopping in Sydney or my father would take me to the cricket ground or the Royal Easter Show. In the season on Sundays, a couple of mates and I would ride our push bikes out to Parramatta speedway and for several years we went to every home game played by Eastwood Rugby Union club at Eastwood Oval, perennial woodenspooners in those days. "Go you Woodies!" we'd chant deliriously as they ran onto the field. "Useless bunch of fat-heads!" we'd cry when they trudged from it eighty minutes later. Fanatical and fickle in one afternoon, the hallmark of many a football supporter I reckon.

As for the western and southern suburbs, we never ventured there and places like Bankstown and Cronulla were as foreign and distant to us as Cloncurry and Oodnadatta. I had never seen a full-blooded Aborigine, or a dingo. I thought Ayers Rock was in Alice Springs, and even if I had heard of it I would have said Marble Bar was a chocolate. By far my longest journey had been on our annual holidays to Avoca Beach for two weeks. After the excitement of making the sandwiches, packing up the car, squeezing in my father's crutches and stopping for a picnic beside Brisbane Waters, it took us most of the day to get there, trundling along the winding Gosford road, my stepmother driving our top-heavy little Austin A40 at twenty-five miles an hour.

"Are we there yet? Are we there yet?"

"No!"

"Well, when are we going to be there, for poop's sake?"

"Don't talk like that, Nicholas!"

Of course I knew the shape of Australia and all about Captain Cook and Matthew Flinders, Bourke and Wills and Blaxland, Wentworth and Lawson. But if someone had asked me to describe the Gold Coast, I would have said it was like Manly and Queenscliff beaches only with Coolangatta at one end and Surfers Paradise at the other. So when you get there and find instead of being only one or two miles apart it is more than twenty miles, it comes as a bit of a shock, especially if you have to hump an unwieldy kit bag! We also hadn't reckoned on hitchhiking being so difficult and frustrating in urban areas. As often as not the lifts were only for a mile or so, and in busy, built-up areas they were few and far between. Three or four days of this, and the novelty of hitchhiking can quickly disappear. Stomachs apart, all that really concerned us was the next bloody lift. If someone stopped, anyone at all, we just got in and worried about where we were going afterwards. Half a mile in the right direction was a result, even if it meant going forty miles sideways to gain it.

Consequently, had our route over the next few days been plotted on a map it would have looked like the gormless meanderings it was. From Ballina we'd got a lift to Bangalow, from Bangalow to Murwullimbah and from Murwullimbah to Coolangatta. It then took us three days just to get to Southport via Mudgeeraba, and we walked most of the way. Eventually we got out of the congestion of the Gold Coast — not as bad as today, perhaps, but it was still pretty bad, with far fewer roads — and made it to Nerang, then to Beaudesert, only to find we had to more or less retrace our steps back to Beenleigh, where we should have gone to from Nerang in the first place.

Fortunately the average teenage boy's mind is just another stunning example of how amazing nature is. Blissfully unaware and wildly optimistic, it is not bogged down with the concerns and worries that so complicate and inhibit the adult mind; things like organisation, patience, forward planning, thinking before they leap and having an awareness of time and distance. With great foresight, the teenage boy's mind has been left completely blank, enabling it to concentrate solely on the important, immediate matters of the day; things like hamburgers, milkshakes, music, cigarettes, sleeping, and what to do with their erection every morning.

Oh, we knew where Magnetic Island was alright. It was off the coast of Townsville, which was north of Mackay, which in turn was north of Rockhampton, which was north of Bundaberg, which was north of Brisbane; what else was there to know? If the sun was more or less on our right in the mornings as we set off, we knew we were more or less heading more or less in the right direction.

The worst day was the fifth after leaving Ballina, or was it the sixth? It felt like the tenth! Although it was late May, at midday it was quite hot and we trudged along, thirsty and increasingly irritable, thumbs ignored by all. Our duffle coats, so comforting and necessary at night, were cumbersome and annoying in the heat of the day.

"Do you have to walk so fast?"

"Do you have to be so slow?"

"I'm not slow."

"Yes, you are."

"No I'm not. Besides, it's hot and I want a drink."

"Well, there isn't any bloody water here, is there!"

"Shit, this bloody frying pan is heavy. Why can't you carry it?"

"Because I'm carrying everything else!"

"Yeah, but it's not as heavy as this frying pan!"

"Will you shut up!"

"No, you shut up!"

"Quick! She's stopping! She's stopping!"

It was midday and we'd left Southport Beach at six o'clock that morning and not had one lift since, so when the Morris Minor pulled up ahead of us we rushed over to it with great excitement and relief.

"Hello, boys," said the elderly lady. "Where are you off to?"

"Magnetic Island."

"Magnetic Island? Good heavens! That's miles away!"

"Yes."

"Well, I'm going to Acacia Gardens, if that's any help."

"Where's that?"

"Well, you go up there to the lights and turn left, then …"

Shit!

The next day outside Nerang was similar. "Jump in boys, goin' to Beaudesert," the driver and his mate grinned down at us. We needed no second bidding. The back of the small truck was empty save for a couple of bales of straw and a lovely black and white sheepdog that got so excited as we clambered over the tailgate that its tail nearly fell off. We stood up behind the cab and hung onto the railings, the dog barking with joy. "Okay?" the driver yelled. "Okay!" we yelled back, and we lurched off. "Where's Beaudesert?" Glen shouted as we picked up speed, his blond hair blowing in the wind.

Shit!

If we weren't near a beach or a river, we discovered the best place to sleep was in parks or local ovals. There we could usually find enough wood to light a fire, make a billy of tea and heat a few tins of food. If it rained there were always the stands, toilet blocks and picnic shelters. A few times our fire attracted the attention of the local police patrol, leading to confrontations that were always a little nerve-racking because we were never too sure what they wanted to talk to us about. To supplement our diet I had begun stealing little items from shops while Glen distracted the shop-keeper, not that he was all that keen. A Kit-Kat here, a Mars bar there, a tin of beans, a pocketful of oranges, a packet of cigarettes, and in one shop in Surfers Paradise I managed to walk out with a loaf of bread and a tin of IXL strawberry jam under my duffle coat. We ate the lot in one sitting. But the police only seemed interested in how old we were, where we'd come from and, more particularly, how long we were staying; on each occasion warning us not to be in the area the following night or they would "Do you for vagrancy." Exactly what happened when you were 'done' for vagrancy, they didn't explain.

So it was that more than a week after leaving Ballina, we were taking cover from the pouring rain on a bench under a picnic shelter in the outer Brisbane suburb of Mt Gravatt. We were here because the previous day in Beaudesert we'd bumped into Ralph, who told us that we could link up with Brisbane's tram service there. He was a soldier going home on leave, and, we discovered, was something of an expert on hitchhiking, having travelled back and forth like that on leave for several years. He was heading in the opposite direction to us, but caught our attention because he had a hand-written sign he held out saying simply 'Newcastle.'

"Does that work, then?" Glen shouted across the road, pointing at the sign.

"Sometimes," said Ralph, and he came across and had a cigarette with us.

"I don't use it in built up areas, puts the locals off stopping. In fact I don't hitch in cities at all if I can help it … just a pain in the arse." Don't we know it, mate! And then we saw he had another piece of equipment that really interested us. As he shrugged his old Army rucksack easily off his shoulders and sat down, we were green with envy. Spacious, comfortable to carry and with various straps to tie up bed rolls, billies and things, and several little pockets to house small items, it was perfect for hitching. "You can get them at the disposal store in Brisbane," Ralph assured us and we knew, somehow or other, we just had to get ourselves one of those packs and get rid of the cumbersome kit bags. Just how we were going to pay for them didn't enter our heads, or at least it didn't enter mine; such things don't when you're permanently locked into 'something will turn up' mode.

By the time we got to Mt Gravatt it was dark and far too late to think about going to Brisbane. The shops would be shut anyway, so we took refuge under the picnic shelter and reviewed our sorry situation. Our last lift had been with an old man in a Ford half truck almost as old as him. Just outside Sunnybank he had a flat tyre, and it had taken us nearly two hours to change it. The back of his truck was full of old engines and axles and we'd had to move them all to get at the spare. Then the jack slipped and we had to chock the vehicle up on wooden blocks. Fortunately he gave us a couple of bob each for helping him, and with that we were able to buy two packs of Smith's chips, two Cherry Ripes, a bag of Jaffas and a large bottle of Shelley's lemonade. We sat on the picnic bench devouring our dinner, looking at the last of the night's trams rattling by in the rain.

Watching them, I was cheered by one thing; it wasn't going to cost us anything to get to Brisbane the next day.

*

Most school holidays and weekends in the summer, a crowd of kids would head either for Bondi or Manly, although Glen rarely came because he wasn't allowed. We liked Manly better, but it wasn't as easy to sneak on a ferry without paying, especially when there were eight or nine of us. Trams, on the other hand, were a doddle as there was always a steady flow of them to Bondi, often one right behind the other, and they were dead easy to jump on and off, or dart around the aptly named running board on the outside avoiding the conductor. The idea was to stay on each tram as long as possible. The first goal was to get from Circular Quay to Bondi on the fewest number of trams. Doing the entire trip on the same tram was the ultimate prize. Not paying for public transport was a challenge, an exciting game and very few of us ever paid a fare or had a problem, apart from 'two knees' Bruce, that was.

Dear old 'two knees', was a really nice, gentle boy but he wasn't the sharpest. Only once did he manage to elude the conductor for the entire trip; the trouble was, he was on the wrong tram and ended up in La Perouse. He'd been given his nick-name by Miss Guy, our form teacher in our second year at high school; the year we were just beginning to get interested in girl's legs and things, although being an all-boys school we didn't get the chance to look at many. How ridiculous is it to have single sex schools? Surely if there is one thing we should all learn at school it is about each other! Anyway, Miss Guy, being only twenty-three, was not only beautiful but had lovely legs. In fact she was a lovely person and a great teacher.

She taught geography and always started her lessons with what she called 'brain warmers'. These were a series of simple, rapid-fire questions, with each child in the class being asked at least one. So fast was she there was no time to think; instant answers were the essence. Hesitate even for a fraction and Miss Guy would be asking the next question, leaving you feeling stupid and inadequate and the butt of much sniggering and finger pointing. We loved it, though. It was great fun, especially when someone got it wrong or couldn't think fast enough, and she tried to make sure we were all caught out eventually. By the end we were left breathless with excitement.

"Barry: what colour is chocolate? Doug: how many eggs in a dozen? Eric: what is your desk made of? Warren: what noise do ducks make? Ray: how old are you? Martin: what school do you go to? John: what day is it? Bruce: how many knees do you have?" It was only for a millisecond, but we all saw it and the class erupted: "He looked! He looked! He looked!" Miss Guy simply smiled indulgently. She was my first love.

In fact, if it hadn't been for Miss Guy, I might not have gone to school at all as it was throughout the second and third years I wagged as many days as I could, becoming quite adept at signing my father's signature. It was the excuses that let me down. *"Dear Headmaster. Nicholas had scarlet fever so couldn't come to school yesterday"*. My ability to recover from serious contagious diseases overnight was never fully appreciated, especially by Mr Unwin, the deputy head, who had a very long cane and very strong arms.

*

My parents divorced when I was four, and my mother went to live in New Guinea. A year later my father married again, and together with my sister and me we moved into the house in Epping. As we had known our stepmother for some time, the transition was quite smooth and I never recall being unhappy, rejected or unloved. Then, when I was about seven, my father was struck down by some sort of paralysis of the legs. The cause was never properly diagnosed, but for the next six years his condition progressively deteriorated. He developed stomach ulcers and huge bed sores, one on each buttock, the result of being left sitting bolt upright in a hospital bed for twenty hours having a blood transfusion. It was felt by some doctors that his paralysis was caused by a defect in his blood, so he just sat there while eight pints dripped intro his arm, at less than half a pint an hour. Just before I turned thirteen he was confined to a wheelchair, and from then until he died three years later he was really quite ill.

Our stepmother was very much younger than my father, who was fifty when I was born. Involvement in one World War can seriously interrupt life, never mind two! So, my stepmother not only had to go out to work part-time to feed us, but spent the rest of her time nursing and looking after him, a task she did with great love and devotion. This meant that although I was loved and well looked after, from the age of twelve neither of them really had the time or the energy to properly supervise and discipline me, and it is easy to be naughty when no-one is looking. Not that I blame them or anything; that was just the situation. Yet it is interesting to observe that Glen, who was severely disciplined and reprimanded at home, passed his intermediate certificate. I, on the other hand, able to do more or less as I pleased, did not; but this was not the only difference between us.

*

One of the mysteries of life is how much of our character and personality we are born with and how much we pick up as we go along. When the two of us were alone, Glen was often as boisterous and loud as me; yet in company he was very reserved and wary. His parents were relatively well off — his father was an accountant and his mother worked in the head office of Qantas — so money had never been a problem. Our sense of humour was similar and we got on really well most of the time, yet when it came to self-confidence and socialising with strangers, especially adults, Glen was often hesitant and unsure. No doubt psychologists would say this was a result of a childhood stunted by anger and violence, but how much of it came naturally?

I, on the other hand, was cocky, loud and cheeky, irritatingly so no doubt. With so much freedom in my early teens I was more streetwise than Glen, more cunning, more cynical. Apart from eleven years in the Army — six in the first war, five in the second — my father had been a freelance writer all his life; not the most secure of incomes at the best of times and when he became ill there was very little money coming in. My childhood was happy and calm, yet by thirteen I had begun stealing money from clothes on the beaches, locker rooms, out of cars or handbags left unattended. It was never much; enough to go to the pictures, or buy some chips and a milkshake. In contrast, Glen had never stolen a thing in his life before we set out, much less wagged school. No doubt psychologists would say such behaviour was the result of a boy left too much to his own devices, a lack of discipline or a cry for attention; but how much of it came naturally? A bit simplistic, maybe, but whatever the answer, the reality was that Glen and I did not have much in common other than our age and, of course, being born Poms.

Now sitting in the dark in this Mt Gravatt park, cold, no food or money, we were at least sharing the same emotion as the precariousness of our situation dawned on us, although we didn't speak of it, or even understand it particularly. Homesickness is a difficult enough state for adults to comprehend, never mind verbalise. Not that either of us actually wanted to go home, although our reasons, like our personalities, were very different. I didn't want to go home because no-one was there; Glen because someone was there. It's strange how sometimes depressing moments can make us see the positive side of things, and we decided we did have one thing going for us; each other. And we held a little ceremony confirming our friendship. Clasping each other's wrists with our hands crossed over like we'd seen Red Indians do in the pictures when they were swearing 'blood brother' allegiances to one another, we made solemn vows to share everything and never part, no matter what happened, devising a plan whereby if we ever got separated we would go to the next town and wait at the police station. It was a pity it was dark as it must have made a touching scene. This decided, we felt much better and fell asleep on the table, snuggled as close together as we could get, as much in friendship as for warmth.

FOUR

Molinari's Cafe

*W*ell before dawn we were woken by council workmen emptying bins. If anything it was even colder, and during the night the rain had been relentless, although it was now bright and clear. Virtually everything was at best damp, so we spread our things out around the other tables to dry. It was the first time since we'd set out that we'd been completely broke — not a biscuit or a tin of food left, and our last packet of cigarettes was a soggy mess. Brisbane and shopping for rucksacks seemed a long way away. We sat shivering under our duffle coats waiting for the sun to come up so we could at least dry out a bit before setting off. And we were trying not to think too much about food.

We were only about fifty yards away from the high street. Early morning trams and commuter traffic was beginning to build. On the other side of the road there was a row of shops, still shuttered and closed but with the lights on. We saw movement inside one, and a moment later an elderly man emerged wearing an apron and carrying a bucket and mop. He leaned the mop up against the wall and proceeded to let down a large red and green awning over the pavement, across which in large black letters was written Molinari's Cafe. Having tied down the awning rope, the man began mopping the pavement, obviously in preparation for laying out the tables and chairs that were stacked up inside.

I'm not sure where the thought came from, but it came in a flash and without a word I was on my feet, running across the park and darting over the road. "Morning, Mr Molinari," I gulped, catching my breath and praying that it was him. To my relief he looked up briefly to acknowledge me, and then did a sort of double-take and peered at me more closely.

"What you name?" he demanded.

"Nick," I replied, slightly taken aback by such immediate interest.

"Nick who?"

"Nick Thomas. Why?" For a moment he stared at me intently and then, just as abruptly, he seemed to lose all interest and waved me away, saying, "No open yet."

"No, no, I know, I'm sorry to trouble you, it's just that ... well, could me and my friend do that for some breakfast?" and sheepishly I pointed at the mop. "We'll do whatever else you want, too," I added hurriedly. "Bring the tables and chairs out, wash up, clean inside ... anything, we're starving ..."

At this he did stop mopping and stood erect, staring at me again for several seconds and then over my shoulder to the park where Glen was standing in the shelter watching us.

"Where you from?"

"Sydney. We're on our way to Magnetic Island but we ran out of money and couldn't get a lift."

"You sleep park!"

"Yes." He gave a little shake of his head.

"How old you?"

Shaking his head again when I told him, he completely surprised me by agreeing to my request but immediately held up his hand in warning and waved his finger sternly. "But you must work, okay? No bullshit, I donna want no bullshit."

My smile of relief and satisfaction that my plan had worked must have been a mile wide. "No bullshit, Mr Molinari, I promise," and I dashed back across the road to get Glen.

For an hour we worked solidly, mopping, sweeping, moving tables and chairs, Mr Molinari hovering over us all the while with a sense of urgency. "Take this, put there. That you put here — no, no there, here! This you do like this. No! No! No! Like that, like this. Si! Si! That better, now you see it, now you see it." There was a sign in the window that stated simply: Breakfast 7am to 9am. Lunch 12pm to 2pm. No Dinner, and Mr. Molinari kept one eye on the clock on the wall as he hurried us along. At 6.45am he went to the front door and moved the little bell above it so that it would ring when the door was opened, and then disappeared into the room at the back, leaving us to finish the last few tables. Moments later he emerged with an armful of red and white check tablecloths and napkins, and proceeded to show us how to spread them out. "Now you see it, now you see it!" he enthused, and happy we were doing it correctly, he left us again, saying, "Soon you finish, come through."

The back room was warm and cosy, although it must have been suffocatingly hot in the summer. Panelled in dark wood, with a large wood-burning stove, it was twice the size of the dining room. Half of it was given over to cooking with the stove, wooden worktops, sinks and plate racks. The other half was a living area, with a dining table and half a dozen chairs, a couple of comfy armchairs and a couch in one corner. There were pictures, plates and maps on the wall, little mementos and figurines dotted about on shelves, and a crucifix in pride of place looking down on the table.

Mr Molinari was at the stove, busy frying eggs and bacon, and he nodded at the table when we came in. "Sit, sit," he commanded. "You like egg, bacon, sausage, fry bread maybe?"

Our cries of delight were cut short when a young couple came bursting through the back door. "Sorry I'm late, papa," the women said, kissing her father and taking down an apron from behind the door, as did the man.

"These boys help today," Mr Molinari said, pointing his egg flip at us, and they both smiled a greeting, but there was no time for further introductions as suddenly the bell sounded. "Let's go! Let's go! Let's go!" Mr Molinari shouted, and the couple disappeared into the dining room.

For forty minutes the bell must have rung every minute or so, and the daughter and the man were constantly running back and forth with the orders and taking meals, which Mr Molinari made with rapid efficiency, belying his looks. Most of his customers were men on their way to work. "Dey know dey getta the good food 'ere," he told us proudly. "Some men come every day." In between orders he managed to serve us a huge breakfast as well, and we were halfway through it when a woman emerged from the stairs that came out in the corner of the room near the stove. She was dressed entirely in black, with thick black stockings, her greying hair tied up neatly in a bun.

"Ah! Bello vederti mamma!" Mr Molinari greeted her. Having been taught to stand up whenever a lady entered the room, we would have done so anyway, but there was something about this woman that made us not just stand up, but jump up. "These boys help this morning," he informed her, waving his egg flip at us again. She hadn't realised we were there, and when she saw us her hand went straight to her chest. "Oh, mio dio!"she gasped, as if she'd had the shock of her life, and immediately she and Mr Molinari launched into a heated discussion in Italian, with much waving of arms, repeatedly pointing at Glen and myself.

Eventually the woman seemed to recover her composure, and I said "hello" as politely as I could. "I'm sorry if we gave you a shock."

"Oh, no you, no you, no you," she said quickly, obviously slightly embarrassed by her outburst.

"Mamma not so happy," said Mr Molinari with a chuckle. "No win lottery." At this mamma again waved her hand dismissively, this time at her husband. "Poosh!" she mocked, and went to the door and took down an apron.

Relieved the uncomfortable moment was over, I was about to

sit down to finish breakfast but was stopped, sort of frozen half-way, when mamma suddenly came over, grabbed my shirt front and sniffed it disapprovingly, screwing up her nose as she released me.

"How long you wear dis?"

"Well … I don't know … I … we did some work …" I pointed lamely to the dining room.

"This no today smell. This old smell. How long you wear?"

"Well … a couple of days, I guess."

"And you!" She turned accusingly to Glen, causing him to leap to his feet again.

"Um … I don't know … the same, I guess."

"You guess, you guess! Where you mamma?" she turned back to me.

"Which one?"

"You have more than one mamma!"

"Yes."

"More than one mamma and still you smell! Come!" She instructed over her shoulder, and without another word went out the back door. Mr Molinari turned and gave a little smile and shrug, holding his hands out as if to say, "Best-a do as she say, boys."

The backyard wasn't very big, but it was made even smaller by the stack of firewood and piles of cartons, crates, boxes and hundreds of old soft drink bottles. In a row down one side were three or four small brick sheds, and at the end a toilet. Beyond that was a patch of grass about five yards square, with a hills hoist in the middle. The grass was about two feet long, and weeds the same height ran all the way down the wooden fence at the side and along the back. The other side of the yard was a dirt driveway leading out to double wooden gates that opened into a lane at the back of the row of shops. Parked in the driveway was a 1938 Chevrolet pick-up with two garbage cans on the back, and the words 'wet' and 'dry' crudely painted on them.

The first shed was the laundry, and we found Mamma inside

sorting out a pile of dirty red and white check tablecloths. There was a large gas-fired copper with steam coming from under the wooden lid, and two concrete sinks, one with an old wooden wringer clamped to it.

"Where you clothes?" she demanded.

"Over in the park."

"Go get."

"What! All of them?"

"Yes, yes. All, all!"

"No this way! This way!" she pointed at the back gates, seeing we were about to go charging off through the cafe.

When we returned she was standing in the doorway of the shed next to the laundry holding two pairs of blue overalls. Behind her we could see a bath, steam rising from the hot water she had just taken from the copper. "Take off clothes," she demanded. "Have bath, put these," and she thrust the overalls into our hands, pushed us inside the bathroom and shut the door. After our bath she insisted on washing everything we owned; or rather, she insisted we wash everything we owned, with the exception of the kit bags and our duffle coats. These she made us beat, turn inside out and shake thoroughly before hanging them on the line to air. Then she disappeared upstairs, reappearing every now and then to see to her washing and other chores.

Breakfast and cleaning up finished, Mr Molinari now took over and kept us working for two hours, virtually non-stop. We cut the lawn, pulled up the weeds, stacked the empty bottles into cases and generally tidied up the yard. "This put here like this, no there, here, that you do like this. No like that; like this. Si! Si! Now you see it! Now you see it!" Then his daughter poked her heard out the door and smiled at us. "Give them a rest, papa," she admonished. "Come and have a cup of tea, boys."

Francesca and Carlo were really nice, and Francesca in particular put us at ease, sensing we'd been a little overwhelmed by her mother and father. Married for only six months, they lived in a flat above a shop just down the road from the cafe. Carlo was studying to be a chef and three days a week went to college; the rest of the time he worked in the café. "Papa is my capo principale!" He patted the old man on the back, and Mr Molinari grinned proudly. Both Carlo and Francesa had been born in Italy but had done much of their schooling in Queensland, so they spoke perfect English, flavoured with that distinctive Aussie accent that only Italians can achieve. "Ow u doin' maiti!"

Mamma joined us for tea, and for an hour we sat together chatting easily, Francesca and Carlo wanting to know all about us, where we'd come from and where we were going. "Gee, hitchhiking to Magnetic Island? That sounds exciting. I'd love to do that," said Francesca.

"Exciting, poosh!" her mother interjected. "Where you stay? Where you sleep!" she demanded.

"It's an adventure, mamma."

"Pish poosh!" exclaimed Mamma. "Errante vagabondo!" and Francesca shook her head and smiled, winking at us.

"Mama lives in a time warp, don't you, Mamma?"

Then the bell in the dining room sounded and Mr Molinari looked at his watch and brought the conversation to an end abruptly. "Let's go! Let's go! Let's go!"

Lunchtime wasn't quite as hectic as breakfast, and Francesca could manage the dining room on her own. This left Carlo free to help with the cooking and food preparation, the whole time being rebuked and praised in equal amounts by Mr Molinari. "No! No! No! Like this! Like this! Si! Si! Now you see it! Now you see it!" Throughout the meal he also kept Glen and I occupied fetching plates and items from the larder, washing up saucepans, peeling potatoes and bringing firewood in. Then Francesca came in with an order for six meals, all the same, and Mr Molinari threw his hands in the air.

"Steak chips! Steak chips! Steak chips! Senza fantasia!" he exploded with exasperation. "Australian eat only for here, never here!" And alternately he patted his stomach and his heart. "In Italia cooking is … how you say … like-a the Michael Angelo. Eating is … gioia, gioia, di celebrazione di Cristo!" and he crossed himself and raised his arms to the heavens. "Here always same, steak potato, fry fish potato, roast beef potato, sausage potato. No flavour, no garlic, no herb, no spice, no inspiriatore! But what we do? We no cook like diss we no make a di money!"

Almost before we knew what was happening we'd been there three days, then four days, then five; sleeping on the couch, which pulled out to make a double bed Mamma made up for us each evening after dinner. At no time were we asked if we wanted to stay, nor was there any talk of payment or how much work we would do. In fact there was no discussion at all. It was as if we'd all just agreed to it; a fait accompli, and before we knew what we were doing, we were doing it. It was obvious they wanted us to stay, making us feel more than welcome in fact. What wasn't so obvious was why?

"I feel like Hansel and Gretel," Glen whispered on the third night when the Molinaris had gone up to bed. "Maybe they're going to keep us here forever!" So it wasn't so much with concern as curiosity that we mentioned it to Francesca the next morning.

"Oh, they can be a bit funny sometimes," she agreed. "But they are lovely people really. If you want to go, just say so, but I know they like having you here. They just want to help you get on your feet again before you set off." Comforting as that was to know, it still left us wondering why!

Every day except Saturday, when he only served breakfast, and Sunday when the cafe was shut all day, the routine was the same. After lunch, when the cleaning and washing up was done and if he didn't have any more chores for us, Mr Molinari would retire upstairs for a nap and Francesca and Carlo would go home. Mamma now took over in the kitchen, making bread, cakes, pastry and preparing the evening meal. Glen and I sat about playing cards and draughts and leaping up whenever Mamma wanted us to do little tasks. At about half past five Mr Molinari would come down, put on a Mantovani record, pour himself a glass of sherry and light a strange-looking, pungent-smelling cigarette wrapped in dark brown paper. Half an hour later Carlo and Francesca would come back, and while she helped Mamma prepare the meal, Carlo and Mr Molinari played dominoes, slapping the tiles down with great glee to win points.

The evening meal was more like an event than a meal and consisted of three, sometimes four courses, spread over two or three hours. All the dishes were small in quantity but different in taste and flavour. They were tastes, flavours and food Glen and I had never seen or experienced before. Exotic fish soup, olives, garlic, sundried tomatoes, lamb pastas with basil, lovely cheeses and fantastic little sweet things like doughnuts without a hole, only much nicer, and they just melted in your mouth. Mamma was not the beaming sort, but she did as she watched Glen and I devour those delicious things. All the dishes were washed down with small glasses of Italian wine, liberally dispensed by Mr Molinari who kept up a steady stream of disparaging comments about Australian diets and eating habits, Mamma constantly admonishing him for giving us too much wine. When Glen and I went to bed each night the room might have been spinning, but we were as happy and content as we had ever been. It felt like we'd become members of another family.

At 4am two mornings a week Mr Molinari set off for the Roma street markets in Brisbane, taking the wet and dry garbage with him and returning with the pick-up laden with fresh vegetables, meat, fish, eggs and cheese, all in time to lay out the tables for breakfast when the day's routine would begin. On the second morning we did get a clue as to why he in particular seemed so keen to keep us there. The last three days of the week Carlo attended college, and although Francesca and Mr Molinari could have handled the work on their own, two extra pairs of hands were very useful. Then on our fourth night, towards the end of the meal, the true reason for their hospitality emerged.

Carlo wasn't there as he had night classes at college, and Francesca and Mamma were beginning to clear up when Mr Molinari turned the radio on for the news. The first headline was about the construction of the Berlin Wall, the second the meeting between Kennedy and Khrushchev in Vienna. Then the announcer began giving details about the trial of Adolf Eichmann, and as soon as his name was mentioned all three Molinaris stopped what they were doing and stared at the radio as if mesmerised. When the reader began to describe a particularly nasty incident involving Eichmann and the Gestapo in a Polish village, it seemed to catch Mr Molinari out and before he could get to the radio to turn it off most of the gory details had been relayed. Mamma let out a little cry of anguish, dropped the plate she was rinsing in the sink, lifted her apron to her face and disappeared upstairs, clearly distressed. The silence that followed was difficult to listen to, with Mr Molinari sitting dejectedly in his chair, his head in his hands. We could only sit, glancing anxiously at each other while Francesca put a comforting arm round his shoulders, giving us a little smile of reassurance as she did. "Okay if I tell them, Papa?" she asked gently, and slowly the distraught man nodded his agreement.

"One day in 1943, near our village in Italy, the resistance blew up a German truck towing an artillery gun," Francesca began, her voice calm and measured as she rubbed her father's neck. "That night, at about midnight, a dozen or so shells landed on the village, straight out of the blue, no warning, nothing. We never really discovered where the shells came from or who fired them, but the next day the Gestapo came to the village and told us if any more vehicles were blown up the entire village would be wiped off the map. The Germans did things like that a lot during the war," she grimaced.

"Nine people were killed, including Mamma's sister, her husband and my cousin. I was only a baby so I don't remember anything, and fortunately our house wasn't hit, but my aunt's house was completely destroyed. When Mamma and Papa got there my aunt and uncle were already dead, but my cousin was still alive. He died shortly afterwards in Mamma's arms." And then Francesca looked at me and smiled gently. "He was fourteen, and according to Papa you look exactly like him. In fact, when he first saw you he thought you were him."

"Ritratto! Ritratto!" Mr Molinari exclaimed, and reaching out, he cupped my face in his hands, tears welling up in his eyes. Even if I'd been able to speak, I wouldn't have known what to say. I still don't.

Mr Molinari got up to go upstairs a few minutes later. "You good boys," he said. "Good boys." Sombre as the mood was, it seemed the right moment.

"I think maybe we should go tomorrow."

"Si, si, I understand," he smiled. "But maybe you stay till Monday, eh? After lunch, okay? Francesca and Carlo no come on Monday. You be good help. I give you money, you no worry."

On Sunday, after Mamma came back from church, we went to Indooroopilly for a picnic on the banks of the Brisbane River. We hired a rowing boat for an hour or so, kicked a football about with Carlo and demolished the fantastic picnic Mamma and Francesca had made that morning. No mention was made of the previous evening, but there was a noticeable difference about Mamma. She seemed calmer, gentler and not quite so intimidating. When we got back from the picnic everybody fussed over us a bit and had ideas about our trip; Francesca and Carlo brought out a map of Queensland and we sat at the table poring over it.

"It's the chance of a lifetime to see the country," Francesca enthused. "You've got to stop and see things, not just drive past," and she rattled off places along the coast where we should go: the Glasshouse Mountains, Noosa Heads, the turtles at Mon Repos beach, "... and the islands!" she squealed excitedly. "You simply have to go to the Whitsundays!"

Francesca's infectious enthusiasm got us thinking differently about our journey, or at least thinking about it, and our moves for the next few days were decided as much by the Molinaris as us. On Monday after lunch the plan was that we would go to Brisbane to look for rucksacks.

"There's a disposal store in the Valley," Carlo told us, "just over the Story Bridge."

"Salvation Army hostel there too," interjected Mamma. "Good place stay, cheap, nice bed."

"Oh Mamma!" cried Francesca. "You worry too much!"

"Ah!" Mamma yelped, as if her daughter had reminded her of something, and she went purposefully over to Glen. "Come," she said, pulling him out of his chair and leading him across the room. Just inside the doorway that led upstairs was a telephone, and she pointed to it. "You ring your mamma. Now!" she demanded. "All mamma worry about their children. I know, I mamma!" Glen had no choice.

Although we all pretended not to listen, it was obvious the call was an ordeal for Glen. "I'm sorry, Mum ... I know ... I just wanted to get ... awe, gee, Mum! What did he do that for? No Mum, I'm not coming home yet but we are alright ... honest we will ... we're heading for Magnetic Island ... near Townsville ... yes, we've got money. We're working in a café ... Mum ... I know, Mum ... we'll be alright Mum, I promise ... love you too."

"Is good you call, yes?" Mamma told him rather than asked, but Glen didn't look too sure.

"Me dad rang the police," he looked at me, grimacing. "Told them we were missing."

"Shit! So what's happening?"

"Nothing. Mum said she'd sort it and she'll ring your sister."

"All mamma worry, all the time, sister too," Mamma scowled at me. "Children no understand," and Francesca gave us a sympathetic smile.

After lunch on Monday we were ready to set off. Mamma had ironed all our clothes and wrapped us some sandwiches, cold pizza and a few of the sweet doughnut-type things in greaseproof paper. Francesca presented us with the map of Queensland, having marked all the places she thought we should visit on the way up to Magnetic Island.

"I'd love to be coming with you!"

Then Mr Molinari gave us £4 each and a small canvas-covered bag, like a wash bag. "Put cigarettes and money," he told us with a wink. "No get wet."

When we looked inside the bag, we found six packets of cigarettes. Cheeks were kissed all round, and Francesca and Mamma hugged us both. "You good boys, good boys," said Mr Molinari, shaking our hands. Tears were not far away from all our eyes. Ten minutes later we were on the tram into the city, and for the first time in my life I paid my fare. It didn't seem right not to, somehow.

FIVE

Milk bar days and wayward ways

R ock 'n' roll came out of the blue, like a huge musical earth-quake. One minute we were listening to the soothing voices of Janette McDonald and Slim Whitman, the gentle tea dances of the big bands, the mighty cadenza of Mario Lanza and the honeyed tones of Guy Lombardo. Suddenly they were gone, wiped away in a flash of Elvis's gyrating hips, the frenetic energy of Little Rich-ard, the decadence of Jerry Lee Lewis, the fantastic tunes of Buddy Holly and the throbbing beat of *Rock Around the Clock*. When we first heard that song, that beat, that rhythm, it was mind -blowing, one of those moments in life where you always remember where you were. It felt like we were involved in some sort of spectacular revolu-tion or coup. Overnight the young had taken control of music. Go, Bill!

> "One, two, three o'clock, four o'clock rock,
> Five, six, seven o'clock, eight o'clock rock,
> Nine, ten, eleven o'clock, twelve o'clock rock.
> We're gonna rock — around — the clock tonight.
> Oh put your glad rags on ..."

We never had a television at home. My father thought he would spend too much time watching it. Not that he was an old fogey or anything. In fact he was quite modern and tolerant; it was just television that he didn't like. I don't recall missing it all that much apart from not being able to see Bandstand, and that I did miss because just about everything in our young lives revolved round that programme. From conversation, clothes and hairstyles, to dance moves, and turning up at the Epping Youth Centre — more widely known as Theo's milk bar — without knowing *all* the words to the latest Number One was social suicide, something the infuriating Brian Watterson understood all too well. Don't get me wrong, he was a nice enough boy, it was just that he was so good-looking it wasn't fair. The rest of us didn't stand a chance, even if we did know the words. Always stylishly dressed with a Frankie Avalon hairstyle and Cary Grant smile, open-necked Mitchell blue shirt, fleck stovepipes and Presley purple socks showing above his ripple soles, Brian knew exactly which buttons to push on the jukebox to push the buttons of the girls, even though I knew he hated most of the songs they liked.

Debra Jackson almost passed out when he sauntered across the floor to her booth, nonchalantly swirling his milkshake as he mouthed the words of Paul Anka, Victor Mature eyebrows working overtime.

"And *they call it Puppy Love,*
  Oh I guess they'll never know,
  How a young heart really feels and why I love her so!"
"Oh, Brian!"
"Oh, Debra!"
  Oh, for Christ's sake!

Not that I didn't try, or wasn't with it. I listened to Bob Rogers religiously every week, owned a pair of blue suede ripple soles, walked like Crash Craddock and used more Brylcreem than Fabian. I got on with most of the girls; I made them laugh, and I know many of them liked me as a friend, but apart from being hugged and kissed on the cheeks a lot that was as close as I got. My penis was convinced my pillow was a girl.

For the vast majority of young teenagers at the time — and for many today too, I suspect — virtually all sex education came from our peers, and in Theo's milk bar the tutors were Barry Wiley and Denise Phillips. Barry was several years older than the rest of us, and nobody liked or trusted him much. He had piggy eyes, and Bronwyn Wilson, who'd gone to the pictures with him once, said he smelt like used underpants. When it came to sex, however, he was listened to with some awe by us boys. Barry had a job and a car and he shaved every day, so obviously he knew what he was talking about, and his much bandied story about him and Christine Martinson 'doing it' on the town's bowling green was the stuff of wet dreams. I suppose the main reason we didn't like or trust him was because we couldn't understand why he hung around with us younger ones, although being credulous and enthusiastic listeners to his sexual exploits was probably one reason.

Christine, of course, strenuously denied ever having anything to do with him, but Allison Silverwater said it was true because everybody knew Christine was a nympho and the town's bike. The cats could be quite vicious at Theo's.

Denise Phillips was also a year or so older than us but she was gorgeous, long legs and a beautiful face. Theo, the Greek owner of the milk bar, was a particular fan, and would always put an extra dollop of ice-cream or a double spoonful of flavouring in her milk-shake — if his wife wasn't looking, that was. Then one day I was mortified when I overheard Denise boasting to some of her friends that she and Theo were lovers, and that he was going to leave his wife and take her on a world tour. I don't know if her friends believed it or not, but I did; nobody as beautiful as Denise Phillips could possibly tell a lie. It was my first taste of jealousy.

The physical culmination of sex — having an ejaculation or a climax — is no more complicated or difficult than going to the toilet. It might be more pleasurable, but it is just as simple and easy to do. The mental aspects of sex, however: love, lust, passion, jealousy, desire and so on, are emotions adults have long found confusing and difficult to cope with, never mind young teenagers. Were it only for these 'natural' emotional difficulties, which after all have been with us forever, we would all have been able to cope; they are part of sex, after all. The problem was that for centuries sex had been ensnared in a web of 'unnatural' emotional difficulties, shrouded in a blanket of fear, guilt, shame and embarrassment. The two World Wars may have loosened our inhibitions a little, enabling us to cope better with those 'natural' difficulties, but in the late 1950s the 'unnatural' difficulties were still as powerful as ever, and an act as straightforward and as simple as sex was *the* most complicated and confusing of all human activities, especially for the young.

On the one hand, music and Hollywood pictures simply oozed sex, we were bombarded with it; yet our parents, or most of them anyway, rarely mentioned or talked about it, as if it was somehow a taboo subject. Girls may have been slightly better informed, simply because of the physical events that occurred to them; but most boys were frighteningly ignorant. Discussing sexual acts or using words for sexual organs in public was seen as so outrageous, so sensitive, so rude that few teenagers dared mention them to anyone outside their peer group. Looking at erotic pictures was thought disgusting, even illegal, and books like *Lady Chatterley's Lover* were still banned. But above all it was the church that so dominated and controlled attitudes, as it had done for centuries, looking down on us with pious indignation and moral superiority.

Mary Stobbbard was fifteen when she had a back-street, knitting needle abortion out near Bankstown, urged on by some of the other girls from her school who 'knew' what they were talking about. Mary was easily persuaded, she was terrified of anyone finding out she was pregnant, especially the nuns. To his credit the child's father, Simon — who was only a few months older than me — went with her. Both of them wagged school for the day, and a few of us wagged as well so we could wave them off at the station — any excuse! Clinging to each other, they boarded the train, tears of anxiety streaming down her face, he, if anything, looking even more distressed. It was fortunate he was with her, however, because almost as soon as they came out of the 'clinic' Mary began to bleed heavily, and Simon said that if she'd had her way she would have just gone to a park and lain down. He took her to hospital and their sorry tale was out, it got into the local paper and a month or so later Mary and her family moved away, lives torn asunder by shame and guilt. For an organisation that espoused love, understanding and compassion, the church sure had a funny way of showing it — and still does.

It was almost as bad at school. There was no such thing as sex education, no discussion, no pictures of sexual organs or how they worked. We taught and explored ourselves in the playground or behind the cricket dressing sheds. The problem was that the web of 'unnatural' emotional difficulties surrounding sex not only confused and frightened people, but created the catalogue of myths, lies and nonsense that always fill the void left by suppression and ignorance.

Bob Stevenson was adamant you could catch syphilis from a doorknob; Barbara Kratz claimed girls could only get pregnant if they had a climax whilst having intercourse; and Eric Wilson said that masturbation stunted your growth and made your teeth go yellow. With no other advice or guidance, the Bobs, Barbaras and Erics of our world were the only source of information. We may not have always believed them, but we were never completely sure; after all, I was smaller for my age than most! Here we were, bursting free of the past with erotic music, outrageous fashion and a totally new perspective on life, yet in many ways we were as repressed, anxious and ignorant about sex as the Victorians had been. We didn't know then that our musical revolution was on the very cusp of setting off another earthquake, this time a sexual one.

The closest I'd come to a sexual encounter happened not long before Glen and I set off. When my father died, my stepmother was distraught. She was still only in her early thirties, and she found it extremely difficult to cope with the loss. By now I, too, was becoming extremely difficult to cope with, and I think things just got on top of her; so much so, that not many weeks after my father's funeral my stepmother set sail to visit her mother in England. My sister, who was five years older than me, had moved into a flat nearer the city some months previously, so suddenly here I was, living every young teenage boy's dream. No bossy parents or interfering older siblings, and a house to myself. Party time!

As might be imagined, things started to go a bit pear-shaped fairly quickly. Several of the older boys liked to play cards, and before I knew what was happening Friday and Saturday became poker nights around at Nick's place. The music got louder, the players got drunker, the neighbours got angrier and when Peter Thorndike caught Graham Salter cheating, the resulting fight smashed one of my stepmother's favourite vases and completely demolished the back flyscreen door. Then one night Dave Anderson's older brother turned up.

Paul Anderson was twelve years older than Dave. In fact, Dave had three siblings all much older than himself. Dave's mother used to say he was 'the mistake of the family', although if the truth be known it was Paul who was the mistake. Widely known as a bully and a thug, the rumours about him and his connections with gangsters and criminals were rife. He drove a black 1954 Rover saloon in which he used to cruise around Kings Cross most nights. One evening, a few weeks after my stepmother left, the Rover pulled into my driveway.

At the time I was working in an office in Sydney as a sort of errand boy. I didn't like the job much, and many days I wouldn't even turn up. Now Paul Anderson made me an offer that was hard to refuse, as they say. If I would allow poker games to be played in the house two or three nights a week, he would guarantee me five shillings a head for every player, plus any tips from the winners. He would organise everything, oversee the games and supply refreshments and so on. All I had to do was empty ashtrays and fetch beers. To begin with, it would only be five or six men, but he was sure the numbers would increase in time. Two or three quid, two or three times a week was twice the amount I was being paid. What was all the fuss about? Paul Anderson was a great bloke!

For a few months things went fantastically well. Some weeks I made as much as £25, and I strutted about like I imagined well-heeled casino operators did, buying new clothes, catching taxis everywhere, tipping the drivers and shouting the milk bar. Some nights a dozen or more men turned up, playing at two or three tables, which at times were weighed down with more money than I thought existed. Occasionally there would be a disagreement or argument, but Paul Anderson controlled things fairly rigidly and there was very little trouble, save from Mrs O'Halloran, our neighbour, complaining about the noise at three in the morning when the games usually finished. Then one night Paul turned up with a girl.

I knew Judy Laverton more by reputation than anything, although I had seen her around town from time to time. Her father had been killed in the war when she was only two or three years old, and she lived with her mother in a council house in Carlingford. I don't know what I expected but she was nothing like the gang-bang tart and slut many called her. Quiet and reserved, she had dark red hair, milky pale skin, freckles and a lovely smile. She reminded me of Pier Angeli the actress, and it was impossible to believe that anyone as beautiful as her could ever be involved in such behaviour. Not that

I'd ever met a gang-banger before; but gang-bang Judy did! I know Paul paid her a few bob to be available every card night. Any 'jobs' she got were her business, although I think she would have come for nothing.

For several weeks we sat on the back veranda together on game nights, smoking and chatting and listening to music as we waited for a call on our respective services. Then one night I asked her with boyish bluntness, "Do you like doing what you do, then?"

"Oh yes," she said unashamedly. "I love being with men. I just like being held in their arms," and she shrugged and gave me a funny little smile. Suddenly I was consumed with emotions I had never experienced before. Here I was, sixteen and completely inexperienced, and there was she, twenty-one and vastly experienced, yet I felt the positions were reversed. She was like a child and I found myself wanting to hold her in my arms, to protect her. Above all it was her smile that got to me. It seemed to say something that I couldn't explain or understand. We sat in silence for a bit, smoking and looking up at the stars, as if she was giving me time to come to terms with these new emotions; Ferlin Husky providing appropriate backing. (That can't possibly be his name! Surely!)

"On the wings of a snow white dove, he sends his pure sweet love ..."

Then Judy asked, "Have you ever done it?"

"Done what?"

"Made love."

"Well ... no."

"Would you like to? I won't charge you or anything, and I'll show you what to do. We could just do it as friends; that would be nice," and she put her hand gently on my knee.

"... a sign from above, on the wings of a dove ..."

"Jude!" Paul's voice shattered the magic moment. And then it struck me. Desperate loneliness, that's what her smile said.

Is it possible to fall in love in twenty minutes? I don't know. All I do know is that the next night I waited for Paul, and especially Judy, to arrive with great anticipation. But they didn't come, nor did they come the next night, or the next. Then, late in the afternoon a few days later a car did pull into the driveway, but it wasn't a black Rover.

For half an hour the two detectives grilled me, initially asking me about why I was there on my own, but their real interest lay with Paul Anderson. How long had I known him? When had I last seen him? Who had been with him? They wanted detailed descriptions of the other men and what make and colour cars they drove. At first I was a bit truculent, but the sergeant very quickly jumped on me. "Look, son, we don't want any bullshit. We know you know him. We know he's been coming here. Now just answer the questions." Satisfied I'd told them all I knew, the other detective went out to the car and returned with a fingerprint pad. "We just need to eliminate you," the sergeant said, grabbing my finger when I tried to object. Eliminate me from what?

"Where is your mother now?" he asked, just before they left, and he and his partner exchanged raised eyebrows when I told them. "Okay, now you listen to me, son! Paul Anderson and his mates are very unpleasant people. Get caught up with them and you're going to get into serious trouble ... understand me?"

"Yes, Sergeant."

"If he or any of them come here again, or get in touch with you, you ring us straight away, okay?"

"Yes, Sergeant." If it had been his intention to scare the shit out of me, he'd succeeded beyond my wildest nightmares.

Fortunately I never saw Paul Anderson again, although I missed the money. Two weeks later I learned from Dave that he and several of his gambling friends had been arrested for the armed robbery of a factory in Glebe some weeks earlier. The robbery had been on the news and in the papers. The factory made microscopes and other scientific equipment, and the thieves had got away with thousands of pounds' worth. Worse, they'd bashed a night-watchman over the head, and although he hadn't died he was badly wounded, so the charges were serious. Dave thought they were probably going to get at least six or seven years in gaol. Unfortunately I never saw Judy Laverton again, either. I missed her, too.

SIX
Jerky Joe and Kangaroo Point

*C*arlo told us trams didn't go over the Story Bridge, so our plan was to get off on the south side of the river at Woollongabba and walk over. As soon as we did, and I saw the sign to 'The Gabba', I knew I had to go and have a look. Glen wasn't so keen, but I was determined and reluctantly he followed me down Vulture Street. Just six months earlier one of the greatest test matches ever played had taken place at this ground, and by the last day the entire nation was riveted; the Melbourne Cup of cricket matches. Listening to the commentary of the thrilling and dramatic partnership between Benaud and Davidson, it felt like the destiny of the world rested on them surviving. Fantastic!

The tied test of 1960 was one of those events where, as Richie Benaud says, "The capacity of the ground could not have accommodated a fraction of the number of people who claimed to have been there." I wasn't, but I heard it all on the radio and I am certain I was just as excited and drained by it as those lucky enough to witness it. As we neared the ground I could feel my excitement rising, and I just knew I had to get inside somehow. There was obviously nothing on that day, and all the gates and doors on Vulture Street were firmly closed. We went around the block to the Stanley Street entrance, but still nothing. I tried to scale the fence at one point.

"For Christ's sake!" Glen pulled me back. "It's only a bloody cricket ground!" Retracing our steps, I was just beginning to despair when a man emerged from a gate opening on to Vulture

Street and he began replacing a poster advertising a forthcoming event on the wall.

"Excuse me!" I yelled, running up to him. "We've come from Sydney. Can we go inside to have a look, just for a minute? Please ... I just want to see the place!" There was obviously something in my breathless enthusiasm that appealed to him, and he grinned expansively. True cricket lovers always recognise one another.

"Of course you can, son," and he looked at his watch. "You've got twenty minutes, then I've got to be somewhere else," and he stood back and let us in. We walked around the dog track and sat in the iconic old stand on the western side of the ground, so often depicted in paintings and photographs with its distinctive red corrugated iron roof. I shut my eyes and could actually hear Alan McGilvray: *"Davidson taps his crease as Hall turns at the Stanley Street end, shirt billowing as he thunders in once more."* When I opened my eyes, I imagined I could see Sobers scoring his fantastic, fast and elegant century and big Norm O'Neill clubbing his way to his grinding century, refusing to be intimidated by the thunderbolts of Hall and Griffiths. Suddenly I found tears welling up behind my eyes and I could see someone else, my father, whose love of the game I had inherited. In fact, one of my last memories of him was listening to the broadcast on that final day with him, his excitement matching my own. And then another image came vividly to me.

In 1954 I had my second memorable encounter with a person who made me all too aware I was a Pom, and as such was viewed as, well, a Pom. I'd arrived in Australia in 1947 so I didn't feel like a Pom, talk like one, or even think like one. Arthur Morris and *Snugglepot and Cuddlepie* were my heroes, and I knew all the words of *My Country*.

My father had taken me to the Sydney Cricket Ground for the second day of the second Ashes Test. He was walking with the aid of crutches at the time, and the most comfortable place for him to sit was on the hill. It was a lovely hot day, the crowd buzzing with expectation, and I was beside myself with excitement as we entered the ground, dragging him around to the hill, frustrated he was so slow. England had lost the first test by a mile at 'The Gabba' a few weeks before, and they'd been bowled out on the first day of this second one for a derisory score. The stage was set.

Arthur Morris came out to open the innings, bristling with nuggety determination and the crowd roared. "That's Arthur Morris, Daddy! That's Arthur Morris!" Frank 'Typhoon' Tyson was the world's fastest bowler, the atmosphere was electric and I wanted to go to the toilet. Tyson was bowling from the M.A. Noble end, beginning his run almost back at the fence, and it seemed to take an age for him to tediously plod back there after each ball.

"Get on with it, ya mug!" bawled a shirtless man sitting on the grass not far from us, as Tyson made his way back for the third or fourth ball.

"Yeah," quipped his mate, "we're only here for the bloody day!" The hill convulsed with laughter.

Hero Arthur survived the ferocious over, Tyson hurtling in and sending down balls so fast the naked eye could barely see them, many of them forcing Morris to duck and weave. The last ball, however, he deftly, almost disdainfully flicked off his legs for two runs and virtually the entire ground stood to applaud and cheer, and the hill went delirious. It was spine-tingling stuff. "Good on yer, Arthur! Give it to the bastards!" bellowed our shirtless neighbour.

The over finished, Tyson came slowly down towards the hill to field at long off, his face crimson with effort, his chest heaving as he mopped his brow with a handkerchief, seemingly oblivious to the jeers and hoots accompanying him.

"Thought you was supposed to be fast, Tyson!" Shirtless yelled mockingly.

"Yeah!" chimed in his mate. "My mother could have faced that over, and she's been dead for a month!" The hill erupted again. So did my father.

Hefting himself to his feet as fast as his legs would allow, he raised his arms above his head and applauded vigorously, his crutches clattering to the ground behind him. "Well bowled, Mister Tyson! Well bowled, sir!"

The hill erupted even more vigorously. "Siddown, ya Pommie bastard!" and my father, roundly booed and hissed, slumped to the ground again. Of course he was as big a hero to me as Arthur Morris, but Arthur was an Aussie to his bootstraps, my father an Englishman to his socks; and I didn't know where to look.

Initially the reaction was just good-natured banter, but then Shirtless suddenly came barging through the crowd towards us and things became much more tense and ugly. Screaming obscenities at my father, the shirtless man's face was contorted with rage and hatred. I had never seen such vicious anger before and I was truly frightened, as I'm sure my father must have been, although he stayed remarkably calm. I don't know if it was the sight of the crutches or because others intervened, but the man stopped several yards from us, chest heaving, and he pointed his finger at my father. "You keep your fucking Pommie mouth shut, arsehole! If I hear you again I'm goin' ta do you, crutches or no fucking crutches!"

Despite most of the people around us being rampant Aussie supporters they objected to the man's attitude as much as we did, and told him to shut up and told us not to take any notice of him. We tried not to, but it was difficult and the rest of the day's play we watched more or less in silence, Shirtless glaring at us from time to time. As it happened England went on to win that test, so I suppose it was fortunate that we didn't go any more days.

"Why did that man hate you so much, Daddy?" I asked, going home on the train.

"Oh, I expect he had his reasons," my father sighed gently, giving me a reassuring smile. "It isn't me he hates. A lot of terrible things happen in wars, and some people find it hard to ever forgive and forget."

I may not have fully understood what he meant, but it was the first awareness I had of what I would come to learn my father was: a man of great humility, compassion and understanding.

*   *   *

"What's the matter?" Glen's concerned enquiry brought me back to the moment and quickly I looked away, wiping the tears from my cheeks. "Nothing."

"It doesn't look like nothing."

"Well it bloody is, alright! Come on, let's get out of here."

"I didn't want to come in the first place, remember?"

"Get stuffed."

"No. You get stuffed! Getting all shitty, what's the matter with you?"

"Nothing!"

"Oh, put another record on, will you!"

We didn't talk again until we got to the road that ran across the Story Bridge. It was early evening, with rush hour traffic filing by and the streetlights had come on. Rucksacks would have to wait until morning. It was also beginning to drizzle, so we needed to find somewhere to stay for the night. We stopped on the corner for a moment to get our bearings, and could see the Story Bridge in the distance to our right. Then from an alley beside some shops to our left a scruffy looking man emerged and came shuffling down the footpath towards us, other pedestrians giving him a wide birth.

He was wearing a pair of battered check slippers, a woollen beanie riddled with holes and an old army greatcoat, covered in grime and stains. The collar of his shirt and the bottoms of his trousers were frayed, tattered and filthy dirty, and as he got nearer the smell got stronger; close up, it was overpowering.

"Gidday, boys. 'Ow youse goin'?" He wheezed. "Where youse from? Not from round 'ere are ya, eh?" He answered himself. "No. Not from round 'ere, I'll bet ya." And he grinned, exposing about five rotting teeth through his straggly beard. Every now and then his left shoulder twitched and his head gave a little involuntary sideways jerk, as if he'd been given a mild electric shock or something. His hands, when not tugging anxiously at the lapels of his coat, trembled uncontrollably and his fingers and moustache were stained nicotine brown. "Travellin', are yer, travellin'. Thought so, yeah, thought so." He answered himself again. "I can tell, see. Wouldn't have a cigarette, would ya. Just one, or a couple would be good, yeah, yeah, a couple would be fine."

It happens naturally with all relationships, I suppose, but without any discussion or planning Glen and I had each assumed certain roles and responsibilities in our day-to-day living. I was more or less in charge of communication, dealing with the public, police etc. while Glen, being a bit more circumspect and careful, was the treasurer and guardian of the goodies. I was therefore a little surprised when he put his kit bag down, took out Mr Molinari's little canvas bag and gave the man a whole packet. "You can have them," he said. The man was so surprised at such a windfall he hardly knew what to say.

"Well! Thanks boys, thanks, thanks! Yeah, yeah, yeah, I got matches, I got matches," he said hurriedly, as if embarrassed by such generosity, and he dug about in his coat pockets with frenzied urgency until he found them. Hands trembling, he ripped open the packet and lit a cigarette, sucking in the smoke like a drowning man suddenly able to breathe again. "You're good boys, I can see that. Yeah, I can see that. Got somewhere to go tonight, have youse? Got somewhere dry? Gonna' be a wet one. Gonna' be a wet one."

"Well ... not exactly, we were going to go over the bridge and find the Salvos ..."

"Salvation Army!" he hissed, spittle flying from his mouth. "Youse don't wanna go there! Nah, get robbed there, ya will. I knows a good place, good place. Nice and dry. Warm, too, got a fire. It's just down there, just down there," and he pointed towards the bridge and made to set off as if leading us there.

Giving him the cigarettes had obviously been some sort of declaration of love on our part, and it was even more obvious we were not going to get rid of him easily. On the other side of the road the neon lights of a cafe winked at us, and on the spur of the moment I nodded at it, saying, "We're going to have something to eat first, mate."

"Oh yeah, yeah, young boys, need yer tucker, need yer tucker," and he followed us across the road and right up to the door of the cafe, so close that it was almost impossible to go in without at least offering to buy him something to eat.

"No boys, no. Don't want nuthin' to eat, nuthin' to eat. Just give us a couple of bob and I'll go down there, down there," and he pointed to a hotel further down the road. Before I could say anything, Glen delved into his pocket and gave the man two shillings. This time I wasn't too sure who was the most amazed, the old bum or me.

"Bit generous, aren't you!" I said, as we ordered steak and chips.

"My mum says, 'when someone's kind to you, you be kind to someone else'." Glen shrugged. "That's how the world goes around, and besides the poor bastard needs it more than we do." I couldn't really argue with that.

This encounter was not a new experience for me, as I suspect it was for Glen. In Sydney, winos and homeless vagrants were common in many of the parks, and some nights in Green Park dozens of them might congregate until they became a nuisance and the police moved them on or arrested them. Some Saturday afternoons, if there was nothing to do, I used to go into town and play chess with them. There was a huge chess board in Hyde Park made out of black and white, two-foot square paving stones; the balsa wood pawns were two feet tall, and having made a move, the player would stand to one side while his opponent stalked around the board, contemplating his response. Often games drew quite large audiences, with people bringing their own chairs and ringing the board. My father had taught me to play when I was quite young, and by the age of fourteen I was a reasonably good player, but there were two or three of those drunken old vagrants I could never beat. The first time I went I was only twelve and the kings and queens were almost as tall as I was, but I suppose because I took it seriously they put up with me. If it taught me anything, it was never to judge their ability, or their intelligence, by their scruffy appearance.

To our relief, when we emerged from the cafe, Jerky Joe, as Glen had christened him, was nowhere to be seen and we set off towards the Story Bridge, only to hear a voice call out behind us.

"Wait up, boys, wait up, wait up!"

Shit!

There was nothing for it but to follow our new friend. Besides, it was beginning to rain quite heavily now and he had said his place was dry. We followed him for what seemed ages down a series of dingy, seedy-looking lanes, and at one stage he ducked into a dark alley and a little hesitantly we followed. About fifty yards down the alley he stopped beside a pile covered in an old piece of tarp. Lifting the tarp, he revealed a dozen or more six-foot-long hardwood fencing posts, and he gruntingly urged us to pick up three or four each while he wrapped the remainder in the tarp. "Good boys, good boys," he wheezed. "This'll keep us goin' all night." We set off again, and eventually came out in the park under the bridge at the end of Kangaroo Point; that narrow thumb of land clamped on three sides by the sweeping bend in the Brisbane River. A grassed area sloped down to the banks, but the dominant features were the two huge pylons supporting the bridge, one near where we'd emerged, the other about sixty yards down the slope, nearer the river. There were no streetlights or anything, but the lighting from the bridge itself — towering a hundred feet above us — combined with the lights of the city on the opposite bank, lit the area up sufficiently to see quite well. Each pylon was in the shape of a large archway, a bit like the Arc de Triomphe, and under the nearer one five men were gathered round a brazier, flames licking from the top of it. All of the men turned and stared at us when we appeared. "It's okay," said Jerky, seeing us hesitate. "Youse have got wood, you'll be okay," and he led us over to the fire.

"These boys is okay," he addressed one man in particular as we approached. "Got some wood, see." To varying degrees they were all as unkempt and dirty as Jerky, and although they didn't look all that happy to see us, none of them said anything; nor were there any introductions, no names exchanged.

"Where youse from," the man Jerky had spoken to demanded after we'd put the wood down beside the fire, as we'd seen Jerky do. He was older than the others, yet somehow he looked more alert, his eyes not quite so vacant.

"Sydney."

"Humph," he said, taking a swig from a bottle wrapped in a brown paper bag. "What are you doin' 'ere?"

"Just passing through. We're heading for Magnetic Island."

"Humph!" he grunted again, and then totally ignored us, as did the other men, and for what seemed ages nobody said anything; it was just becoming uncomfortable when Jerky pulled a bottle out of his coat pocket and offered it to us. "Have a drink, boys, have a drink."

"No thanks," I said.

"You don't drink, you don't stay here," said the older man, and he glared at me, his eyes hard and uncompromising.

"Best youse have a sip, boys," Jerky encouraged, nodding his head knowingly, and again he offered us the bottle. "It's pretty good stuff, pretty good stuff."

Now the other four men were also watching us, as if daring us to defy the older man. By now it was teeming down, the wind blowing the rain in under the bridge from time to time. The fire was nice and warm, and under the arch it was bone dry; it was obvious we could have a reasonably comfortable night here, there didn't seem much choice in the matter, so I took the bottle and gingerly had a sip.

To my surprise Jerky was right, it was 'pretty good stuff' — sweet, smooth and warm in the stomach. We discovered later that it was port, and although drinking it didn't instantly make us all the best of mates, the hostile atmosphere eased a little.

"Go get the cardboard," the older man said to nobody in particular a few moments later. Without a murmur, Jerky and another man went around behind the pylon and emerged carrying several, six foot by two foot lengths of thick cardboard. These they gave to the old man, who sat on one and handed one each to the other men, who sat down on them to form a ring around the fire. "You two sit over there," he commanded, pointing to an area a few yards just outside their ring.

"Why?"

"Because I told you to go over there. You don't like it, you don't have to stay," and he took another swig from his bottle and looked away, expecting his orders to be obeyed. Again Jerky Joe sort of came to our rescue, shuffling across. "Here's a good spot boys, good spot," he enthused, scraping the ground near the sides of the pylon with his slipper. "Youse can sleep here, no worries." So we spread out the ground sheets we got from 'Uncle' Alf when we first set out and we sat down. It seemed the sensible thing to do. A few minutes later another scruffy, unkempt figure emerged from the direction we'd come from and stood looking at the group.

"Couldn't find no wood," he said, clasping his coat.

"Too bad," the old man snapped. "You know the rules — fuck off!"

For about an hour we sat there, smoking and sipping port, not daring to do otherwise really. Glen and I were getting very little benefit from the fire ten yards away, and eventually, courage no doubt emboldened by the port, we picked up our ground sheets and moved them closer. "We did bring some wood!" I countered the old man's glare, and to my relief he didn't say anything and Jerky winked as he handed us the bottle again. There wasn't a great deal of conversation, more like occasional mutterings, and at one stage two of the men exchanged sharp words about something but it didn't last long after the old man glared at them. He dictated just about everything that went on around the brazier; only he stoked the fire, and he made sure everybody was stoked with port, bottles of which appeared as if magically from various coat pockets; firewood and port were obviously the keys of entry to this club. Then one of the men began to sing quietly.

"My Bonnie lies over the ocean, my Bonnie lies over the sea ..."

None of the others joined in, and for what seemed like ages he sang the song, over and over again in a surprisingly melodic, soporific deep voice. Warm fire, port and a lilting lullaby, we were nodding off to sleep. Then the singer was interrupted by the sound of loud voices coming from down near the waterfront. Getting louder and louder, a group of about eight Aborigines appeared under the pylon below us. They were all drunk and engaged in a monumental argument which raged for about ten minutes before, one at a time, they slumped to the ground and sat in a bad-tempered circle, shouting and yelling at each other even as they passed bottles of beer about.

It was illegal to supply Aboriginals with alcohol; they weren't allowed into pubs, and only a few years before the famous artist Albert Namatjira had been sent to prison for giving alcohol to his own family, so where they'd got their beer from was anyone's guess. They took no notice of our group sitting by the fire sixty yards away.

It was as if we weren't there at all, and other than looking down every so often when their voices were raised, we totally ignored them. It was surreal; sitting under an enormous structure, a group of black drunks arguing and squabbling, totally ignoring a group of silent, dishevelled white drunks sixty yards away, the fire flickering in their bedraggled, gaunt faces. *"Oh bring back, bring back, bring back my Bonnie to me, to me. Bring back, bring ..."*

Suddenly the old man turned to us and demanded, "You blokes ever had a fuck before?" For several moments nobody said a thing, least of all Glen and myself. We were so stunned we could only stare stupidly at him, the strains of *Bonnie* fading away.

"Didn't think so," he said, nodding to himself. "Hey, Alice!" he shouted down to the Aborigines, a smile now playing round his lips. "Couple of young virgins up 'ere, never done it before, got a bottle of port, yours if you want to show 'em a good time!" The silence that followed this was excruciating, to put it mildly, and both Glen and I were struck dumb with embarrassment.

"Guess they're not interested, Alice!" the old man shouted again, and the others all chuckled and chortled at our discomfort, including Jerky, although he was a little more sympathetic and came over, offering us the bottle again.

"Wot's the matta, white boy!" a shrill voice rent the night. "Think black sheilas is no good, eh!"

Looking down, we could see an Aboriginal woman had detached herself from the group and come about a quarter of the way up the slope towards us. Suddenly she lifted up her dress, not that we could see anything as she was blacker than the night.

"See!" she shouted. "We ain't no different to no white sheila," and she let her dress fall down and turned back to the group, all of whom were now chuckling. Then Alice shrieked out, "We's all pink inside, white boy! We's all pink inside!"

At this, everybody under the bridge except Glen and I fell about with laughter, with Alice's shrill cackle reverberating around the metal girders of the bridge. Never had a bottle of port been so comforting.

Half an hour later, both groups had settled down and were once again studiously ignoring each other. Glen and I were just beginning to doze off when the lights of a vehicle splashed onto the grass and a paddy wagon, followed by a police car, came speeding down the track, past us and straight across the grass to the Aborigines, many of whom had by now flaked out and were asleep in the dirt.

"Don't worry," Jerky held out his hand, motioning for us not to move. "They ain't come for us." One or two Aborigines were awake, including Alice, and she ran from the scene shouting obscenities as the police vehicles skidded to a halt. Alerted by her, the others began to stagger to their feet but were too slow and no match for the four or five policemen who leapt from the vehicles, batons raining down indiscriminately. It was all over in minutes and half a dozen Aboriginals, yelping as they were hit and prodded with batons, were bundled unceremoniously into the back of the wagon. The little convoy left far more sedately than they'd arrived, driving slowly back up the hill and seemingly not the slightest bit interested in us. They passed by only yards from our fire and both Glen and I detected just the slightest nod from the sergeant in the passenger's seat, the old man acknowledging him with an even slighter flick of his finger. "Same every night, same every night," said Jerky, handing us the bottle again. "Them black fellas never learn."

It was the traffic noise that woke us, and we sat up gingerly, holding our heads. "Jesus, I feel awful!" Glen moaned. After the police left we'd had a few more swigs of port and neither of us could actually remember much after that, although I did recall getting up in the night and vomiting copiously into the bushes behind the pylon. The sun was shining brightly and the roar of morning traffic filled the air but the place was deserted, even the brazier and the sheets of cardboard were nowhere to be seen. Spotting a tap down by one of the park benches, I went stumbling down to it; I'd just put my head under when I heard Glen let out a cry of anguish, and looking up could see him flinging stuff out of his kit bag.

"It's gone! The fucking thing's gone!"

"What's gone?"

"The bag! The bloody bag and all our money!"

For ten minutes we searched our bags and rifled frantically through each other's clothes and pockets, unable to believe it had happened.

"It's that fucking Jerky bloke! "

"I reckon it's more likely the old man," said Glen.

"Does it matter? Come on, we might catch up with the bastards!" And quickly we stuffed everything back into our kit bags and retraced our footsteps of the night before, running up lanes and down alleys. Finally we emerged breathless onto the road leading over the bridge and stood for a second contemplating which way to go; then I saw the police car.

"Hey!" I yelled, and rushed out into the traffic in front of it, waving them down. "We've been robbed! We've been robbed!"

Looking anxiously in his mirror, the driver was forced to pull up quickly and angrily he wound down his window. "What the hell are you doing, you stupid bastard! Get off the road and go and stand over there!" And he swung the wheel hard and pulled the car to the side. His mate was getting out and putting on his cap as I got there.

"What's your name?"

"Nick. We've been robbed! We were sleeping under the brid ..."

"Full name!"

"Nick Thomas ... what the fuck does that matter! We've been robbed!"

"Yeah, I heard you the first time, son," the policeman said. "Now just calm down and don't swear at me again."

At this point Glen, who'd been left standing on the other side of the road when I darted out, came running over in time to hear me say, "I'm not bloody well swearing at you, we've been robbed!" By now the second policeman was also out of the car, and suddenly I found myself being shoved hard up against the side of it. "You were told not to swear any more. Now you shut your mouth! What happened?" He turned to Glen.

"He's right, we were robbed," said Glen.

"And what's your name?"

"Glen Olsen."

"Who robbed you?"

"We're not sure but there were some old drunks and some Abos, under the bridge ... we were sleeping ..."

"Some old drunks and some Abos! Got any names?"

"Well ... no, they didn't tell us ... but ... it couldn't have been the Abos ... your blokes must have seen us when you picked them up!"

"What did they steal?" asked the first cop, ignoring Glen's comments.

"All our money and cigarettes, they were in a little black bag in here." Glen indicated his kit bag.

"What time was this?"

"I don't know, last night some time, after you picked up the Abos."

"How much money?"

"Six pounds and four packets of cigarettes."

"Why were you under the bridge? Where do you live?"

While Glen explained our circumstances I was left beside the police car, getting more and more exasperated. What did they want to know all this crap for! We'd been robbed!

"So, let's get this straight. You were robbed under the bridge some time last night, but you don't know when, by some drunks whose names you don't know?"

"But one of them was really distinctive," said Glen, getting agitated himself now. "He had a really old Army greatcoat and a beanie with holes in it, and his head jerked a lot … and there was an older man who seemed to be the boss," he added.

"So, what do you want us to do about it?" the policeman asked, and I could hardly believe I'd heard him and pushed myself off the police car.

"What do you mean, what do we want? You're bloody policemen, aren't you. We just want our bloody money back!"

This time I was flung against the side of the car, the policeman's forearm pressing into my neck, forcing me back. "I told you not to swear any more. Now you listen to me, both of you. We'll make some enquiries, but … !" And he pressed his arm into my neck again, sensing I was about to say something else, which I was. "The chances of finding your money are about as slim as finding a polite teenager!" And saying that, he grabbed my chin in his hand and vigorously shook my head. "You with me!" Satisfied I was subdued; he eased off the pressure a little but kept his forearm leaning on my chest. "We've got a fair idea who it might be, but by now he'll have got rid of all the money and probably sold the cigarettes to his mates. It will just be your word against theirs, and there's no way in the world you'll get any of it back, or even prove it was stolen, so if I were you boys I'd forget it, put it down to experience. You shouldn't have been sleeping down there anyway." Again I was about to object, but he simply pressed on my chest. "There is nothing we can do!" That this was the last word on the subject was obvious by the black look on his face, inches from mine, so I slumped back, defeated and dejected. "Now I suggest you go home or find somewhere decent to sleep. Either way, I don't want to catch you hanging round these parts again, understood?"

"Piss off, you arseholes!" I yelled at the departing police car; but if I was frustrated and annoyed, Glen was almost in tears. I'd never seen him so angry, and suddenly he exploded.

"Shit! Shit! Shit!" He kicked his kit bag so hard it flew about ten yards across the pavement, pedestrians having to leap out of its way. "Why are you always so fucking lippy!" he yelled at me. "If you hadn't mouthed off they might have helped us!"

"That's fucking rich! We wouldn't have needed any bloody help if you hadn't shown your jerky mate our bag!"

"He's not my mate!"

"Well, it looked like it, giving him cigarettes and money!"

"Oh! So it's my fault, is it?"

"I didn't say that!"

"Yes, you did!"

"No, I didn't! But you did show him the fucking bag; he could probably see everything that was in it!"

"Well you can piss off too, if that's what you think!"

"Yeah, well I just might!"

"Good! Tell you what," he added, glaring at me and delving into his pockets. "Here's half the money left, now why don't you just fuck off!"

"Okay!" I yelled back. "I fucking will!" And I snatched up my kit bag, pausing long enough to pull out the frying pan. "I won't be needing this fucking thing!" And flinging it down, I marched across to the southbound side of the road and we stood opposite each other shouting obscenities across the traffic.

"Stupid prick!"

"Arsehole!"

Forty minutes later, we were still standing there. It was towards the end of morning rush hour, the hitchhiker's nightmare time and everybody ignored our outstretched thumbs. After a while we calmed down a bit but continued to glare at each other, neither wanting to be the first either to get a lift or give in. The whole time the frying pan stayed on the ground where I'd flung it, Glen refusing to look at it, much less pick it up, as if somehow even to acknowledge it would be a sign of weakness. Then a semi-trailer pulled up in front of him and all I could see were his feet moving across to the cab door until a tram rattled past in front of me, and for half a minute or so I couldn't see the other side of the road at all. When the tram went by the truck had gone but Glen was still standing there. "Do you really want to go home?" he shouted.

Dodging the traffic, I ran back across the road.

We didn't speak, there were no apologies or handshakes; Glen just pulled the plates and mugs out of his kit bag and gave them to me, then he bent down and picked up the frying pan. "I'll carry this for a bit if you like."

We walked across Story Bridge in silence, and jumped on the first tram heading north and made it all the way to Chermside before we had to run for it, whooping with glee, the conductor shouting abuse behind us. It was the first time Glen had ever done anything like that and he obviously enjoyed it, quickly mastering the art of constantly but casually moving about the tram to avoid the conductor without drawing attention to himself. When we finally stopped running and sat down on a bench in a park we were breathless and flushed with the excitement that being naughty brings. Bloody cops! We'd show them!

We were now in the northern outskirts of Brisbane, and getting a good lift was much more likely so we sorted ourselves out a bit and devised a plan of action. Fortunately Glen had kept the change from the meal the previous night and I had a few bob in my pocket, so we still had about eighteen shillings, a fortune a few weeks before, so financially we were okay; as for food, all we had to do was get out of the city to a police station in some country town up ahead and get another voucher. Thinking of food, we both suddenly realised we hadn't eaten since the previous night so we tucked into mamma's wonderful sandwiches and cold pizza. As for the plan of action, it was the same plan as before; head for Magnetic Island, only now getting there had suddenly become much more important, a hurdle we were both determined to get over for our own satisfaction and self-esteem; not that we said so to each other.

Dumping my kit bag down after escaping from the tram, I'd noticed one of the seams was beginning to part and it reminded me of Francesco and Carlo's plan for us. "I guess we've got to forget about rucksacks for a bit," I said, as much to myself as anything.

"But mousie, thou art no thy lane
In proving foresight may be vain.
The best laid schemes o'mice an' men
Gang aft a-gley
An' lea' us nought but grief a' pain
For promised joy!"

"What!"

"Me mum's Scottish," said Glen, grinning and getting up. "She used to read Robbie Burns to me every night. Come on, let's go to Magnetic Island!"

Just when you think you know somebody!

SEVEN

Grandfather, mountain retreats, Mr Willard and bloody Gympie.

When my parents first split up, our mother took us to live with her parents who managed a pineapple plantation just outside Nambour. They farmed a dozen or so acres of their own, and ran a few sheep with the help of their lovely kelpie dog, Koorie. There were watermelons, persimmons and mangoes, and sometimes I ate so much pineapple my mouth hurt. There were chickens and geese and an old ram called Henry, whose job it was to keep the grass short around the house. My sister and I often tried to ride him, but like most rams he was erratically bad-tempered which didn't help but if you've ever tried to ride a sheep you will know how difficult it is, even if it's good-tempered. Their fleece wobbles about so much it is almost impossible to stay on.

Much of the work around the farm was still done manually and Cobber, my grandfather's mighty old draft horse, worked tirelessly pulling sled loads of pineapples at harvest time. He was a wonderfully good-natured old horse with big, sad eyes, and I loved him dearly and spent many hours riding on him. When my father first read me *Animal Farm* a few years later, I imagined Boxer was Cobber's father. He was so big I had to stand on packing cases if I wanted to get on him. But he just stood there, solid and island-like, patiently waiting for me to clamber up and ignoring the fact that I was almost pulling his mane out.

My grandfather, although kind enough, was a fairly blunt,

uncompromising sort of man. A stickler for protocol and table manners, he always dressed for dinner and shouted at anyone who was late, including our poor grandmother, and woe betide anyone who spoke with their mouth full. A New Zealander, he taught my sister and me to fish and swim in the Maroochy River, which in my case consisted of strapping two sealed-up biscuit tins around my chest and chucking me in. Gruff and stern he may have been, but from him we gained an insight and knowledge of agriculture, animals and nature we might never have got living in the city, even if in my case it was perhaps more a subconscious insight. I was only four and five years old at the time so I don't remember a lot, but I do remember going into the chicken coop to feed the chickens; I didn't have a shirt on and suddenly the rooster, for some reason taking a dislike to my presence, came screeching down from his perch, landing on my back. I've still got the scars to prove it. I ran screaming from the coop, leaving the gate open and all the chickens got out.

Another vivid memory is of sitting on the dunny one day, legs swinging freely as I couldn't touch the floor. Our grandfather had built the entire thing himself, dug the huge hole and made the wooden bench that covered it, and the wooden, hinged toilet seat in the middle that I was sitting on. Above my head was a shelf, and looking up I noticed a large cardboard box; somehow, by standing on the bench and reaching on my tiptoes, I managed to knock the box down and in it discovered three-dozen toilet rolls. Then I had an idea. For half an hour, holding the end of the roll, I let each one spiral down into the smelly depths. When it hit the bottom I tucked the end of it neatly under the toilet seat to hold it in place, and then let down another roll. By the time I'd finished it looked like an inverted white maypole, much prettier than a black hole. I was very proud of it. My grandfather was not amused.

I remember, too, him plucking chickens and the pungent smell when he dunked them in boiling water first. The most memorable bit, though, was when he chopped their heads off with an axe. My sister and I watched in amazed fascination as they ran about — just like headless chickens! It still amazes me. "Can we do another one, Grandpa! Can we do another one?"

* * *

"Bullshit!" said Glen.

"No it's not. Fair dinkum, they used to run around with no head!" But no matter how hard I tried to convince him, I don't think Glen ever believed me. City kids rarely see such sights, and it is hard to believe such a thing if you haven't seen it. It was three nights since we'd left Brisbane, and we were sitting beside our raging campfire on the top of one of the Glasshouse Mountains — those strangely shaped rocky outcrops Captain Cook named as he passed by all those years before. They were more like big rocky hills than mountains, but it was a great place to camp with a fantastic view and we imagined we were there two hundred years earlier and could see his ship passing way out to sea. We could also see the towns of Maroochydore and Mooloolaba in the distance, and the town of Nambour wasn't far away.

From Brisbane we'd got a lift with a Buttercup Bread delivery van taking a load of bread to Caboolture. There we'd gone straight to the police station, but found it was shut. In the general store they told us the local cop was off sick, and that if we wanted a policeman we should go to Nambour. Glen thought that's what we should do to conserve our funds, but I disagreed. I wanted to buy some food now, so we could go and see the Glasshouse Mountains. I was determined we should at least try and see some of the sights Francesca had mentioned. We were discussing it fairly heatedly when the Buttercup man came out of the store. We had already told him of our adventures in Brisbane, and when we mentioned the Glasshouse

Mountains he immediately became very animated. "Oh yeah, you'll like it up there, used to camp up there meself, sausages over the fire, camping under the stars, ya can't beat it, great views too. Tell you what; I got a delivery to make in Beerwah. I can take you there. Some of the mountains is fairly steep so you might want to stay a few days. I can give you a couple of loaves of bread, buy some sausages and beans and you'll be laughing." That settled it, Fires, sausages and camping under stars have always attracted young boys, and by the time the Buttercup man finished talking even Glen was raring to go. We had plenty of tea and sugar left so we bought half a dozen eggs, two pounds of sausages, a few tins of beans and potatoes, four large tins of fruit, a packet of Cornflakes, two tins of condensed milk, some broken biscuits, a few bags of sweets and two packets of cigarettes. The whole lot only cost us about fifteen shillings, which still left us with three or four bob ... she'll be right mate.

In the end we camped up there for four nights, and only came down because we ran out of food.

The biggest problem was water, although after Southport, when we'd got so thirsty, we had found a couple of old screw-cap lemonade bottles and filled them with water, making sure we refilled them at every opportunity. The water didn't last long with cooking and everything, so we devised a routine where we would go down the hillside early in the morning, have a wash in the creek and fill up the bottles and our billy. The return trip from the top to the bottom took us about two and a half hours, one hour down and an hour and half back up. But we barely noticed it, pretending we were early explorers — Glen was Leichhardt and I was Mitchell. We were back playing cowboys and Indians along the banks of the creek at the bottom of my garden in Epping. Sometimes in the summer holidays we were allowed to camp down there, building a shelter from branches and leaves like Robinson Crusoe. Now we did the same, only this time it was for real.

There were plenty of signs that others had camped up here before us, and on the first afternoon we discovered the remains of a makeshift shelter, tucked in under an overhanging rock. A few more branches and palm leaves on the roof, some ferns and leaves on the ground to make the bed more comfortable, a roaring fire at the entrance and hey presto, we had a nice, cosy camp. Luckily it only drizzled briefly on a couple of nights, but we liked to think we would have stayed dry even if it had poured. We spent the days exploring and climbing about our mountain retreat, and although we had seen many of the animals before it was the first time either of us had really been close up with them, living in their own environment. Rock wallabies and goannas, carpet snakes and black cockatoos and at night we fed the possums and bandicoots that came to explore our camp. We were two excited boys on holiday discovering something new each day. It was only hunger that drove us down on the fourth day. We hadn't realised how far it was back to the highway, and it took us most of the day to get there, by which time it was nearly dark and the little village of Beerwah was quiet and deserted with nothing open. Not since the first night had we hitched at night, but now hunger forced the issue and we realised we had to at least try and get to the next town so we wrote 'Magnetic Island' on the inside of the Cornflakes packet and stuck it out, stomachs rumbling.

Much to our delight, the first car that came along a few minutes later stopped and the driver leaned across and opened the passenger window. "I can take you to Gladstone, will that do?"

Gladstone! Wow! That would be the best lift we'd had for days. Would it do? We almost ripped the doors off!

"One in the front, one in the back, please." The driver held his hand up, seeing we were both about to pile into the front bench seat with him. "And don't slam the doors!"

The car was a Triumph Mayflower, the poor man's Rolls some

called them, although we called them butterboxes because of their peculiar square shape.

Inside it was immaculately clean and tidy; the mahogany dash positively glowing under the interior lights, and the leather seats smelled and looked like they too had only just been polished. Turning the radio down so you could only just hear it, the driver offered me his hand as I got in. "I'm Mr Willard," and he turned and nodded a greeting to Glen. "Can you put your bags on the floor, please." When he was happy things were organised just how he wanted them, he engaged the gears with great care and slowly set off, gripping the wheel with both hands, shoulders hunched.

As everybody over twenty-three looked old to me, I had no idea what age Mr Willard was, but reckoned he must have been at least fifty. He had grey hair, glasses and was wearing a woollen cardigan; in fact he looked just like someone would who owned an immaculate Triumph Mayflower and drove it with pedantic caution. All he lacked was a hat. Whenever a vehicle travelling in the other direction came into sight he would slow down. On one corner he almost came to a complete standstill. Then he suddenly turned the radio up. "Oh! I quite like this one."

"I looked into the muddy water and what could I see? I saw a lonely, lonely face lookin' back at me. Tears in his eyes and a prayer on his lips; and the glove of his lost love at his fingertips. Moody river ..."

Back at Theo's milk bar, if a boy put a Pat Boon record on the jukebox he got stuff chucked at him. If a girl played him, we all pretended to vomit. I glanced back at Glen with an open-eyed grimace, only to find him hiding behind the driver's seat, crossing his eyes and pulling a grotesque face; it was all I could do to stop myself bursting into laughter. But the dulcet tones of Pat seemed to calm Mr Willard and gradually he began to relax, as if the further he went the more confident he became. He didn't say much himself, but Glen and I ... well, mostly me, relieved and excited to at last be getting somewhere, regaled him with our story. Other than the fact he was going to Gladstone, we learned nothing more about him. Then Glen yawned and lay down on the seat, causing Mr Willard to look back quickly, and for a moment I thought he was going to tell him off, but he just smiled and asked "Tired?"

"Yeah." Glen yawned again. "Been a long day." We drove on for a bit in silence, and I began to feel myself nodding off.

"Tell you what," Mr Willard's voice broke through the fuzz, I wasn't sure how long later. "How does a mixed grill and a night in a comfy bed sound? I'll pay."

"What?"

"A proper bed for the night and a good meal," he repeated. "I was going to try and get to Maryborough tonight, but I'm getting a bit tired myself."

"Gee, that sounds great!" Glen piped up from the back. "I'm starving!"

"Fine," said Mr Willard. "There's a motel with a diner in Nambour. We'll pull in there." And then he put his hand on my leg and gently squeezed my upper thigh. "We might even have some ice cream, how about that!" he smiled, his hand giving my leg a final little squeeze before returning to the wheel.

I may not have yet discovered the mysterious delights girls had at the tops of their legs, but I had discovered the goings on at the tops of my legs whenever I imagined the tops of Denise Phillips' legs. So I suppose I knew I wasn't a poofter, although I wasn't entirely sure what poofters did or were, other than they liked other poofters. Barry Wiley, on the other hand, was very knowledgeable about them and it was from him we learned that Mr Reynolds, our school science teacher, was one, as was Mr Watson in the paper shop. How he knew this, he didn't explain, but he was adamant that all poofters were arseholes and if one ever came near him he would kick his head in. As everybody else agreed and seemed to know all about poofters as well, I didn't say anything in case they thought me naive and unworldly. That was a situation to be avoided at all costs as being thought of as naive and unworldly in Theo's milk bar was the ultimate humiliation.

Thus it was, as we entered Nambour, that I was still fairly ignorant about sexual matters, and despite his hand on my leg, it didn't enter my head that Mr Willard might have plans for us in that way. Such thoughts and fears are the preserve of the experienced and the knowledgeable; nevertheless, I knew there was something about him that made me feel uncomfortable. I wasn't scared or particularly worried, in fact if anything I found myself getting annoyed because Glen was fast asleep in the back and not sharing my discomfort.

Even after we'd stopped outside the motel Glen continued to sleep, so I jumped out and shook him awake. "Get up!" I hissed. "This bloke's a weirdo!" That was all I could say, however, for Mr Willard opened the other back door and started organising us.

"Leave your bags in the car," he told us. "We'll go and get something to eat first, and then I'll check us in."

Suddenly my imagination went berserk and I convinced myself that Mr Willard didn't want Glen and I to be alone together for some reason, even, I was sure, positioning himself between us as we walked across to the diner. Now I *was* beginning to worry, but throughout the meal it was impossible to say anything, or get Glen's attention as he was so busy devouring his food; besides, Mr Willard had seen to it that he was sitting opposite me and could watch my every move.

For a while, relieving my hunger pains made me forget the situation and I too tucked into the meal. Then Mr Willard got up to get another cup of coffee. "He's weird!" I hissed. "I'm not staying here with him."

"Why not? He's okay, he bought us this, didn't he?"

"I don't care! I'm not staying. When I say go, we run for it, okay?"

"But our bags are in the car."

Shit!

We could say no more. Mr Willard had returned.

"We'll just get the one room," he told us, finishing his coffee and preparing to get up. "It's got three beds and it's cheaper like that. I'll just go and pay for this first."

As soon as he turned his back I nodded at Glen and, trusting he would follow, leapt up and darted out of the restaurant; as I did, I snatched Mr Willard's cigarettes and lighter, stuffing them into my pocket as I ran. I'd worked out that we should have enough time to get to the car, grab our bags and be away before he would know what was going on. And so it turned out; he didn't even get to the door of the restaurant before we had reclaimed our bags and were running back out onto the road. "Oi!" he yelled. "Come back here!"

We ran down the highway towards the town centre as fast as we could, desperately looking for somewhere to hide. Two or three hundred yards from the motel a large semi-trailer was parked off the side of the road in semi-darkness, and chucking our kit bags up on top of the canvas load we clambered up and lay as flat as we could. Moments later we saw Mr Willard's car come out of the motel and drive slowly towards us. "See, I told you he'd come after us," I hissed.

"He wouldn't have if you hadn't pinched his bloody cigarettes!"

"Bullshit, the bloke's a weirdo, he grabbed my leg! Quick! Get down!"

Three times Mr Willard went slowly back and forth up the street, and we could see him peering out looking for us. We dared not move, and it was well over two hours after his last pass before we plucked up the courage to come down. By then I had managed to convince Glen that we had been in some sort of danger, although I still didn't really understand what sort. Had it just been my uncontrolled imagination? I didn't know, but deep down I really didn't believe so; that's why I'd stolen his cigarettes, to teach him a lesson. We climbed down, every headlight causing us to duck and dive for cover. It was obvious we had to get off the highway and out of the town centre. Mr Willard might come back at any time.

With no sort of plan other than to get away from the highway, we jogged and ran, weaving our way through the back streets of Nambour for twenty minutes, eventually coming to a bridge. For a moment we rested, leaning over the handrail to catch our breath and there, only six feet or so below us, were the wagons of a goods train. Forty or fifty yards away we could see the engine stopped at a red signal, letting off the steady and subdued chuffs that steam locomotives do when they are stationary. We didn't need a discussion about it, a look was enough. Bye, bye Mr Willard.

* * *

Jumping from the bridge, we landed in a clump of lantana growing on the bank beside the tracks. Ever been in a clump of lantana? Bloody stuff! Luckily we had our duffle coats on which protected us a bit, but our faces and the backs of our hands got badly scratched. Then we stumbled along in the dark beside the train for twenty minutes trying to find somewhere even half comfortable to ride. The wagons were either empty coal tenders or flatbeds carrying a variety of heavy material and equipment. Eventually we found one with two, thirty-foot long, four-foot diameter concrete pipes strapped to it, and climbed inside one of them. It was pitch black and we sat there for what seemed ages before the train finally jerked into movement. It wasn't long before the repetitive clickety-clack and gentle sway of the wagon had us fast asleep, lying head to foot along the pipe.

It was the quiet and stillness as much as anything else that woke us, and scrambling up the pipe we stuck our heads out. All the wagons of the train had been left on a side track and the engine, hissing and huffing, was pulled up next to a brightly-lit station a hundred yards away. Our wagon was stopped next to an old signal box and we dug out Francesca's map and lit a match.

"Shit! Bloody Gympie! That's only an inch!"

At the pictures on Saturday afternoons, whenever a cowboy or hobo jumped a freight train, they always seemed to find an empty box car, usually with a comfortable straw bale in the corner, then they'd spend four or five days travelling across America before they got hungry, had to go to the toilet or reload their 45s. We'd been on this bloody thing all night, crammed inside a concrete pipe, and only gone an inch, and every time we licked our lips we got a mouthful of grit. We sat at the entrance of the pipe for a moment, pondering what to do; the eastern skyline was just getting light and we were both getting restless.

"I need a shit."

"Yeah, so do I."

Using the station toilets was out of the question as there were several men standing about next to the engine, talking and smoking. Of course we could have gone in the bush like we usually did, but hanging your arse over a log and wiping it with leaves isn't the most comfortable thing to do and if we could find a proper toilet it was preferable. So, clambering up a bank and over a fence, we followed our noses into town and down the deserted main street, looking in vain for a toilet. It was still quite dark and our need was just becoming dire when we passed the main entrance of a hotel and I suddenly remembered our conversation with Ralph, the hitchhiking soldier in Beaudesert.

"In country towns I go into pubs for a shit."

"We're too young, we're not allowed in."

"No, not in the bar; upstairs, in the guest's toilets; especially early in the morning, there's never anybody about."

Of course! I pushed the door; it was open, and I was in and up the stairs before Glen could complain. I waited for him at the top, silencing his objections with an urgent wave and pointing to the sign 'Ladies & Gents Bathrooms' with an arrow pointing down the dark corridor.

"What if someone comes?" Glen hissed, looking round anxiously.

"We're only going to the bloody toilet!" Even so, I too whispered and we tiptoed down the corridor, creeping past bedroom doors like real criminals. The floorboards creaked loudly, and by the time we got to the bathroom our hearts were in our mouths, making our need even more desperate and we each charged into a booth. Amazing how having a shit can be such a wonderful experience sometimes.

When we came out it was the first time since the diner in Nambour that we'd been able to see each other properly, and immediately we burst into suppressed giggles, hissing and exhorting each other to keep quiet. Glen looked like something out of the Black and White Minstrels who'd been in a fight with a cat. The scratches on our cheeks and hands were far worse than we'd realised, and our faces, hair and clothes were covered in grit and soot. There were three or four shower booths next to the toilets, and using them just seemed the natural thing to do.

While we were at it we washed our clothes as we washed ourselves, the shower soon awash with black grit, and I was just beginning to wring out my trousers when I heard someone come into the bathroom. I froze, but Glen in the booth next to me kept whistling quietly to himself, his water still running. I held my breath, silently screaming at him to shut up, but whoever it was went into a toilet and clicked the latch.

"Gee, that was good!" enthused Glen cheerily as his water stopped. Instantly I hefted myself up so I could see over the partition.

"Shut up!" I mouthed, and pointed frantically to the toilets. The silence that followed was probably more incriminating than any noise we might have made, but to our relief when the man came out of the toilet he just washed his hands and left the bathroom.

Wrapping our wet clothes in our towels, we got dressed as fast as we could and tiptoed back up the corridor and out into the street, unseen.

The sun was beginning to come up and we found a park and spread our wet clothes out on some benches. On the way we passed both the police station, with a sign outside informing us that it opened at 9am, and the grocers, where we could cash in our voucher, thoughts of which only reminded us how hungry we were. Even so, comforted by the knowledge we would soon have the vouchers, we spent the last of our money on a packet of cigarettes. We got to the police station just on opening time, to find a beefy-faced police constable standing in the doorway, tucking his crisply ironed shirt into his equally crisp trousers, grimacing slightly as he tightened his belt around his substantial beer belly.

"Mornin', boys! Had a bit of a disagreement, have we?"

"What? Oh!" I put my hand to my cheek. "Lantana, we ended up in some last night."

"As yer do," he chuckled. "What can I do for you?"

"We're hitchhiking from Sydney to Magnetic Island, and we want some food vouchers."

"Sorry," he shook his head. "Don't do them any more," and he turned to go back into the station, Glen and I following, alarm bells clanging.

"What do you mean, you don't do them any more?"

"I mean we don't do them any more," and he went around behind the desk and began busying himself with papers, getting ready for the day's work.

"But that's impossible! We haven't got any food, we're starving. Where do we get the vouchers from?"

"You don't," he said flatly. "Food vouchers were phased out last year in Queensland."

"But what are we supposed to do? How do we get food?"

"Like everybody else, I guess, son. You get a job."

"But we're hitchhiking, we're bona-fide travellers, we're unemploy ..."

Laconic benevolence fading slightly, he interrupted me. "It doesn't matter how bona-fide you are, son, food vouchers are finished. If you're unemployed you have to go and register to claim benefits. Rockhampton is the nearest office on your route, so I suggest you get yourselves up there and register."

This was a disaster neither of us had been prepared for, and for a moment we could only stare incredulously at the policeman.

"Look," he said, seeing our dismay. "I can probably help you out with a couple of bob from petty cash to get yourselves enough tucker to get to Rocky. Other than that ..." and he held his hands out sympathetically. We left the station almost in a state of shock. True to his word he gave us two and sixpence each from his petty cash, but it was only enough to buy a few tins of food and we still had hundreds of miles to go to get to Magnetic Island. We went back to the park and sat, dejected, hungry and squabbling furiously.

"I said we shouldn't have spent our last money on those bloody cigarettes!"

"Get stuffed! You wanted them too!"

We spent the following two hours sitting apart in the park, ignoring each other while tempers cooled and clothes dried, but we eventually got together again, as we both knew we had to; unity was our strength.

I didn't discuss it with Glen, because I didn't really plan it as such, it just sort of happened and before I realised what I was doing, I'd done it. No doubt I had an idea of what I was going to do subconsciously, because I made sure our water bottles were full and our clothes were dry before we set off; I didn't want to have to come back for them. The money the policeman had given us was enough to buy the basics — tea, sugar, flour, a few tins of baked beans and maybe some broken biscuits — barely enough for one meal, never mind getting us to Rockhampton; so, kit bags packed with clean, dry clothes, we headed for the shop.

In many country towns the general store was also the local produce store and sold various grains in bulk, along with flour, tea, sugar, salt, cooking oil and other staples that were weighed or measured out from sacks, tins and drums, often directly into customers' own containers. Like the majority of stores, the Gympie shop had these larger items stored on racks in a large room out the back, and as soon as we entered and I saw there were no other customers and only one lady behind the counter I knew what I was going to do. Motioning for Glen to go and buy the items we'd decided we could afford, I sort of hovered in the background behind the two rows of grocery shelves that ran down the middle of the store, and when the shopkeeper turned her back to go and weigh out our flour and sugar I ran along the aisle stuffing as many tins, bottles and packets of things into my kit bag as I could. When I got to the other end the lady still hadn't returned, so I grabbed a couple more things without looking and by the time she came back I was standing nonchalantly in the shop doorway, my now bulging kit bag tied up between my legs. It couldn't have been easier, even Glen had no idea what I'd done.

As we left the store I tried to be as casual as possible, but when we were out of sight a few hundred yards down the road I began to run, calling back. "Come on! Quick! I've pinched some stuff, and as soon as she sees it's missing she'll call the cops!"

"Ah! For Christ's sake!" Glen yelled with exasperation, but he didn't really have much choice other than to follow me. For ten minutes we ran, looking back all the time to see if we were being followed, Glen abusing me all the way. Eventually we got out onto the highway heading north, and darted up the first track we came to. Three hundred yards down the track we spotted an old lean-to, fifty to sixty yards away under some gum trees. Jumping the fence, we ran across to it.

"Jesus!" exclaimed Glen, as he saw the things emerge from my kit bag. Even I was amazed. There were five tins of bully beef, two of baked beans and two of spaghetti and meatballs; one Irish stew and one mixed vegetables. There was a bottle of tomato sauce, a tin of golden syrup, a packet of aeroplane jelly, two tins of sardines, a bottle of orange squash and roll of toilet paper.

"You're mad!" said Glen.

"Yeah, but I'm also hungry," and I began gathering firewood. "You don't have to eat any of it!"

"Oh, I'll eat it alright, but that doesn't mean you're not mad!"

The only disappointing things were the tins I'd grabbed blindly at the end. All of them were broad beans, and if there was one thing I hated it was broad beans. The other problem was the orange squash; it was concentrated juice, impossible to drink without water, and as we only had two bottles we couldn't afford to use any of it for that so I stuffed the juice right down in the bottom of my kit bag and we began to make lunch.

On the morning after we had broken down with 'Uncle' Alf, apart from warning us of the perils of putting a tin of beans on the fire without opening it first, he'd shown us how to make dampers, wrapping the dough round a stick and holding it over the fire. "Staple diet in the bush during the Depression," he told us.

The ingredients may have been simple flour and water, but with a bit of imagination a damper could be the basis of a reasonably tasty meal, or at least keep hunger at bay for a while. Our first effort was a bit of a disaster, and nothing like the one 'Uncle' Alf had made. It was all gooey and blobs fell off the stick and into the fire, which was way too hot, burning most of what was left. But we did manage to make a reasonable one eventually, and it was quite nice with golden syrup spread on it. Tins of corned beef were another one of Alf's tips as the meat always came covered in a layer of fat, dispensing with the need to cart cooking oil about. "Nothing better than a fried corned beef damper sandwich, maybe with a dollop of tomato sauce," he'd winked. He was right. Even the broad beans tasted okay when fried with the meat.

After stuffing ourselves, we sorted the food out and split it between us. There was enough for three days, probably four if we rationed things; more than enough to get us to Rockhampton. We decided it might be best to lie low and stay in the lean-to for the rest of that day and night, as we thought the police were less likely to be out on the highway first thing in the morning. Our prospects suddenly looking much rosier, we settled back with a cigarette, surveying our little home and at peace with the world — and each other — once more. The influence our stomachs have over our emotions is truly remarkable.

Next morning at first light we set off, keeping well into the light scrub and trees at the side of the highway. At the end of the first long, straight stretch we sat behind a large gum tree, from where we could see what was coming a mile off. A couple of vehicles came our way but they were obviously locals, and waved apologetically when they saw our Magnetic Island sign, indicating they were turning off soon. Then in the distance we saw a car coming but stayed hidden; it had a strange livery and something on the roof, not that it really looked like a police car, but the guilty always see trouble where none exists. Only when the car was a hundred yards from us were we certain it wasn't the police, and we stepped out and held up our sign.

EIGHT
Auntie Marge and Constable Waring

"Sorry, mate." I poked my head in the window when he stopped. "Didn't realise."

"That's okay," the man grinned. "I'm not for hire, but I am going where you want to go. Hop in."

Yes!

His name was Mal Dixon and the taxi was a brand new EK Holden, still giving off that lovely leathery aroma only brand new cars have. He was the owner driver, he explained; taking his new taxi back to Townsville, where he'd lived and worked for over thirty years. "I could have waited for her to be sent up on a transporter," he told us, patting the dashboard affectionately, "but I wouldn't have got her for another month, and me old taxi's buggered so I went down to Melbourne on the train and picked this up myself from the factory. Kids might have left home, but I still need to pay the bills," he smiled. "I'll be back at work again in two days. Anyway, enough about me, what are you two doing?"

Excitement dampened somewhat by the knowledge that we wouldn't be able to go all the way with him because we had to stop in Rockhampton and sort our finances out, we were still glad to be on our way again and mightily relieved to have escaped from Gympie unscathed. Consequently, as we had with Mr Willard, we babbled away for the next twenty minutes about our adventures and problems, although leaving out the stealing bit. He was obviously very proud of his new car and drove it with great care, never going more than forty miles an hour because he was running it in; but Mal Dixon was no Mr Wallis, and he listened to our story with interest, good humour and no little astonishment, grinning and shaking his head in wonder.

"Quite an adventure," he smiled. "What are you going to do on Magnetic Island?"

"Pick coconuts."

"You're joking!" He looked at us. "You're not joking." He shook his head.

"We heard you could sell them to the tourists."

Again he looked at us, this time a little sympathetically. "Sounds like a fine idea, but I don't know you'll make too much money at it; there are a lot of coconuts on Magnetic Island, they're not difficult to come by."

"Is there any work there?"

"Well," Mal began, obviously not wanting to disappoint us further. "I haven't been over for a while, but I know there are a few small farms and businesses. I have to be honest, though," and he paused, grimacing slightly. "If I was looking to make good money, I'd head for Mount Isa, not Magnetic Island."

Subdued might best describe our mood for the next few miles.

We soon cheered up in Miriam Vale, though, when Mal bought us a couple of pies, a lamington and a drink while he ate his sandwiches and had a coffee from his flask. We didn't stop long, and an hour or so later, having left Gladstone behind, we dug out Francesca's map and realised we were doing the very thing she said we shouldn't, drive straight past everything. Not that there was a lot to stop for. We were at least forty miles inland now, and the countryside was very brown and parched. Mal told us it hadn't rained in these parts for months. Mile after mile went by without us encountering another vehicle, and apart from the odd kangaroo there was very little to see except bush and scrub; we were getting an inkling of just how big, remote and uninhabited Australia was, and still is. Out here the radio was the long distance driver's best friend, and although Mal preferred Perry Como to Eddie Cochran we all joined in with Jimmy Dean.

"Ev'ry mornin' at the mine you could see him arrive,
He stood six foot six and weighed two forty-five.
Kinda broad at the shoulder and narrow at the hip,
And everybody knew you didn't give no lip to Big John, Big John,
Big Bad John ..."

We arrived in Rockhampton at about six o'clock. Mal had told us he was going to stay with some friends about ten miles out of town. "Can't offer you a bed," he said apologetically. "I can offer you a feed, though, how about that?"

We stopped at a roadhouse on the southern outskirts of the city and ordered mixed grills with the works. Over the meal Mal showed us on a map of the city where we needed to go to register for unemployment benefits the next day. Then he got up and went to the toilet, and when he came back he had a piece of paper in his hand.

"Might be your lucky day. I found this pinned on the notice board." And he handed the piece of paper to us.

"Workers wanted," it stated simply. "Help clear yard. Four or five days; twelve bob a day. Mrs. Hayes, Lammermoor," and there was a phone number.

"Where's Lammermoor?"

"Out near Yeppoon," Mal pointed. "Only about thirty miles away. I can drop you out there if you like. Twelve shillings a day is pretty good money. You'll only get about five bob a day on unemployment benefits and you'll probably have to wait a week for it to come through. I know her. Everybody does up this way. Want me to give her a call?"

It was as simple as that. A brief phone call, and Mal had got us a job and arranged for us to meet Mrs Hayes by the War Memorial in Yeppoon at 9 o'clock the next morning. At eight o'clock that night, having shown us where the memorial was, he dropped us on the promenade by the beach in Yeppoon, where we planned to sleep. Only then did it strike us that this was the first time we'd seen the sea since leaving Southport, which seemed ages ago.

"Gee!" said Glen, "no surf!"

"You're on the barrier reef now, boys," Mal grinned. "Good luck. Look me up when you get to Townsville. I'll be on the main cab rank," and with a handshake he took his leave as we jumped down onto the sand to make our bed.

The next thing I knew my shoulder was being firmly prodded with the end of a pick handle and a torch shone in my face. "Oi, you two, wake up!" a terse voice commanded, and blearily we got to our elbows. There was a figure standing on the wall above, shining a torch down on us. "What are you doing here?"

"Trying to sleep."

"Don't give me any lip, son. Just answer the question."

"What for, who are you?"

"The police," said the voice firmly. "Now get up here," and once more I was prodded with the pick handle.

Shit! The shop in Gympie!

We clambered up the wall and stood nervously in front of him while he shone his torch, first over us and then down on our kit bags on the sand.

"You," he poked his stick at me. "Go down and bring your gear up here."

Anxiously I tossed our kit bags up as gently as I could, hoping the squash bottle wouldn't make a noise, and as I scrambled back I tried to give Glen a warning look through the darkness.

"Where are you from?"

"What?"

"From! Where are you from? Where do you live!"

"Melbourne," Glen said suddenly, completely flooring me with the sincerity of his lie, and instantly my mind was in turmoil as I desperately tried to think of an address in Melbourne. For a moment the policeman was silent, shining his torch from one to the other of us. "Where have you come from today?"

"Townsville," I blurted, hoping I sounded as convincing as Glen and determined to put us as far away from the shop as possible.

"How old are you?" he asked Glen.

"Eighteen," said Glen, again with such utter conviction that for a second even I believed him, and again I was thrown into a panic; if I said the same, the policeman would probably laugh.

Fortunately he didn't ask me. Instead he stepped back a pace and pointed to the police car parked nearby. "Get in," he ordered, surprising us both.

"What! What for?"

"Get in the car!"

We got in.

The police station was also the policeman's house, a small, unlined, fibro bungalow made even smaller by the fact that one of the two front rooms was being used as the office. We stood in front of the desk as he took down our names and false addresses in Carlton, the only football team I could think of. Glancing up briefly, he raised his eyebrows when we said our parents were not on the phone. "I take it none of your aunts, relatives or neighbours are on the phone, either?" he asked cuttingly.

"Yeah, but how are we supposed to remember their numbers!" We were not endearing ourselves to him.

"What were you doing in Townsville?" he suddenly asked, giving us a penetrating look.

"Not a lot," we shrugged. "Just hitching about, then we saw the job advertised at Mrs Hayes and thought we'd come and apply."

Our kit bags were in the corner where we'd put them and I was sure I could see out of the corner of my eye the orange squash bottle flashing brightly. But as time went by and his questions concentrated on our movements in Townsville, we grew increasingly certain that he wasn't interested in the contents of our bags. Getting ever more cocky, we elaborated on the story about coming from Townsville, each of us abetting the other with little lies about how we'd hitched a lift down the day before. So sure of our ground were we becoming, that when he suddenly came around our side of the desk and handcuffed the two of us together we were completely taken aback. In fact it happened so fast we didn't even have time to object, and just stared down in amazement at the handcuffs.

"Go out of the door and turn down the hall," the policeman ordered.

"What for? What have we done?"

He prodded us down the hall, out the back door and a few yards along a path to a brick shed at the end of the little garden. It had two solid-looking iron doors side by side, and he opened one and pushed us in, removing the handcuffs. There were two canvas camp cots with a pillow and blanket folded on each, a toilet bucket and an enamel wash bowl and jug of water in the corner, and precious little else.

"You can stay in here until the morning, while I make some enquiries," he told us, and he slammed the door shut, bolting it firmly.

"But we haven't done anything!" we cried after him. There was a tiny window next to the door, no glass, just bars and fly-screen mesh, and we stood staring at the policeman disappearing back into the house, both of us too stunned to say anything more.

Half an hour later we heard the door being unbolted and the policeman stood outside. Behind him was a lady carrying a tray, and he stepped aside and allowed her into the cell. Her motherly presence immediately reassured us, and when she put the tray down and smiled our relief was palpable.

On the tray was a jug of ginger beer and two glasses, along with some bananas and a dozen arrowroot biscuits. "Just a little something," she smiled again, "I know how hungry you boys can get," and she fussed about, fluffing up the pillows, laying the blankets out and chatting away as if we were her nephews. "Now, if you have a problem in the night, just call out through the window. Our bedroom's just at the back there, so we'll hear you."

All the while her husband fidgeted at the door. "Come on, Marge," he sighed eventually, unable to keep the impatience out of his voice, and reluctantly Marge left, repeating again that we should call out through the window if we wanted anything. As he bolted the door, we heard him say to her, "For God's sake, Marge, they're bloody criminals!"

"Oh don't be so silly, Arthur!" she chided. "They're so young! They couldn't possibly have done it!" Done what? We asked ourselves anxiously, as we downed the ginger beer. It was three o'clock in the morning; we were obviously involved in a bizarre dream.

A few hours later we discovered it was anything but. Marge bought us a huge breakfast at about eight o'clock, but this time she was on her own and we seized the chance. "Why are we in here? We haven't done anything!" we pleaded with her.

"I can't talk to you about that, boys," she shrugged sympathetically. "Constable Waring will be over shortly to speak to you."

"But we haven't done anything!" For a moment she looked at us, smiling gently. "No, I don't believe you have. You just tell Constable Waring everything and it will be alright," and then she paused, as if unsure how much she should say. "He might look a bit severe," she smiled reassuringly again, "but he's a good man, and he'll see you get a fair hearing."

An hour later we were sitting side by side on one cot, with

Constable Waring sitting opposite on a chair he'd brought with him. Three times he made us go over our movements after leaving Townsville, each time exposing one of our little lies.

"I thought you said you left at ten o'clock?"

"Well, it was about then."

"Last night you said you got a lift in a blue Zephyr, this morning it's a Consul?"

"Well, it was a Ford! For Christ's sake! Does it matter?"

Ten minutes later he folded his notes and stood up, his face, if anything, even more firm and official. "I'm afraid, boys, I'm going to have to charge you. This means that from now on you don't have to say anything, but if you do ..."

"Charge us! What do you mean? What with?"

I was vaguely aware that we had certain rights in these circumstances, not that I knew what they were, and I wasn't really listening — preparing instead to demand those rights — when the constable began reading out the charges and suddenly we were riveted to the cot with gut-lurching attention. Breaking and entering, burglary, arson, assault, grievous bodily harm, the list seemed to go on and on as we stared stupidly up at him. "Three days ago, two boys closely matching your descriptions were seen running from a caravan park in Townsville. Four caravans were set alight, a number of items were stolen and an elderly man was burnt, quite badly I ..."

"But we didn't do that! We weren't even ... !"

"I'm sorry, boys," he cut us off, and for the first time he looked half-sympathetic. "It's out of my hands now. Rockhampton CIB is going to come and interview you." Then from his bag he produced something I instantly recognised, a fingerprint pad; refusing wasn't an option. When he'd finished, carefully rolling each of our fingers over the ink pad and pressing them onto the special piece of paper to record the imprint, he looked at us as if he was making up his mind about something.

"Look, boys," he sighed. "I don't know what's going on with you two, but a couple of words of advice. From now on be very careful what you say. If you're not eighteen, don't say you are; under eighteen you're still legally minors and have certain rights. Secondly, I'd try and get my story straight if I were you. Mrs Hayes didn't advertise her job anywhere in Townsville."

As he bolted the door behind him, Glen and I could only stare at each other, the anxiety in his face no doubt mirrored in mine.

"Why did you say we came from bloody Townsville!"

"Well, you told him we lived in Melbourne!"

"You agreed!"

"No, I didn't!"

"You bloody did!"

Shit!

Several times that day and night Mrs Waring kept popping back to see how we were, bringing with her little tit-bits of food and drink, but she never had any news and we just had to sit there, biting our nails and blaming each other for our predicament. On the second morning she arrived at the cell empty-handed and stood in the doorway for a moment, looking gently at us. "Now I want you to promise me, boys, if I let you out over to the house for breakfast you won't run away." Constable Waring had gone to Rockhampton to fetch the detective, she informed us, and would be back later that afternoon. We sat in her small kitchen-come-dining room after breakfast, playing Monopoly while Mrs Waring did her washing and other housework. Mid-morning she came into the kitchen and made us doorstopper peanut butter sandwiches washed down with her wonderful ginger beer, and again we tried to find out what was going on but she was adamant she couldn't talk about it. "It's police business," she said. "I'm not supposed to get involved. In fact I shouldn't really have let you out. You'll just have to wait until the detective comes. I'm sure if you explain properly what you were doing in Townsville it will be alright."

"But we weren't ever *in* Townsville! We made that up because we stole some food! We got a lift with a taxi driver in Gympie, and he rang up Mrs Hayes when we got to Rockhampton!"

"Oh, for heaven's sake, boys!" she sighed, wiping her hands on her apron and sitting down. "You'd better tell me the truth."

At twelve-thirty we went back to the cells and Mrs Waring locked the door. "Just tell the detective what you told me, and everything will be alright," she assured us. But it was a nervous wait, and an hour later we heard the constable and Mrs Waring having a furtive but heated debate outside their back door. We glued our ears to the fly screen.

"For Pete's sake, Marge," we could just hear him hiss. "You can't go round letting prisoners out like that. They could be dangerous!"

"Oh, don't be so silly, Arthur," she said dismissively. "Of course they're not!" A further explosion of exasperation from the constable was cut short when a large man in a suit came out of the door and joined them. Then, with Mrs Waring behind them waving encouragingly at us, the two men came along the path together and we quickly moved away from the window.

Constable Waring's stern countenance was positively uncle-like compared to this new man's scowl as he came into the cell, standing menacingly in the middle of it.

"This is Detective Sergeant somebody or other," Constable Waring told us. "For your own sakes, I'd tell him the truth," and rather ominously he left the cell and shut the door. For an hour the detective grilled us at length, barking out sharp questions and making us go over our story again and again, occasionally interrupting us with shouts of "Bullshit!" or "What time was that?" We went from being frightened and speechless to angry and insolent and back to frightened again, the detective's disposition growing ever more hostile as we stuck to our story; which was fairly easy to do as now it was the truth, not that he ever looked like believing us.

Again I was vaguely aware that we had rights and that he probably shouldn't be doing this to us, but when I mentioned it he got so angry I shut up. At one stage he put us in separate cells, going back and forth, trying to convince each of us that the other had admitted being in Townsville. Then he put us back in the one cell and went away for two hours or so, when he returned it was obvious he'd been drinking.

If we'd been frightened before, now we became scared stiff as he removed a foot-long truncheon from inside his jacket and tapped it in his hand; later we discovered it was a section of a bicycle tyre tube, filled up with sand and the ends sealed.

"I want some answers from you bastards, and this time I want the truth, understand!" and stepping forward a pace, he jabbed the end of the truncheon up under my rib cage. The pain was excruciating and sucked the breath out of me for a moment.

"Right! Let's start again. What time did you leave Townsville?"

"But we didn't come from Townsville! We came from Gympie, the orange squash we took is still in the kit bag if you don't believe us! Do you think we'd tell you we took it if we hadn't?"

"Where's the radio?" he demanded suddenly, and for a moment we were both speechless, although I noticed Glen had been getting increasingly agitated and annoyed and suddenly he shouted out, "What fucking radio! We weren't even there, you stupid prick!"

In one movement the detective crossed the cell and hit Glen a thumping blow in the ribs with the truncheon, much harder than he'd hit me, the force of it doubling him up.

"The radio you stole from the caravan park! We'll find it eventually. Your fingerprints will be all over it! Now I'll ask you again. Where's the fucking radio?" By now I was too terrified to say anything, and Glen couldn't as he was on his knees gasping for breath. I decided that at the next opportunity I would yell as loud as I could to alert Mrs Waring, at the same time kicking the detective in the shins and hope Glen joined in, which I was sure he would, despite his condition.

Mercifully at that moment there was a tap on the door, and quickly putting his truncheon away beneath his coat, the detective snapped, "What is it?"

"Mrs Waring's just been on the phone to Townsville," said Constable Waring, opening the door and surveying the scene with a frown, Glen still on his knees. "She spoke to a taxi driver there who says he picked the boys up in Gympie and dropped them here three days ago. Mrs Hayes has confirmed she spoke to him."

Now why hadn't we thought of that! Good old Auntie Marge.

The detective left the cell immediately, barging passed Constable Waring and instructing him to charge us, not just with the theft in Gympie but for giving false evidence and wasting police time. "These little pricks have just fed us a pack of lies!" and he stormed up the path, Constable Waring hurrying after him. They disappeared into the house locked in heated, arm-waving debate. Meanwhile Glen sat on the cot, clearly distressed and holding his ribs. When the constable came back twenty minutes later he was still sitting there.

"Jesus!" he cursed, more or less to himself when Glen lifted his shirt to show him the bruise.

"The bastard had a little truncheon thing! He hit me, too!"

"Is he allowed to do that?" Glen demanded, voice trembling with emotion. "Isn't there something we can do?" And then something seemed to snap in him and he cried out, "I'm sick of bullies! Fucking sick of them!" and burst into tears.

It was an outcry of such intense, naked anguish that for a moment the constable was at a complete loss as to know how to respond, as was I. Although I remember thinking, young and naive as I was, that this was some sort of seminal moment in Glen's life, that it was truly important for him to say those words out loud and with such anger and bitterness. Constable Waring obviously had similar thoughts, and he looked at Glen with great sympathy, sitting on the cot wiping his eyes on the sleeve of his shirt, trembling slightly and visibly straining to control his emotions. "You have every right to be angry, son, and I apologise for it happening in my cell." His own anger was plain to see, but then his face softened slightly. "For the moment, though, I'm going to get the doctor to come and have a look at you both. You can come over to the house while we wait for him."

I was alright, just a bit of redness, but Glen was in a much worse state. Although no ribs were broken, his lower chest was badly bruised and the doctor strapped him up as a precaution, then he spoke to the constable and Marge, who'd been clucking over us since she heard what had happened. "I think he's suffering a bit from shock, he should take it easy for a bit. I'll come back in a few days and see how he is."

As it turned out, by hitting us the detective had done us a favour. We would probably have remained locked up for a few more days anyway, while the police sorted out what was going to happen to us. The Townsville charges may have been dropped, but we were still technically under arrest for the Gympie thefts, giving false evidence and wasting police time; so having to spend a few more nights in the cell was no great hardship, and as the doctor had ordered Glen should take it easy, the next few days were more relaxed than they might have been. We weren't locked in at night, and during the day we were allowed out for walks. On the third morning Glen was feeling better, so we went for a swim in the sea. Mrs Waring plied us with great meals and lots of ginger beer, and made sure Glen took his Bex powder every four hours as instructed. On the second night Glen asked if he could ring his mother and I was able to talk to my sister, although we didn't tell them everything, just that we'd been arrested for something we didn't do and that otherwise we were alright. Mrs Waring spoke to Glen's mum briefly to confirm this. By the time the doctor came back and took the strapping off Glen was more or less back to his old self, and although the bruise was a nasty yellow colour, it didn't hurt so much.

It was gone five o'clock on Friday evening by the time the doctor left and it looked like we might have to spend a few more days in the cell, as everything came to a standstill over the weekend. Then Constable Waring called us into his office, his face set as firm as ever we'd seen it.

"Wrong as it was, and unhappy as I am about what happened in the cells," he began, "I have to say boys that any trouble you've found yourselves in is entirely of your own making. Giving false evidence and lying to the police are serious offences, and if stupidity was a crime you'd be sent to gaol for the rest of your bloody lives!" He glared at us. "You're not in Sydney now, you know! How many other pairs of young Pommie teenagers carrying kit bags have you seen wandering about? My colleague in Gympie knew it was you the moment the shopkeeper reported the goods stolen! It was only a matter of time before we picked you up. Out here you two stick out like dogs' balls!"

"But we were hungry ..."

"I don't give a stuff if you were starving to death — which you weren't, because the constable in Gympie gave you five bob, more than enough to get you to Rockhampton! You didn't need to steal anything, much less get yourselves into serious trouble by lying and wasting police time!"

By now we, or perhaps I should say I, was at last beginning to grasp the notion that keeping my mouth shut more often than open was a good idea, so the room was silent for a moment as the constable shuffled his papers about, collecting his thoughts.

"I have spoken to my colleague in Gympie, who says the shopkeeper will not press charges against you so long as you pay for the goods stolen ..."

"But we haven't got any ..." I began, instantly breaking my latest resolution.

"I'll come to that in a minute," the constable cut me off. "She says the items you stole come to fourteen shillings and sixpence, and if she receives payment for them nothing more will be said. Now then," and he paused once more, obviously choosing his words. "As to the other business, the detective says he will drop all the charges against you so long as you say nothing more about what went on in the cells. Now I know!" He held up his hand once more to stifle our objections. "The man was totally out of order and should at the very least be reported. But if you do, he will throw the book at you, about Gympie, lying, giving false evidence and wasting police time, and as you are plainly guilty of all of those charges the result will mean that although the detective may well be hauled over the coals and could even be demoted, you two will end up with criminal records, and that is not a good thing to have, believe me!"

It was all a bit much to take in, I suppose, and for a moment neither of us really had a clue what to say.

"I understand how you feel," he looked at Glen sympathetically, "and if you really want to make a formal complaint against the detective I will help you and give evidence for you, as will the doctor. I just thought you should know the situation before you make that decision. By rights I should either be charging you now or letting you go, but as it's Friday I'll give you a couple of days to think about it. I just want your word that if I release you, you won't piss off anywhere," and he accepted our nodded agreement without further comment, although it was obvious by the look on his face that he hadn't finished with us yet.

"Regardless of your decision, it is my duty to officially warn you about your behaviour in the future while you are in Queensland. This means that if you get into any more trouble with the police, and I mean anything at all!" and he stabbed his finger onto his blotter, "you will be in big trouble, and the punishments will be much harsher because of this warning. Do you understand me?"

"Yes, Constable."

"Okay. Now, as for paying back the Gympie debt, I suggest you go and see Mrs Waring in the kitchen. There's someone there who wants to meet you." And he waved us away.

We couldn't get out of there fast enough.

NINE

Mrs Hayes

"Gidday, boys!" Mrs Hayes greeted us brightly, shaking our hands but not getting up from the kitchen table where she was sitting drinking tea with Marge. "Been havin' some adventures, I hear!" and her craggy, parchment-like face split into an enormous grin. Even sitting down, it was possible to see how tall and thin she was and her handshake, although strong and firm, was very bony. She was wearing a pair of tough grey trousers, a man's check shirt and work boots, and her white hair was tied up tightly in a bun. Tough and stern might have been words to describe her were it not for her grin; it lit up the room, not just her face.

"Still lookin' for work?" and Glen and I looked at each other, a little subdued from our dressing down by Constable Waring.

"Well … yeah, we guess so."

"Okey-dokey," and she slammed down her empty cup and got up, plonking a battered, sweat-stained slouch hat onto her head. Two black and tan kelpie dogs that we hadn't seen lying at her feet leapt up in excited unison. "Let's get goin' then! Thanks for the tea, Marge. See ya next week."

Parked outside the police station was a very battered Second World War US Army Jeep with a faded white star on the bonnet. There were no doors, just a canvas roof and windscreen, and there was only one seat. Without prompting, the two dogs leaped into the back with practised ease. Marge came out with us to say goodbye, and kissed both Glen and I on the cheeks. "Look after yourselves, boys." She smiled her motherly smile and spontaneously, if a little self-consciously, both Glen and I gave her a hug. 'Auntie' Marge stood waving at us until we were out of sight, Glen sitting on the floor next to Mrs Hayes, me in the back with the dogs and kit bags, the bolts and ridges of the metal floor digging into my backside, the dogs licking my face in sympathy as we bumped along.

It was dark by the time we got to her place, and although the house was silhouetted against the night sky all we could really see from the headlights were the front steps leading up onto a veranda. But we didn't stop, and drove on for another fifty yards or so, bumping across rugged ground until we came to a large, open-sided shed and Mrs Hayes positioned the jeep so the headlights shone inside. Parked in the middle was an old tractor, and at one end there was a small caged room. Leaving the engine running, she got out, opened the padlock on the mesh door and went inside.

As soon as her back was turned the dogs were off, barking excitedly and obviously chasing something they'd seen or smelt in the dark. Moments later there was a loud whirring noise and a diesel engine thundered into life. A dull light came on in the shed, and one above the steps on the veranda of the house. When Mrs Hayes came out and saw the dogs gone she swore softly, stuck her fingers in her mouth and gave a shrill whistle. "Jessie!" she yelled above the noise of the generator. "Get here!" Almost immediately both dogs returned, eyes and heads lowered, acknowledging their naughtiness. "Go sit!" she commanded, pointing back up towards the house, and they ran off as she got back into the jeep. By the time we got back to the house the dogs were sitting on their hessian bags at the top of the steps as if butter wouldn't melt.

"Which one's Jessie?"

"Both of 'em," Mrs Hayes patted one of them on the head. "We've had two dogs called Jessie for over forty-five years, all related to the original."

"Don't they get confused?"

"Don't seem to," she shrugged. "They've usually been mother and daughter, like these two, so they do everything together anyway; it just makes life easier having one name. Besides, it always feels like the original Jess is still with us," and the two Jessies looked up, panting adoringly at their mistress, knowing she was talking about them.

Even in the dark we could see the house had seen better days, but it was still a lovely example of a 'Queenslander', up on stilts with shuttered windows and a wide veranda that ran right the way around. The front door was opposite the steps, but instead of going inside Mrs Hayes walked off round the veranda. "I'll show you your beds first," she said over her shoulder. Halfway down the side of the house the veranda had been enclosed with a waist-high fibro wall and flyscreen all the way around across the top. Opening the flimsy door, Mrs Hayes went inside and lit a kerosene lamp hanging from a butcher's hook.

"Don't you have electricity?"

"No!" she said emphatically. "Oh, I could have it," she went on, waving dismissively outside. "The bloody pole is sitting outside waiting for me to tell them to come and connect it. I just don't like relying on somebody else. I get by good enough, and the blackouts don't bother me," she grinned. "Anyway, make yourselves comfy. Pillows are in the cupboard. I'll go and rustle up some tucker. Oh, and I'd keep this door closed if I were you. Midges can be bad out here sometimes." Lying head to foot along the wall of the house were two settees with bright, homemade patchwork quilts, and beyond them a small cupboard and two little cane chairs. Making ourselves comfortable consisted mainly of having a spontaneous wrestling match to decide who got which bed (Glen won), and then bouncing up and down on them for five minutes to test the springs; doesn't everybody do that? They were nice and soft, though, as were the pillows, even if they did smell of stale mothballs. Then Mrs Hayes called from inside the house. "Come and get it, boys!"

Her kitchen was as basic as our bedroom. There was a simple pine table and four chairs, a small wood-burning stove, two or three little pine parlour cupboards with flyscreen mesh in the doors, a large concrete sink and an old 'Silent Night' kerosene fridge. Mrs Hayes was at the stove filling a big brown teapot from the kettle.

"Help yourselves," and she nodded at the table, on which were three enamel plates and three mugs, a loaf of bread, some butter, two opened tins of corned beef, three boiled eggs and a few condiments and sauces. The whole scene, including Mrs Hayes, looked like something out of an old cowboy picture. "Not up to Marge's standards, I'm afraid," she smiled, "but I've never been one for fancy tucker." This she said with no hint of apology. It was just a statement of fact, and having poured the tea she took out a bottle of whisky from one of the cupboards and sat down, pouring a generous shot into her mug. "Right then! Let's hear a bit about you two."

Marge had obviously filled her in on the trials and tribulations of our journey, but Mrs Hayes seemed more interested in our family life back in Sydney. She was not the slightest bit condescending or judgmental, and her earthiness and simple sincerity somehow made you want to talk to her. For once Glen seemed comfortable and at ease in the presence of an adult, and he babbled away like I'd never heard him. Within an hour she knew just about everything there was to know about us both.

"Was your dad in the war?" she asked Glen at one stage.

"Yeah, he was in the British Navy, twice the ship he was on got sunk but he doesn't talk about it much."

"That's probably the trouble; the war, I mean, and not talking about it." Mrs Hayes nodded. "Oh, it doesn't excuse his behaviour. But it might explain it. Wars and women," she smiled. "They do strange things to men." And she poured herself another stiff whisky.

There was an uncomfortable silence for a moment, and then Glen asked, happy to change the subject: "Do you live here on your own, then?"

"Yes," she nodded. "Clem, my husband, went seven years ago. No, he didn't die." She saw the look on our faces. "He just went, buggered off, or to be truthful I told the bastard to bugger off!"

"Sorry ... I didn't mean to ..."

"No, that's okay, everybody knows about it round here. He had an affair with a barmaid from Rockhampton; no asparagus veins and bigger tits," she shrugged, taking another mouthful of whisky. "'Course it didn't last long," she went on, not noticing our reaction, or if she did, ignoring it; adults talking about bums and tits still made us giggle. "It was never going to, but the damage was done. Unbeknown to me he'd mortgaged the property and given her a chunk of money, and we never really recovered. I don't mean the marriage," she looked up quickly to make sure we didn't misunderstand. "That had long been dead in the water; no, I mean the farm never recovered, and after Charlie died I couldn't manage on my own so I had to sell up. I still own the house, but only just."

"Who's Charlie?"

"My son," and she nodded to the photograph of a young man about twenty years old on top of one of the cupboards. "He was killed in a motorcycle accident three years ago. He never got over his dad leaving, and I've never got over him dying." The whisky was now plainly having an effect, and she continued almost as if we weren't there. "Oh, don't get me wrong. Clem was a good farmer. He knew what he was doing and God knows he worked hard enough." Then she sighed heavily. "This used to be such a lovely house, and Hayes Farm was one of the most successful in these parts before the war. We had twelve full-time staff and any number of casual workers, so Clem was exempt from military duty. Not only that, he was also almost forty when the war started but the silly bastard still insisted on joining up. He went out west where nobody knew him and signed on at a mobile recruiting office, told them he was thirty-three; they didn't ask too many questions in those days. He was sent to North Africa and I didn't see him again for two and a half years. When his leave was over he wanted to go back, but I went to the authorities and told them who he was and how old he was. They discharged him that day, and I don't think he ever forgave me." She paused again and took another sip of whisky, looking reflectively at the photograph of her son. "Clem was a different man after that. I hardly knew him and things were never the same; *we* were never the same. He couldn't cope with Charlie as a child, used to get very angry and drank a lot. He never hit us or anything, but we never got back to the days before the war. By the time fancy pants at the pub got her claws into him he was an easy target, and she knew it!" Suddenly Mrs Hayes seemed to realise where she was and what she was saying and she came back to the moment, her moment of reminiscing over. "Not that I expect you two to know much about sheilas yet, do you? Just be warned, some of us can be very cunning. Trouble is you blokes make it so easy for us! As my mother used to say, 'A man's principles and his penis are like curtains in the wind. When one gets up, the other goes straight out the window.'

From somewhere in the house the chimes of ten o'clock rescued us from having to find somewhere to look, and knocking back the remains of her whisky, Mrs Hayes got up, if a little unsteadily. "Past my bed time; and yours," she added, ruffling my hair and smiling at the looks on our faces. "We've got an early start in the morning."

When we got to the door Glen stopped and looked back, frowning slightly.

"What are asparagus veins?"

Mrs Hayes smiled again, but she didn't explain, just lifted up her trouser leg and showed us.

The rooster woke us just before dawn, which was just as well because moments later Mrs Hayes called out that breakfast was ready and by the time we stumbled bleary-eyed into the kitchen she had already eaten her Cornflakes and was putting slices of Kraft cheese on her toast and marmalade.

"Morning," she greeted us, getting up to pour the tea.

In the daylight it was possible to see just how run-down the house had become. Much of the veranda on the opposite side to where we were sleeping had rotted away, and the kitchen ceiling was covered in brown water stains, tell-tale signs of a leaking roof; and many of the floorboards had sprung. As was usual with 'Queenslanders', the inside rooms were all quite dark, even in the middle of the day, and not having a reason to go into them, we didn't see much of the inside except the hall and kitchen. Immediately outside the kitchen and at the side was a bathroom and laundry — obviously a later exten-sion — and next to it were two huge rainwater tanks. At the back of the house was a small fenced-off area with some flowerbeds and a vegetable patch, both of which were reasonably well tended. Beyond the garden, stepping stones led across the grass to a corrugated iron dunny, and not far from the dunny, under a tree, was a small, well-kept patch of ground surrounded by a foot high picket fence with a simple little sign. 'JESSIE' it read, and planted inside were a dozen or more little wooden crosses with nothing on them but a date.

The main yard was at the front of the house and must have been at least twenty-five acres, a three hundred metre wide, rectangular piece of land, fenced and sloping down to a dam and chicken coop several hundred yards away. The house was at the top of a slope, which meant that from the front veranda we could see the ocean and the hills of Keppel Island in the distance, but we didn't have long to admire the view.

"Right, let's get started!" Mrs Hayes came out, hat and gloves on, and set off down towards the largest of the barns. "We used to own most of what you can see," she said, waving at the surrounding area of gentle slopes stretching into the distance, the majority, save for one or two paddocks, covered in pineapples. "Sold most of the land a few years back, the bit the bank didn't own, that is." She made no attempt to hide her irony. "Now this yard is all that's left." A small flock of seven or eight sheep, startled by us, went charging off down the slope, the dogs obviously bursting at the seams to chase them but not game while Mrs Hayes was about. "Don't own them, either," she informed us. "Belong to a neighbour; he lets me run them here to keep the grass down."

Over breakfast she'd given us a quick run-down of what she wanted done. The job she had originally advertised for, clearing her yard, had been done while we were in gaol by two local men, but now she wanted the largest out-building furthest away from the house cleared out. This she was going to lease to a neighbouring farmer who wanted somewhere to park his tractors and other farm equipment. It was an enormous iron shed, fifteen to twenty feet high and open-fronted like the generator shed but twice the size. Inside it was stacked to the rafters with a mountain of old pallets and packing cases and heavy wooden sleds like my grandfather used to use to pull pineapples from the fields. There were bales of hay and no end of old equipment, empty diesel drums, coils of rusting barbed wire, tractor implements, sheets of roofing iron, dozens of old tyres and the chassis and other bits and pieces of at least two old vehicles. Clearing the place looked a daunting task, and for a few moments we stood contemplating it.

"Bit of a mess, eh!" Mrs Hayes conceded, coming as close as she would to apologising for anything. "But we won't get it shifted by lookin' at it!"

For seven days solid we worked, not that we could complain; Mrs Hayes worked just as hard right alongside us most of the time, although it was obvious she had to rest a lot and we had plenty of tea breaks. At lunchtimes — corned beef and tomato sandwiches and tinned peaches, every day — we stopped for an hour while Mrs Hayes listened to *Blue Hills*.

On the first evening, after a bath and dinner — fried corned beef, boiled potatoes, tomatoes and peas most days, if not it was sausages and the above — Mrs Hayes gave us fifteen shillings each. "Man does a day's work, he deserves a day's pay. Besides, you might get sick of it tomorrow and want to bugger off."

"Constable Waring told us we had to stay in the area."

"I know." Mrs Hayes nodded.

"Are we under arrest here, then?" Glen asked.

"Christ, no! That's why I'm paying you — if you want to go, you can! But it might not be a bad idea to stay until the constable says you can go."

It was only then that we began to understand that our being here had been arranged between the constable and Mrs Hayes.

By the fourth day the shed was two-thirds cleared and stacked outside were three separate piles: one of usable stuff she was going to keep, the second rubbish to be taken to the tip, and a third mainly of scrap metal, tyres and empty drums that a dealer from Rock-hampton was going to come and collect. Then, late in the afternoon, Mrs Hayes went up to the generator shed and started up the 1947 Fordson Stegamajor and we roped up the two vehicle chassis and she towed them out into the yard. She was about to take the tractor back to the shed when she paused and looked at us for a moment, before sliding off the seat.

"Ever driven one of these?"

Glen might have beaten me to the best bed, but he wasn't going to beat me onto that tractor and I was up and sitting in the iron seat before you could blink.

Not a lot of other work got done after that, as Glen and I took turns to drive the tractor up and down the yard. Having satisfied herself that we knew vaguely what we were doing, Mrs Hayes left us to it and went back to the house, where she sat on the veranda having a cup of tea, getting as much delight and pleasure from watching us whooping with joy as we were getting from driving a vehicle, never mind a tractor, for the first time in our lives. We might not have been allowed to bash into anything, but it was ten times more fun than the dodgems at Luna Park and we didn't have to pay! The dogs loved it too, although the poor old sheep got seriously confused.

Each evening, after a bath and dinner, we sat on the veranda for two or three hours, talking and smoking while Mrs Hayes sipped her whisky. One night our run-in with the detective had come up, and both Glen I were still keen to pursue the matter, despite what the constable had said. The threat of a criminal record didn't really seem all that big a deal to us.

"So what," Glen argued. "Small price to pay to get that prick!" But Mrs Hayes, like the constable, urged caution.

"Oh, don't get me wrong! If it was me I'd report the bastard straight away. He's a bad egg, that one, well known round here, he is. Such a pity, too, because most country cops are pretty good blokes. They understand how people live out here. But," she shrugged "I'm a grumpy old bat, so it wouldn't hurt me if I got a record. You two, on the other hand, have got your whole lives in front of you. If you've been given the chance not to have a criminal record, I'd take it with both hands! Forget the detective. He'll get his come-uppance one day."

So it was that by the time Constable Waring arrived a few days later we had made up our minds and he accepted our decision to let the matter rest without comment, simply nodding his head approvingly. We gave him the money we owed the shop in Gympie, and he told us we were free to go. Then he and Mrs Hayes exchanged a few words before he turned back to us. "Just remember what I told you in the office, boys." He opened the door of his car, and for the first time since we met him on the beach, which now seemed ages ago, he smiled. "And keep your bloody noses clean!"

"There goes a good man, and a good cop," said Mrs Hayes as he drove out of the yard, and she looked at us. "You know he stuck his neck out for you, don't you?"

"Well, yeah, he let us off."

"That's not the half of it!" Mrs Hayes said fairly sternly, determined we should fully understand. "Marge letting you out of the cells was a serious breach of police protocol, and he would have been in big trouble himself had you wanted to report the detective. Despite that, he was prepared to give evidence for you. You don't know how lucky you are that he was the policeman who originally caught you!"

By the following weekend we'd finished clearing the shed and on Monday morning Mrs Hayes hitched up an old trailer to the Jeep and we took a load of rubbish to the tip. By the time we returned it was too late to make a second trip, so we loaded the trailer ready for the morning. The tip was on the way to Rockhampton, and after dinner Mrs Hayes suddenly had an idea. "I know what we'll do, boys! Tomorrow after we've dumped the rubbish, we'll leave the trailer at the tip and go on into town for lunch. The baker makes lovely pies, how about it?"

In Rockhampton Mrs Hayes did a bit of shopping, went to the bank and one or two other offices, with Glen and I feeling a bit like her children tagging along behind. As we walked about, virtually every second person stopped to say hello to her, many asking how she was and saying how good it was to see her up and about, and in the baker's the lady behind the counter positively beamed when we walked in the door. We ate our pies and finger buns sitting on a park bench, with Mrs Hayes obviously happy to sit down for awhile.

"Have you been sick?"

"Yeah, I was crook for a bit there, but I'm better now," and a few moments later she got up, as if to prove the point. "Come on, one last chore."

As soon as we walked into the Army Disposals Store we saw the rucksacks hanging up. "This what you were after?" she smiled.

When we got back from Rockhampton, Mrs Hayes suggested we wash all our clothes. It was a nice warm afternoon and they soon dried, and that evening we packed our new rucksacks and afterwards sat on the veranda, Mrs Hayes sipping her whisky as usual. To our surprise she gave us fifteen shillings each for that day as well.

"But we hardly did anything today!"

"Never mind that!" She dismissed our protests, which in truth were not all that vociferous. "You worked hard enough the first few days."

In all we'd earned twelve pounds six shillings in the seven days, and Mrs Hayes had paid for the rucksacks. We'd spent about a pound in Rockhampton restocking with food and cigarettes, and we'd paid off our dept in Gympie, so we still had about ten pounds left. It was the richest we'd ever been, and this time we were determined not to part with it so easily or quickly.

Magnetic Island was still our goal, and despite not feeling quite so confident about what we would find when we got there, both of us still felt that if we didn't get there the trip would be a failure somehow. Mrs Hayes was her most emphatic self when we mentioned this.

"Oh, you've got to have faith in your dreams, boys. Goals and dreams are important, never mind what the rest of us think of them. They might not always work out, but I reckon if a man goes through life doing what he feels is right, as often as not he will be right. Air and water might keep us alive, but goals and dreams are what get us out of bed in the mornings," and her parchment-splitting grin lit up the veranda.

Next morning she drove us out to the Bruce Highway, and on the way told us about a lady called Mrs McDonald who was the secretary of the Proserpine Show and chief hirer and firer of the casual labour used over the week the show took to set up, run and dismantle. "It starts in a few days, I think, there's usually plenty of work. Call in and look her up. You can mention my name." After this Mrs Hayes was silent as she drove us up the highway for a few miles, almost as if she was as reluctant to part with our company as we were with hers. Eventually she stopped and we got out and stood beside the Jeep. "Take care of yourselves, boys." She extended her bony hand and we could still hear the two Jessies barking their farewell when the Jeep was long out of sight.

TEN

The Proserpine Show: Jimmy Sharman and Carol

*Y*eppon had left its mark on us, physically and mentally, not that we could have explained the mental bit. We weren't sad or pissed off or anything, but we sat on our new rucksacks beside the road in contemplative silence for over two hours after Mrs Hayes dropped us off, not one vehicle passing by in either direction. Strangely, the atmosphere seemed to match our mood; it wasn't particularly hot but there wasn't a cloud in the sky or a breath of wind, and once the noise of the Jeep and the barking Jessies faded away it was almost eerily still and quiet. The silence seemed to press down on us, and I am certain both Glen and I experienced the same feeling; that we were somehow suddenly completely alone in the world, cut off from society. When a crow squawked in the distance it wasn't a harsh, unpleasant sound but a comforting reassurance, and we both looked in the direction it had come from.

"You okay? You've gone all quiet again."

"Yeah, I'm fine, just thinking how different everybody is," and Glen looked at me in astonishment.

"I was just thinking something like that!"

I don't believe we were gratuitous about it, and we certainly didn't plan things around it or play on it; more it was instinctive, I suppose, but the further we went it was impossible not to be aware of the effect we had on people. Constable Waring was right. Young, seemingly homeless Pommie teenagers hitchhiking about the country were not exactly an everyday sight. From 'Uncle' Alf to Sergeant

Pearce, the Molinaris and 'Aunty' Marge, and just about everyone in between, it seemed that people were not only surprised when we turned up on their doorsteps or got into their cars, but most were helpful, generous, even concerned about us. Of course, being well-endowed with teenage disdain for concern about anything, we were rarely worried about ourselves, but we were increasingly conscious that the concerns of others helped us enormously, and that without this help we would never have got as far as we had and would probably have turned back weeks before. We didn't speak of it, but so common was this generosity and help that when somebody didn't buy us a meal or offer us a bed it was conspicuous.

Which is why Sam Barker stood out a bit; not that he was nasty or anything. In fact, he was as chatty and friendly as anybody we'd met so far. I suppose the reason he didn't fawn over us or wasn't particularly surprised by what we were doing was because he had led a disjointed, nomadic existence for much of his life himself, starting as a child during the Depression. When Sam was eight his father had 'hit the roads', as many had at the time in search of work. What was slightly more unusual was that Sam's dad had taken his entire family with him: his mother, his wife and three children.

"Slept many a night under the stars," Sam told us. "Me and me little sisters loved it. We thought it was a great adventure, but I don't think me mum and gran was too keen." He grimaced. "Oh, I remember being hungry a lot and sometimes real cold, but I guess because we were all together it wasn't so bad. 'A trouble shared is a crisis spared' me gran always used to say. Me dad got work eventually, but it was never permanent and we moved about a lot, living in barns, renting shacks. One way or another I've been on the road ever since," he grinned. "Still am, I guess," and he waved at the suitcase on the back seat of his car and the shirts hanging from the back window. Not that he was a bum or vagrant or anything; his clothes and car told us that. It was an immaculate black 1954 Chrysler Imperial sedan, and pulling up in front of us he'd cleared the bench seat next to him of papers and things and flung open the door with a cheery welcome: "Gidday boys, goin' to Mackay, hop in!"

Sam Barker was a one-man advance party for Bullen's Circus. His job was to go to the towns and cities ahead of the circus, organise dates and venues and put up posters and billboards advertising its coming. The back of his car and the boot were stuffed with posters and other literature, the majority of the posters showing elephants performing various feats and acts. "Elephants are our big attraction," Sam explained proudly. "Mr Bullen and his sons have bred and trained them for years. There's not many in Australia know more about elephants." He and his wife, who also worked with the circus as the clown's make-up artist and ticket seller, lived in a caravan on site. "I'm not home much. Sometimes I'm weeks, even months ahead of them, then I'll go back and stay for a while before I set off again. I'm always on the road. Not that I mind," he grinned. "I love it," and he turned up the radio as the roomy Chrysler flashed through the Queensland countryside, gliding smoothly over the bumps like only the cushioned absorbers of those lovely 1950s American cars allowed, with Dion providing the rhythm.

"… *and when she asks me, which one I love best?*
I tear open my shirt I got Rosie on my chest.
They call me the wanderer, yeah I'm a wanderer,
I go around, around …"

At his suggestion, Sam dropped us off near the railway yards in Mackay at about five that evening and we headed straight for the truck stop cafe opposite. There were plenty of trucks parked in the yard, and one of them was bound to be going our way. The woman who ran the cafe was called Molly. Plump and matronly, she was known to all the truckies as 'Good Golly', and she more than made up for Sam's lack of surprise and concern about us.

"Sydney! My, you are a long way from home. What are you doing way up here?"

After we'd eaten she came across to our table to clear the dishes away. It was beginning to get dark, and she looked outside.

"Where will you sleep tonight?"

See! It wasn't any of our doing! She asked!

Within an hour we were settling down on two mattresses she put on the floor for us in a store room behind the kitchen. Not only that, but on hearing we wanted to get to Proserpine the next day she'd arranged a lift with a driver she knew was going there in the morning, and pointed his truck out to us.

"He's staying the night in the hotel down the road. You've got to be by his cab at four o'clock in the morning. I'll wake you," she smiled. Then she took her leave, saying over her shoulder, "If you want a drink or anything during the night, just help yourselves."

"Good Golly Miss Molly, sure like to ball!"

Good Golly Miss Molly … !"

There were still two days to go before the Proserpine Show opened, but as we neared the ground the following afternoon and saw the hive of activity — the Ferris wheel and rides of the funfair, the marquees and tents being erected around the main arena, and the horse floats, cattle trucks and other vehicles waiting to get in — the excitement and anticipation came flooding back.

* * *

The mother of all agricultural shows, of course, was the Sydney Royal Easter Show and for weeks before it we used to save every penny we could get our hands on, or in my case steal the pennies if the opportunity arose. Mostly, though, we scrounged as many tips as we could from our paper rounds, scoured the suburb for empty lemonade bottles to return, or collected old newspapers for the fish and chip shop, three-pence a bundle they would give you. By the time show time came we might have fifteen or sixteen shillings, maybe even a pound, although it never seemed to last long and half way through the day we would have spent everything. But it was exciting with the show bags, the wood chopping, the Grand Parade and of course the sideshows and funfairs, the helter-skelter and knock 'em downs, the fattest lady in the world, the dwarves, the man with three legs and the incomparable, the one and only 'Jimmy Sharman's Boxing Troupe'.

Before each show all the boxers would line up in their glittering dressing gowns on a ten-foot high catwalk erected along the front of the gaudy marquee, the canvas of which was daubed with dreadful paintings of past Australian boxing legends.

At the end of the catwalk a huge Piltdown of a man in a shiny red dressing gown constantly beat a large bass drum. His days in the ring may have been over but he still looked terrifying, his nose and ears bent and squashed, as if taped to his head. Then the canvas behind the catwalk was flung back and the sartorial, flamboyant Jimmy Sharman emerged to much fanfare, coils of smoke rising from the fat cigar he never seemed to smoke.

"Roll up! Roll Up! Roll up!" he shouted to make himself heard over the boom of the drum and the blaring music from the merry-go-round next door. "Go three, one-minute rounds with any of these champions and win ten shillings! Six boxers! Six weights! Six world champions!" he exaggerated without batting an eyelid, and Piltdown man almost burst the drum-skin in his enthusiasm.

"Yes, ladies and gentlemen, I give you six of the world's greatest boxers. At the far end, weighing two hundred and forty pounds, the unstoppable! The mighty! The unbeatable! Brute Brabazon!"

To a fearsome pounding by Piltdown man, Brute stepped forward, scowling down at the crowd now rapidly being drawn to the spectacle. Shaking his fist and beating his chest, he strutted above us, looking every inch the hard, mean bastard he undoubtedly was yet unable to conceal his flabby stomach, or the fact that he must be at least forty-five.

"Six hundred professional bouts and never beaten!" Jimmy enthused, his nose visibly growing longer. "Five hundred and seventy knockouts, thirty …"

"I could take 'im in one!" shouted a voice, cutting Jimmy off, and the crowd wheeled around, gasping at the audacity.

"Yessir!" shouted Jimmy gleefully. "Ladies and gentlemen, we might have our first contest. How much do you weigh, sir?"

Conveniently the man, who looked like Brute's twin brother, was also almost exactly the right weight, and having given his details he was ushered inside the marquee to prepare for his bout. Meanwhile the crowd grew ever larger as Jimmy introduced the rest of his troupe: middleweights, welterweights, lightweights, all of whom were eventually challenged to a fight by someone in the crowd.

The first night I went, I thought it was the most magical and exciting thing I had ever seen. I had no idea it was in any way stage-managed. It cost a shilling to get in, and with funds tight, a couple of us boys snuck round the back and managed to crawl under the side of the tent, only to be spotted by one of the bouncers who grabbed us by the scruff of the neck. He was about to chuck us out when Jimmy appeared.

"Caught them sneaking in, Mr Sharman," the bouncer explained.

"Let 'em be," said Jimmy. "Come 'ere," he commanded, and as we got to him he gave each of us a clip on the back of the head.

"Sit down there and don't let me catch you again."

We had the best seats in the house, on the floor right next to the ring; we could reach out and touch the boxers!

The ring was not raised up like a normal boxing ring and just two ropes enclosed it, with an inch of sawdust covering the hard dirt floor. Overhead a huge rectangular, grubby lightshade hung over the centre, a pale orange light filtering through the thick cigarette smoke. Completely encircling the ring were tiers of rickety wooden benches, five or six rows high, the top rows so close to the sloping roof of the tent that the people sitting up there had to lean forward. By fight time the tent was packed to the rafters, literally, and as the first boxers emerged the atmosphere was electrifying, with shouted bets and money changing hands all around the ring.

The referee was none other than Piltdown man, who was booed mercilessly when the first fight was stopped in the first round. Everybody wanted the challengers to win, obvious plant or not, and by the time the massive Brute Brabazon and his equally large challenger emerged the crowd had become restless. Most of the other fights had finished within two rounds, with the challengers being beaten easily or appearing not to try. Heated words were exchanged and Jimmy's bouncers looked concerned. The two huge men entering the ring diverted attention for a moment, but soon cries of "Rubbish" and "Av-a-go ya mug" rang out as they spent the first two rounds locked in a blubbery embrace.

In the third round they came out snorting and snarling, the crowd by now baying for action. Suddenly Brute swung a wild haymaker that hit the challenger a glancing blow on the shoulder. Instantly he crashed to the sawdust as if pole-axed and lay there, eyes tightly shut but lids fluttering, like a child pretending to be asleep. This was too much. The crowd went berserk, screaming their disgust as much at the dreadful acting as anything else, some demanding their money back, and for a moment a riot looked to be on the cards but the bouncers moved in, rough and menacing, and the revolt was quelled. Besides, the highlight of the show was about to start.

Ernie Watson came into the ring and was greeted with a roar of cheering and applause. Outside, Ernie had been presented as a young country boy from Wilcannia, a half-caste Aboriginal who had never had a fight in his life. As if to highlight this amateurish status, Ernie didn't have smart shiny shorts on like the others; he was still wearing his trousers, rolled up to the calf above his bare feet. By the end of the first round, however, the crowd sensed the stable boxer had a fight on his hands and expectation turned to excitement.

"Come on, Ernie, show these bastards how it's done!"

Like the first, the second round was fairly even, although right at the end Ernie caught the stable boxer with a ripper, right on the button, and the excitement became pandemonium.

"Come on, Ernie! Come on, Ernie! Come on, Ernie!"

The last round was frenetic, punches being thrown wildly by both young men right up to the bell. It was close, but the crowd was sure and they let Piltdown know in no uncertain terms. He took an age to decide, his stubby pencil repeatedly going over his sweat-soaked notes. Eventually he made up his mind and lifted Ernie's arm in the air. The crowd went mad, all else was forgotten and forgiven and Jimmy Sharman magically appeared in the ring, handing Ernie his money while soaking up the acclaim.

"Can I play a crowd or what?" his toothy grin asked as he circled the ring with the victorious Ernie, waving his fat cigar, knowing that the next time Ernie fights the crowd will be different and few will recognise him.

There was no doubt Jimmy Sharman understood the art of the showman, but his show was by no means all a sham and many challengers were genuine people from the crowd. Years later I discovered he did a great deal for boxing generally in Australia, especially helping young Aboriginal men whom he claimed were "born to fight". Like many things from those days, Jimmy Sharman is no more, but boy, it was fantastic! Brutal at times, maybe, farcical at others perhaps, but always it was pure, magical, unadulterated theatre.

*   *   *

The truckie who'd given us a lift from Mackay dropped us off right outside the showground gates, and as we jumped down we were confronted by a large sign:

'Absolutely no admittance without a badge or pass on set up days'.
Two gate officials were making damn sure the rule was obeyed to the letter, causing a mini traffic jam. Isn't it strange how officious gate officials always seem to get? Anyway, to avoid a confrontation we snuck in behind a truck.

"Oi, you two!" yelled a distinguished-looking older man we hadn't noticed hovering in the background. His hat, tie and smart tweed jacket hosted a vast array of official-looking badges and agricultural paraphernalia. "Where are your badges?"

Shit!

"We've been told to report to Mrs McDonald," I said, and just for a second he was taken aback slightly and checked his clipboard.

"Are you signed on as casuals?"

"Yes."

"So where are your badges? What are your names?" he demanded, looking down at his clipboard again. I was trying to think up a plausible answer when Glen came to the rescue.

"Mrs McDonald is going to give them to us."

Being able to lie with the utmost sincerity is as necessary for survival as a warm coat for those living on the margins of society. It was a skill Glen was obviously beginning to master, not that it cut any ice with old Badges. He didn't believe a word of it. Fortunately, at that moment a lorry driver who'd been waiting to get in for some time came to our rescue, hooting impatiently, and the old man was obliged to see to him.

"I'll check with Mrs McDonald, mind!" and he waved his finger at us. "And if I catch you about without a badge you'll be for it, understand!"

We didn't hang around any longer, and headed for several large marquees that looked like the main administrative area of the show. Halfway there we passed a stockman covered in dust and carrying a saddle on his shoulder. He was obviously not the slightest bit official, giving us a cheery wink and "Gidday, boys," greeting, so I took the opportunity.

"Don't know where we can find Mrs McDonald, do you?"

"Ah! Barnyard Betty!" he exclaimed with a grin. "Sure, she's in the dining marquee there. Yer can't miss her! Calf-bearing hips and tits yer could camp under! Better be careful, though. She eats boys like you for breakfast!" And chuckling to himself, he swung his saddle onto his other shoulder and went on his way.

He was right; Mrs Elizabeth McDonald truly was unmissable! She was wearing a bright woollen tartan skirt and heavy brogue shoes, but without doubt her most noticeable feature were her enormous breasts, a frilly blue blouse only emphasising their size. The most amazing thing was that they appeared to be virtually flat on top. It was as if she had a large tray strapped under her blouse and it was all we could do not to ogle them as we introduced ourselves.

"Ah, been expecting you two," she said, adding to our amazement. "How was Mrs Hayes when you left her?"

"Well ... okay, I guess. She got a bit tired sometimes."

"Yes, I imagine she did," and she shook her head in silent sympathy for a moment. "Now then," she abruptly changed the subject. "Six shillings a day, all you can eat for breakfast, lunch and dinner and a straw bed in the boy's barn."

It wasn't so much an offer as a statement of fact, and neither of us knew what to say and could only stand there, desperately trying not to look at her heaving bosom.

"Good," said Mrs McDonald, interpreting our silence as accepting the deal. "You can start tomorrow," then she looked around the tent and called to a girl about my age who was spreading tablecloths out on trestle tables as fast as two men erected them. "Carol, can you take these two boys and show them where they'll be sleeping?"

"Yes, Mrs McDonald," said the girl dutifully, and as she came skipping over to us, smiling prettily, she reminded me of someone.

"Come on, then!" she chivvied, amused by our nonplussed looks, and she set off briskly.

"When you're settled, come straight back here!" Mrs McDonald called after us.

"Is she always that bossy?" I asked, running to catch up with the girl.

"Oh she's alright. She just likes things to run smoothly."

The 'boy's barn' was one end of a disused stock shed, the rows of waist-high wooden pens with a couple of straw bales chucked into them being the bedrooms. The 'girl's barn' was at the other end of the shed, separated by a hessian screen.

"You can have any one of the pens without gear in it," said Carol, and made to dash off.

"Do you sleep in there, then?" I asked, nodding to the other end, hoping to prolong the conversation.

"No, I have to look after the General," and she smiled her lovely smile and skipped away before I could say anything else.

"She's alright, isn't she," I said, watching the girl running back to the marquee, her simple floral dress swishing in the breeze.

"Yeah, I suppose so."

"I wonder who the General is?"

"Search me. Come on, we'd better get sorted and go back."

"Hands out, please," Mrs McDonald demanded as she walked down the line inspecting us. There were about a dozen of us, mainly teenagers, lined up outside the Show Secretary's tent near the main arena. One or two were fully grown men and women but she spoke to us all like we were ten-year-olds, and Glen and I were not the only ones admonished for having dirty nails and told to "do something about them before I see you again tomorrow!" Then Mrs McDonald informed us we were free to go until six in the morning, when we would be dispatched around the show to do any job required for the first few hours. After that our main tasks were either to be waiters and waitresses serving lunch, morning and afternoon teas to the members and their guests, or helping in the kitchen washing up and clearing away before, during and after those events.

Morning teas were served between 9am and 10.30am; lunch from 12pm to 2pm; and afternoon tea from 3.30pm to 5pm. "Having cleared away after afternoon tea, your time is your own until six the next morning." Mrs McDonald finished the briefing. "Any questions?" No-one dared say a word. Then she handed us each an apron, blue for boys, pink for girls and told us that when serving we were to wear them at all times. "And don't get them dirty!" she commanded. "Report back here at six o'clock in the morning!"

Despite being a bit of a tartar and the butt of many a joke — not that anybody was game to say boo in her presence — Mrs McDonald was a big softie at heart really. She wouldn't stand for any nonsense and told us off roundly if we were late, and she made sure we were as tidy as our wardrobe allowed, but all in all she treated us well and we had a pretty good few days at the Proserpine Show, even if we didn't get paid much. The food was great and there was plenty of it, and we got the occasional tip from farmers celebrating with a few bottles of champagne at lunchtime after their precious bull or rooster won a prize. At night, as promised, our time was our own, and Glen and I must have gone on every ride, tried out every dodgem car, thrown every coconut and seen every sideshow half a dozen times, the majority of which we didn't have to pay for after we got to know the staff a bit better. Unfortunately there was no Jimmy Sharman, but there was wood chopping and at night either a rodeo or some other spectacle in the main arena. We had a great time, and the work was never really that taxing.

To my disappointment I discovered that Carol wasn't a casual labourer like us; her father was a show official, farmer and pig breeder, and one of the other girls told me that she worked with him most of the time and had only been helping to set up the dining marquee. Once or twice I caught sight of her, but either she was busy doing something or we were working, so it wasn't until the end of the second last day of the show that I caught up with her again. Glen and I were heading back to the 'boy's barn' about six o'clock, having finished the afternoon tea clear up. It was getting dark and we were earnestly discussing what rides we were going on that night when through the gloom I spotted Carol in the distance, heading purposefully towards one of the large animal sheds and carrying something in her hands. I left Glen standing as I ran across to her.

To my surprise, the something in her hands were five toffee apples.

"Like them, do you!"

"They're not for me." Carol smiled, and suddenly I knew who she reminded me of; or rather *what* she reminded me of. It was the feelings I'd had when Judy Laverton had smiled at me.

"They're for the General, he loves them."

"Who is this General?"

"You can come and meet him if you want."

Yes!

General Eisenhower was lying in his pen, nuzzling the soft straw that cocooned him. He was an enormous large white pig, although I thought he looked more like a hippopotamus than a pig; I'd never seen such a massive animal before, and my astonishment had Carol smiling with delight, which had my stomach turning over with delight. God, she was lovely!

"We call him Ike," said Carol, bending down so he could sniff one of the toffee apples and immediately the huge creature hefted himself to his feet with surprising agility, gobbling the apple down in one mouthful. The other four didn't last much longer, and afterwards he stood there looking at her dolefully and licking his lips.

"He'd eat a hundred if I gave them to him," said Carol, looking lovingly at her charge. "Wouldn't you," she said, bending down to hug his massive head, an embrace the huge beast was obviously used to.

"But we have to be careful how much and what we feed him," and taking the sticks of the apples away so Ike didn't eat them as well, she went into the pen beside him.

It was just like the 'bedroom' Glen and I shared, only Carol was there on her own.

"You sleep next to him!"

"Pigs need a lot of looking after, especially at show time, and we don't want anybody getting to him. Oh, he farts a lot and shits everywhere, but I don't mind, I love him really, and he should at least win Best in Breed I hope."

The long shed was full of a variety of animals with their minders and there wasn't much privacy. Carol sat down, retreating into the seclusion of her walled pen and indicating I should join her. Next to her pillow at the top of her sleeping bag was a portable forty-five record player with a pile of records beside it, and she rifled through a few.

"Who do you like?" she asked. "I've got Connie Francis, Doris Day, Cliff Richard, Ricky Nelson, Pat Boon ... do you like Pat Boon?"

"Oh, yeah!" and I sat down, as close to her as I could.

"Really! Most boys I know hate him!"

"No, I think he's great. I've got most of his records at home."

I don't know how long we sat there, chatting away like life-long friends while we listened to the music. She was easy to talk to, unpretentious and bubbly, and we laughed a lot.

"Oh, I'd love to go to Sydney!" she gushed, when I told her about Sydney Harbour and Manly. "I did go to Brisbane once, but I was only five."

"Have you finished school, then?"

"Yes, two years ago when I was fifteen. Dad doesn't think girls need to go to school after that. He says education is wasted on them as they'll only go and get married and have kids. Besides, Mum died when I was thirteen and he needs me to help him on the farm." And she shrugged and put on another record.

Her father owned a property near Monto where they grew fruit, vegetables and grains mainly, but he was also one of Queensland's leading pig breeders.

"We go to most of the shows around the state."

Just then a man arrived at Ike's pen and went in, patting his rump.

"Oh, hi Dad. This is Nick."

"Hi Nick," the man grinned, leaning across to shake my hand. "Any problems?" he asked his daughter, bending down to inspect the General's ears.

"No. He's fine."

"I guess I should go," I said, standing up.

"Come back again tomorrow after you've finished if you want. We could listen to some more records?" said Carol.

"Yeah, sure," I agreed instantly, and was about to say my farewells to her father when she leant across and kissed me quickly on the cheek, whispering in my ear as she did: "Good. I like you."

"On a day like today, I pass the time away
Writing love letters in the sand ..."

Great singer, that Pat Boon!

By the time I got back to the boy's barn I was so tall I could hardly fit through the doors, although my euphoria was short-lived.

"Where have you been?" Glen asked accusingly, and I felt like I'd cheated on him somehow. The next morning he was still obviously annoyed, although there was something about his mood that wasn't just annoyance and he barely said two words to me all day. I didn't take too much notice, however; all I could think about was Carol and her soft lips on my cheek. Normally Glen and I went to the showers together after work, but this evening I went charging off and was finished long before he got there, having used plenty of soap and spending ages combing my hair. I was going on my first date!

General Eisenhower was looking very pleased with himself, standing in his pen surrounded by balloons, coloured ribbons and rosettes. Not only had he won Best in Breed but he'd come second in Best in Show, and a group of eight or nine farmers was gathered around, listening intently as Carol's father explained the virtues of his wonderful beast. Winning Best in Breed was not just a thrill and a reward for the all the hard work and effort they'd put into Ike, but it would be financially rewarding as well, and both Carol and her father were beaming with pleasure.

With the men obviously engrossed in serious business discussions, Carol and I were sidelined a bit, not that we minded; and a few minutes after I arrived, she called out, "Dad, Nick and I are just going for a look around, okay?" and he waved at her in recognition and went back to his dealing. On the wall of the pen beside her bed there were several keys hanging from a hook, and she took one down and grabbed my hand. "Come on. I know where we can go." I didn't need any persuading, and followed her as she skipped up and out of the shed. Outside she continued to hurry, leading me across to another shed, at one end of which was a padlocked door. She opened it and we went inside. It wasn't a very big room; there was some straw on the floor, obviously recently used by someone as a bed, but what caught the eye were all the harnesses, saddles and bridles hanging on every wall.

"It's a tack room," explained Carol, bolting the door behind us. "I've taken over from the girl who used to look after it. She went home this afternoon; nobody will come in here now," and she turned and stood in front of me, smiling. "Well?"

"What?"

"Aren't you going to kiss me?"

Jesus!

I suppose the biggest surprise was the electrifying, almost desperate urgency that consumed her. In all my most erotic dreams I had never imagined a girl would be like that; so uninhibited, so hungry, but above all so knowledgeable. She must have realised from the beginning how inexperienced I was, but not once did she make me feel embarrassed or anything. I might have been a novice, but a little something in my trousers understood fully what was going on and was literally bursting at the seams to get out and into the action. I'm not sure how long we stood there kissing, my tongue emulating hers, and she must have felt me pressing into her, digging into her more like. Suddenly she broke away and stepped back a pace, as if to catch her breath.

"I can't go all the way," she panted apologetically. "Not 'til I'm married. I promised Mum."

For a second I didn't have a clue what she meant, and could only gape stupidly at her.

What is she talking about? All the way? Mum? All the way where? "But your mum's not here," was all I could blurt.

"I know, silly," she giggled beautifully, and in one quick movement she pulled her dress over her head and stood in front of me completely naked. "But that doesn't mean we can't have a good time," and she pushed me gently down onto the straw.

Jesus!

It was only much later that it struck me she must have planned what we were going to do long before I got there; she'd come prepared, as it were. The word premature might be pertinent here, but it wasn't really any of my doing. She undid my trousers and released me and for a second I couldn't believe it was mine, it was so huge and engorged, I was quite proud of it. Carol seemed to like it too, and she knew exactly what to do with it. I may not have lasted very long, but boy it was fantastic.

When I recovered, she lay back on the straw. God she was

gorgeous, pert little breasts and hard nipples, and she guided my head down onto them.

"Just lick them and flick them with your tongue," she sighed, as instinctively my hand went between her legs, but I didn't really know what to do when I got there, other than poke my fingers inside. She was all wet and warm, and then she placed her hand on mine and gently guided my fingers where she wanted them to go.

"Not there; here. Yes … that's it … there … now put a finger inside me as well, yes that's it … like that … now together … oh yes … like that … like that … harder … harder … oh yes … yes! Don't stop! Don't stop!" And when her cries turned almost to screams and went on and on, I had visions of her dad pounding at the door.

Afterwards we lay in each other's arms for twenty minutes or so, nuzzling and kissing, and then she looked at her watch. "Shit, I better get back. Dad will be wondering where I am."

"Have you done that before?" I couldn't help asking as we got dressed, and immediately kicked myself, realising what a dumb question it was.

"Oh yes," she said. "I often have to tug the General off to get his spunk." Then she saw the look on my face. "But that's just like milking a cow," and she smiled and cupped my face in her hands. "It's not like this. This was beautiful. Thank you."

She was thanking me!

We strolled back to her pen in the dark, holding hands and kissing and hugging every ten yards. "Why don't you come down to Monto," she asked. "I'm sure Dad could find you and your friend a job on the farm." When we got back to the General's pen her father and his business friends were gone and the General was lying down, opening one eye in acknowledgment when he heard Carol's voice as she gave me her address.

"Can I see you tomorrow?"

"No," she sighed. "We're leaving at five to go home." Then she pulled me down into the pen and kissed me, her dress riding up above her thighs. "But you could come to Monto!" I floated back to our shed, consumed by one thought. If it was that good when you didn't go all the way, what must it be like when you did!

Glen was lying on his side, his back to my bed, but I knew he wasn't asleep. I didn't say anything, just got under my duffle coat and lay down, my mind a whirl. Could we go to Monto? After about ten minutes I sensed Glen half turn towards me. "Did you do it, then?"

For a moment I didn't say anything. I'm not sure where it came from, but suddenly I was certain the answer to that question was crucially important to our relationship.

I was aware my going off with Carol had pissed him off, but initially I just thought he was jealous; now something told me it was much deeper than that. It was as if I'd breached his trust, broken the oath of loyalty we'd sworn to each other in the bus shelter at Mount Gravatt.

"No," I said eventually, which was partly true, adding, "She goes home tomorrow," as if that would somehow make him feel better. I knew that if I even suggested going to Monto it would be the end of us. The problem was I also knew that had Carol walked into our pen right then and asked me to come with her, I would have gone like a shot. It was my first lesson of just how powerful an emotion sex is. It was a long time before I fell asleep, with two visions swirling about. First the image of Carol's gorgeous body, and then Mrs Hayes sitting in her chair, whisky in hand, warning us about a man's penis and his principles ...

The next day was our last at the Proserpine Show, a great deal of it having already been dismantled and exhibitors and animals on their way home. I knew it was stupid, but I just couldn't resist the urge to duck over to the General's pen, just to make sure she'd gone, an action that didn't improve my relationship with Glen. It was obvious that going to Monto was out of the question. Perhaps I could get there one day, but there was no way I could go with Glen. Nor could I just up and leave him. Like it or not we were in this together, whatever *this* was, and the least I owed him was to see it through together. Magnetic Island was *our* goal; Monto would have to be *my* dream.

At five-thirty that evening all the casual workers were lined up outside the show secretary's tent, where we'd been summoned to be paid. The half dozen or so of us who'd worked in the dining marquee had become quite friendly over the show days and a certain camaraderie had built up, us against the formidable Mrs McDonald as it were, so there was a slight air of sadness that it was all over, that the next day we would all be going our separate ways. The talk was all about where and what people were going to do next, and addresses were swapped and invitations made. Most of them, including Mrs McDonald, had long since known about our plan to go to Magnetic Island, which, we were to discover, was why we were the last to be called in to receive our money.

"Ah, boys! I've kept you until last as I have a proposition to put to you. How would you feel about staying on and helping the maintenance staff clear up? Nothing too taxing, picking up rubbish, bit of humping and shifting, should take about a week. You can stay sleeping in the barn."

I suppose we'd been readying ourselves for the final push to Magnetic Island, so at first we were a little hesitant.

"As we won't be feeding you, we can pay you ten shillings a day each and you can use the showers and the cooking facilities in the kitchens. Also at the end of the week I can guarantee you a lift to Townsville. What do you say?"

It was the lift to Townsville that did it. At least we could now be certain of getting there in one go. So it was we stayed on at the Proserpine Show for seven more days, three of them spent simply picking up rubbish. It's amazing how much mess accumulates at an event like that. It must take a fortnight to clear up after Sydney!

ELEVEN

Dunny carters, public bars and Mr Personality

*R*ay Cooper's dad drove the dunny cart and very few children ever let him forget it. He was a few years ahead of me in primary school so I didn't have much to do with him there, but I know he was the butt of constant taunts and jibes. The boys in his class wouldn't play marbles with him, and the girls used to change their skipping song whenever he came near them in the playground.

"I'm a little Dutch girl dressed in blue
These are the things I like to do
Salute to the Captain
Bow to the Queen
And hold my nose when the dunny man's been!"

And they'd stop skipping, hold their noses, screw their faces up in disgust and scream at him to go away. Gee, kids can be cruel! We might have taunted him when he was young, but as he got older no one was game to say a word to him or his dad.

Jack Cooper was the first of the trio of people who never let me forget I was a Pom. He was a huge, unimaginative brute of a man with massive hands and a violent temper. An ex-soldier, like Mr Archer he'd been incensed when "That cunt Churchill and those Pommie arseholes!" initially refused to let the Australian Army go home from North Africa to defend the country after the Japanese invaded New Guinea. Trouble was Jack Cooper had few, if any, of

Mr Archer's finer characteristics to offset this bitterness, and as the Coopers only lived four or five doors away from us it was difficult not to cross paths with them occasionally. When we first arrived in the street I was four and Ray, who was nine or ten, sort of befriended me for awhile, I suppose because he could boss me about and be the main man when we played Cowboys and Indians. It was a few weeks after we moved in that I went to his house for the one and only time.

"What's that fucking Pom doin' here! Get him out!" Mr Cooper yelled when he found me in the kitchen eating a chocolate biscuit Mrs Cooper had given me, and for a moment I thought he was going to grab me and chuck me out himself.

"He's only a kid for Christ's sake!" Mrs Cooper screamed back at him, getting between us.

"I don't give a stuff! I won't have any of those cunts in my house!"

Of course I was far too young to understand why he was so angry. All I knew was he frightened the life out of me, and I ran home in tears. Such was his hatred, I'm surprised he ever stopped at our house to take our dunny can away.

The dunny cart wasn't really a cart, it was a truck, but I suppose the name stuck from when, not so many years before, the job was done with a horse and cart. The back of the truck was split into two horizontal levels, like an upper and a lower deck. When the truck left the sewerage depot at four in the morning the lower level was empty while the upper level was full with fifty or more empty dunny cans. Each truck had a crew of three — a driver and two carters — and their round might consist of several streets, returning to base at intervals to get rid of the full cans and bring back a load of empty ones. It was an indescribably awful job, yet there was always a queue of fit young men waiting to do it as it paid quite well and they were usually finished for the day by half past ten.

The driver had the best of it as he always remained in the vehicle, driving it slowly up the road as the carters jogged from house to house, taking an empty can and returning with a full one which they slid onto the lower level. As was the norm, most dunnies were in the back gardens of houses and each empty can had a lid with a special hinge which clanked loudly as the carter ran, giving ample warning of his approach; this lid was to clamp on the full can before they picked it up. It was prudent to know what day was dunny day as shit carters stopped for no one, and would more or less take the full can from under you and replace it with the new one as you sat there, if you happened to be in situ when they arrived. They always carried the cans, full or empty, on their shoulders, draped across which were pieces of canvas like a sort of poncho to protect their shirts. By the end of the first truckload of the morning this canvas sheet, and the protective cloth caps they wore, would be wet and stained brown as the lids never fitted securely and the contents sloshed about, slopping out as they ran. By the time a dunny cart was full the stench around it was ripe, to put it mildly. The stench around the dunny carters was pretty ripe too, but nobody dared say so, and certainly not to Jack Cooper when he was in his domain: the public bar of the Epping Hotel, where he held court most evenings.

For five years I did an afternoon paper round on my bicycle, and when I finished I spent an hour or so outside the Epping Hotel selling papers and "Pix" and "Post" magazines. In the late 1950s the public bars of Australian hotels had long been male-only bastions, and for a decade and more after the war they were like barometers of the stresses and strains that bedevil all societies after major conflicts; victor or vanquished, trauma doesn't discriminate. Always raucous, often vulgar and usually intimidating, violent arguments, fist fights and even all-out brawls were common events in many pubs, especially in the larger cities. Nothing has changed, you might feel; the difference, however, was that fifty years ago the perpetrators were grown men in their thirties, forties and fifties, self-medicating away their terrible memories and seeking the comfort and assurance of understanding comrades. Today it is young people in their eighteens, nineteens and twenties, self-medicating away their youth and seeking the comfort and assurance of understanding policemen. Adding to the mix in the 1950s were the plethora of peculiar licensing laws in place at the time, including women being banned from entering public bars — although it was difficult to imagine any woman actually *wanting* to go into them — but there were two other equally contentious laws.

As it happened, the first and last years of my paper round coincided with the ending of those two laws, and the first, repealed in 1955, was one of the most amazing licensing laws ever imposed anywhere in the world; a law so incomprehensible and silly that it was known universally as "the six o'clock swill."

This law demanded that all pubs had to shut for an hour between six and seven in the evening. It was introduced in 1910 in the belief it would force men to go home after work for dinner, or at least go home. What happened, of course, was precisely the opposite, a situation merely exacerbated by war. Evening commuter trains returning workers to the suburbs from the city spewed out men intent only on one thing, getting in as many schooners as possible before the deadline. With ten minutes to go men would order two, three or even four more schooners, lining them up on the bar. By the time six o'clock came they'd have consumed twice as much as normal, drunk it three times faster than normal and when they were kicked out into the street they took their unfinished schooners with them. By half past six there were probably as many drunk men stumbling along the gutters of the nation's city streets as sober ones sitting at their dinner tables.

The other law, which was in place until 1960, was that all hotels had to stay closed on Anzac Day, supposedly as a mark of respect but truth be known it was simply because the authorities were terrified at the prospect of tens of thousands of old soldiers roaming the streets pissed out of their heads. As it turned out, they were right to be wary. On that first Anzac Day after the law was changed, the dignity and solemnity of the Dawn Service had long been forgotten by sunset in many pubs, monumental piss-ups being the order of the day.

Although public bars may have seemed like a seething cauldron, to us young boys they were fascinating places full of drama and excitement, and we couldn't wait until we were old enough to drink. Of course, paper boys weren't supposed to go into the bar but we frequently did, ignoring the curses, avoiding the vomit and ducking the clips round the ear from the landlord. It was worth it though, as the tips were usually much bigger, drunk men being far more interested in hearing the end of the latest crude joke, or continuing their argument than bothering with a few pennies change.

When tempers flared in the Epping Hotel Jack Cooper was more often than not in the thick of it, even if the argument or fight didn't involve him. In time I got used to his abuse, and by the age of eleven I realised he was never going to do anything other than shout and yell. In fact I found his ravings quite amusing, strangely enough. The same couldn't be said about his son, though. By the time I was eleven, Ray Cooper had not only inherited his father's size and imagination but his violence and hatred of Poms, and whenever he saw me he would either push me in the gutter or take my bike and dump it in the storm drain or in the bush somewhere. I always got it back, but for many years until they moved away I was petrified of Ray Cooper and used to make complicated detours to avoid going near his house or meeting him in the street.

* * *

In size and demeanour, Colin Tucker reminded me of Jack Cooper. He wasn't as bad-tempered and abusive, nor did he smell like a dunny carter ... well, not quite as bad. Glen and I had spent our last day at the Proserpine Show helping to dismantle the fences and jumps in the equestrian arena. It turned out the majority of them had been borrowed from the Townsville Showground and, the night before, a battered old Bedford Commer flat back truck that was a bit like 'Uncle' Alf's only in much worse condition had arrived from Townsville to pick them up. The driver was Colin Tucker. Like Jack Cooper, he was a mountain of a man; bare footed, he had massive arms and hands and his beer belly made his very short rugby shorts appear even shorter, and stretched his much worn and battered 'Townsville Brothers' rugby league jumper to bursting point. On the doors of the truck, the words 'Tuckers Transport Townsville' were crudely painted in large faded letters, the colour matching his jumper. Beneath this in smaller letters, but similarly crudely done, it said 'Colin Tucker Proprietor'.

The truck was not fully laden so the load had been split in two, the metal stands and supports over the rear axle, the wooden planks and poles stacked hard up against the back of the cab. In the middle was a four or five foot space where a few spare tarps and empty hessian sacks were stacked. At first, after Mrs McDonald had introduced us and asked Colin Tucker if he could take us to Townsville, he didn't seem all that keen and just continued tightening the ropes of his load; then he grunted, without looking at us.

"They'll have to ride up there," and nodded to the back of the truck.

We were actually standing by the open door of his cab and could see there was no passenger seat at all, just a mess of his belongings, including a badly rolled up sleeping swag, completely filling the space.

"Yeah, fine," we agreed.

"Six o'clock outside the main gates," he muttered, and went around the other side of the truck, the conversation obviously terminated.

It turned out Colin Tucker had been working for the Townsville Showground for years, and bringing the borrowed fence planks and poles down for the Proserpine Show for as long as anybody could remember.

"He owns the truck himself, "Mrs McDonald explained. "Bought it just after the war with some compensation he received from the army, but I'm told he is almost incapable of running a business, or getting any work. If the Townsville Showground doesn't need him, he just sits in the pub all day, so I believe."

"Is he alright?" Glen asked. "He looks a bit dodgy to me!"

"I agree he's not exactly Mr Personality," she smiled, "but I know he has to get the fences back to Townsville before the weekend, and that is where you want to go, isn't it? I doubt you'll have any problems. He's harmless enough. Just don't expect him to entertain you!" And she smiled reassuringly again.

That day she was wearing a frilly pink blouse, which if anything made her breasts appear even larger, when she sat down her entire front quivered, like an enormous pink blancmange.

"Now then, boys, how much do we owe you?"

Apart from cigarettes and the odd hot dog we'd hardly spent any money at the show, so we still had most of what Mrs Hayes had given us, and with this extra ten pounds ten shillings to put in the kitty we were rolling in it. We were also raring to go, and well before six o'clock the next morning were waiting expectantly outside the gates for our lift. One more day and we'd be there: Magnetic Island at last!

*　*　*

In the end it took us nearly fifty hours to get to Townsville, despite it only being about a hundred and sixty miles. True, the road was pretty bad in places and the truck was laboriously slow, but at one time we thought we would never get there, so often did Colin Tucker stop. Being in the back didn't help, as it severely restricted conversation so we could never find out his intentions, but even when we did stop he rarely spoke to us or told us anything. Of course we could have left at any time and taken our chances on the road, but because we were never too sure what was going on, or how long he was going to be, it was difficult to know what to do; besides, there wasn't that much traffic and he was a definite lift right to Townsville.

The first time we stopped was in Bowen, mid-morning on the first day. He just parked in a truck stop near the salt flats outside town, jumped down from the cab and disappeared down the street without a word. We were left sitting in the back like lemons, expecting he would return at any moment and arguing about what to do when he didn't. When he did come back over two hours later it was obvious he'd been drinking but he said nothing, just climbed into the cab and roared off.

The next stop was in Home Hill. It was just getting dark as we pulled up, but this time he did at least tell us we would be there for awhile and that we should go off and get something to eat. In the end we spent the night there, as he was so drunk when he came back he could hardly open the cab door, never mind drive. He yanked his swag out of the cab, cursing and struggling with it, then he just let it drop to the ground and collapsed on top of it, not even bothering to get into it. Within a minute he was snoring his head off. There wasn't much else we could do but make up a bed for ourselves on top of the tarps and sacks, which was surprisingly comfortable.

Next morning he didn't wake up until gone eight o'clock. We'd been up for hours, and as he stuffed his swag back into the cab we asked him if we would get to Townsville that day.

"Dunno," he shrugged, and then he had a "dingo's breakfast" — a yawn, a leak and a good look around — and set off without another word. We only got as far as Ayr before he stopped again, and as he climbed down, mumbled, "Get yourselves some breakfast" before setting off.

This time we followed him, and sure enough he went straight into the first pub he came to. Glen and I found ourselves standing outside in the street debating what we should do. In the end we did as he suggested, went and had breakfast, but we still couldn't make up our minds. One minute Glen was all for leaving the weird bastard and getting another lift, next minute I was, then suddenly Glen got up. "I'm going to go into the pub and ask him," he said. "I mean he could be in there for hours, couldn't he! It's not fair on us!"

I wasn't so sure, but Glen set off before I could argue.

We stuck our heads round the door and saw Colin Tucker sitting at the bar with several other fairly rough-looking men, their filthy black clothes identifying them instantly as cane cutters.

"Excuse us, Mr Tucker," Glen called across as politely as he could. "How much longer do you think you'll be?"

For a second you could have heard a flea fart. Everybody, including the barman, just stared at us in astonishment, and then to a man they burst into howls of laughter.

"Ooooo!" One of the men howled, mimicking Glen. "Excuse me, Mr Tucker, but how much longer do you think you'll be!" and they all fell about in hysterics again.

"Give him a chance, son, he's not pissed yet!" shouted another man, and Glen's face went bright red as the howls rang around the bar.

Fortunately Colin Tucker didn't seem the slightest bit concerned by our interruption. I think he quite liked being addressed as Mr Tucker and as we exited he shouted, "Won't be long, just finish this," and held up his glass. The raucous laughter followed us up the street.

An hour later, he returned.

"Let's go!" was all he slurred.

By six o'clock that evening we were only fifteen miles or so from Townsville, but to our amazement he stopped again at a pub near

Alligator Creek and without a word disappeared inside. We wandered about the place for a bit, never letting the pub or the truck out of our sight in case he came back and went off without us. Wandering round Alligator Creek wasn't a taxing task; if you blinked when you passed through, you'd miss it. We ate the last of our tins of food and then went and stood outside the pub for awhile having a smoke. We could see him sitting on a stool, waving his arms about. It didn't look like he was ever going to come out, but there was no way either of us were going to go in and ask him, so we just went back to the truck and made up our beds. This time when he returned he was so drunk we had to help him get his swag out of the cab.

At three o'clock in the morning the roar of the engine startled us awake and we were lucky not to be thrown off the back when the truck lurched violently, the rear wheels catching the edge of the road as we set off.

"Jesus!" Glen shouted, grabbing his rucksack as it was about to fall off. "The bastard's fucking mad!"

We eventually rolled into Townsville about five o'clock in the morning, having spent over fifty hours doing a trip that a push bike could do in twenty. Still, mad or not, he had got us there, Townsville at last, so as we jumped down we were feeling grateful as well as relieved. "Thanks," we yelled up to him.

"Yeah, see youse," he grunted, and without so much as a glance he drove off.

We'd met a few strange people on our journey so far, but 'Mr Personality' Colin Tucker was certainly right up there with the strangest. Although no doubt he thought we were pretty weird, too.

As it was so early, we took the opportunity to have a shower and wash our clothes in the bathroom of the first likely looking hotel we came to. Having done it once, it wasn't quite such a nerve-racking experience, but we still didn't breath easily until we were outside, clean underpants and shirts wrapped in our towels. Drying them was our first priority, and not far from the hotel we saw a sign: 'Castle Hill Lookout' so we set off up the fairly steep road. It looked like a good place to get our bearings, and we weren't disappointed. The view was just fantastic. Laid out before us was the city and harbour of Townsville, and there in the distance, rising out of a shimmering aqua green sea, was Magnetic Island. We could barely believe it. We're here! We've made it! Whoopee! There was another reason for rejoicing too, or at least going down into town and having a T-bone with the works — it was my seventeenth birthday.

TWELVE

Magnetic Island

*T*he day we arrived in Townsville was exactly nine years after the most disappointing thing that had ever happened to me occurred. The day before my eighth birthday, a parcel — the first I'd ever received actually addressed to me personally — arrived from my grandfather in Queensland. I was at school when it was delivered, and when I came home it was sitting on the dining table. It was a large parcel wrapped in brown paper with a birthday card stuck under the string, and although it was a strange shape it was quite heavy and I knew instantly what it was. Mainly because for weeks I'd been banging on to anyone who would listen that the one present I really, really, really wanted was a Meccano set. And here it was! Yes! Yes! Yes! I was so excited I almost wet myself, and then did wet myself at the other end with frustration when my stepmother said I couldn't open it until the next day.

"Why not!" I flounced. "It's my present!"

"Yes, but it's not your birthday yet and birthday presents are for *birth* days, not the day before!"

"OOOOOH!! Poop! Poop! Poop!"

"Don't talk like that, Nicholas."

Fortunately the next day was Saturday, and on non-school days we were allowed to open our presents at breakfast instead of waiting until we came home. For the rest of that afternoon I didn't go out to play as usual but lay on the dining room floor, staring up at my parcel. By the time I went to bed I'd designed a dozen things I was going to build, foremost among them a crane. It took me ages to go to sleep.

Next morning at breakfast, my father, sister and stepmother gathered about expectantly as I ripped open the brown paper, heart pumping. Then, after the stifled exclamations, stunned silence reverberated round the room and we all stared down incredulously at the wooden toilet seat. The next hour or so has always been a bit of a blur. I was completely devastated, and have no idea how long I cried. I think my father was as upset as I was, although he would have better understood that my grandfather, being a fourth generation Kiwi farmer, couldn't help himself. Like many of his kind, he was shackled with that obtuse disposition country New Zealanders like to think is a sense of humour. In fairness, though, he could never have known how disappointed his gift would make me; it was just his way of reminding me of all those rolls of toilet paper I had so assiduously dropped down his dunny.

*   *   *

Of course, Magnetic Island wasn't the immediate, crushing disappointment of the toilet seat; more it was a gradual, deepening disenchantment, but it stemmed from the same error. By the second day I think we both realised, even if we couldn't have explained it, that we'd made a mistake; not in going there, but in placing so much importance on *getting* there, like it was the culmination of our journey, rather than just another place along the way. Magnetic Island had become our Holy Grail, our Meccano set, and when we got there and found it wasn't we gradually became more and more discouraged.

It was so quiet and peaceful, there was no such thing as a 'pace of life'; 'morgue of life' might better describe it. There was absolutely no work and very little to do other than touristy things like swim in lagoons, go for walks in the bush, build sandcastles and take in the wonderful views. Of course up on the Glasshouse Mountains there had been even less to do, and nobody at all lived there; but we'd expected it to be like that, and at that point all our goals and dreams still lay ahead of us. Now, suddenly, we didn't have a clue what to do next or where to go. We had no goal, no dream.

Quite a few people did live on the Island, but they were scattered about on smallholdings or perched up on the hills in their weekenders. It did get a little busier on the weekends, as people came over from Townsville for the day. During the week, however, there were very few people about and they were mostly older, or families with young children; the whole time we were there we barely saw another person our age. Oh, we explored the place alright, marvelled at the fantastic coral reefs, the strange fish and squadrons of birds and we saw our first wild koalas, lots of them in fact — how did they get over there? We climbed Mt Cook, walked virtually right around the island and gorged ourselves on the fruit we pinched from the orchards of the smallholdings. But, pinching fruit apart, those are all occupations for which teenagers have notoriously short attention spans.

Such an enigmatic emotion is boredom! It doesn't manifest itself like anger and humour, for example; they are obvious more or less straight away. Boredom dispenses its poison in little doses. Hours take days to pass by, restlessness becomes frustration, squabbles become heated arguments, tempers get shorter, and fuming silences longer. By the time you realise it's boredom that you're suffering from, you've been crippled by it for days. Had it not been for Harry Melling, Glen and I may well have split up and gone our separate ways from Magnetic Island.

* * *

Harry Melling might as well have had 'salt of the earth' engraved on his forehead, so obvious it was; solid build, a lived-in face, reassuring serenity and hands worn and battered by decades of manual labour. He'd been visible long before the ferry reached Picnic Bay, standing out like a beacon at the end of the jetty in his outrageously lurid Hawaiian shirt. "Welcome to Magnetic Island, folks!" he greeted the handful of passengers as we alighted. "I'm Harry, and that's Doris," he grinned, pointing to a gaudily painted old bus parked at the entrance to the jetty.

Doris was a 1946 Ford long nose 'jail bar', so-called because of the vertical bars in the front grille. Now seriously rearranged to carry more luggage, it seated about twenty-five passengers. It did have a roof, but that was about all; there was not one window, save for the windscreen, and what was left of the bodywork was painted all over in a complete mishmash of bright colours — a bit like Harry's shirt.

Twice a day the bus took those wanting to go to the beaches and holiday shacks on the other side of the island, bringing back those returning to the mainland on the return journey; each trip, roughly an hour long, timed to meet the morning and afternoon ferry. There was no charge, as the bus was owned by the same people who ran the ferry service and one ticket covered it all. Back in Townsville the day before, we'd stocked up on provisions and waited around for a bit to see Mal Dixon at the taxi rank. It was one of his driver mates who'd told us the best place to camp was Horseshoe Bay, so we followed the half dozen or so other passengers and clambered aboard Doris.

"Okey-dokey Doris baby! Let's hit the road!" Harry yelled, climbing into the driver's seat, then he whistled and called out "Bing!" and a blue kelpie, panting with excitement, came rushing over and leapt into the bus, taking up a position on the floor next to the gear lever. "First stop Nelly Bay! Then all stations to Horseshoe Bay," and Doris rattled into life. For the first couple of miles the track hugged the coastline, Harry giving us a running commentary as we went through Nelly Bay and Arcadia, but it wasn't until we began climbing into the hills in the bush above Alma Bay, engine roaring in protest, that he began to sing at the top of his voice:

> *"Oh I love to go a-wandering*
> *Along the mountain track*
> *And as I go, I love to sing*
> *My knapsack on my back."*

Then he turned briefly into the bus, one hand on the wheel with the other arm vigorously urging everyone to join in, and soon we were all singing as gustily as Harry:

> *Val-de-ri; val-de-ra*
> *Val-de-ri; Val-de-rah-ha-ha-ha-ha-ha-ha!!*
> *Val-de-ri; Val-de-rah*
> *My knapsack on my back"*

Once started there was no stopping him, and for the rest of the journey the bus rang out with boisterous renditions of half a dozen popular tunes, the last, as we came down into Horseshoe Bay, being a song by his favourite singer. "Always like to finish a trip with my lovely Doris!" he informed us.

> *"Oh the deadwood stage is a-headin' on over the hills*
> *Where injun arrows is sharper than porcupine quills*
> *Dangerous land, no time to delay!*
> *Whip crack away, whip crack away, whip crack away!"*

Harry was right, of course. Doris Day was lovely! 'Wet dream Doris' we used to call her.

Having dropped all the other passengers off in the main area of

Horseshoe Bay, Harry went out of his way a bit to take us as far as he could to the western end where Mal's taxi mate had told us was the most secluded place to camp. We chatted on the way and learned he was retired and only drove the bus part-time, sharing the job with his neighbour. "One week I'll do the morning run and he does the afternoons, next week we swap about. Works out pretty good," he smiled, as Doris squeaked to a halt at the end of the sandy track. "Far as I can go, boys. There's a track down to the beach just up there. If you need anything just give us a shout. I live about half a mile over there," he pointed inland. "Can't miss the place." He patted the vibrating dash. "Doris will be parked in the front yard," and he roared off, Bing in the doorway wagging his tail in farewell.

The first few days were okay as we were busy exploring the area and building our camp. Not knowing how long we were going to stay, we'd bought a couple of pieces of old tarpaulin and some rope from a junk shop in Townsville, just in case we needed more shelter than banana leaves and palm fronds. It took us nearly two days to gather all the material and build our camp, tucked in under the rocks right at the end of the beach. We were quite proud of it, even if the construction had been interrupted by our increasingly ill-tempered, petty arguments.

In three days we only saw half a dozen people, four of whom had strolled up to our end of the beach one evening, coming from the other end where most of the holiday accommodation was situated. We'd just lit our fire and were preparing to cook dinner when the two couples stopped about a hundred yards away and stared at us. Glen was opening a tin so I gave them a wave. One of the ladies did wave back but it was with some reluctance, as if we were two scruffy teenagers from Epping and they might catch something if they got too friendly.

I was tempted to yell out, "What are you looking at!" but mumbled it instead.

"They're only curious," said Glen.

"What about? How would they like if we went down there and stared at them?"

"Jesus, you're touchy!"

"No, I'm not!"

"Yes, you are! Go and get some more wood!"

"No. You go and get the fucking wood!"

We did eventually get around to eating, but it was a silent affair.

A couple of mornings later we were running out of food so we caught the morning bus back to Picnic Bay with Harry and bought some bread, eggs, sausages and a few other things in the little general store. Then we went to the fish and chip shop to buy lunch; the chocolate bars sitting on the counter were too much of a temptation and while the shopkeeper was distracted I whipped two or three of them into my pocket.

"What's the matter with you?" Glen seethed as we emerged. "Can't you go into any shop without stealing something?"

"You don't have to eat them!"

"Oh fuck off!"

"No! You fuck off!"

We sat apart on the harbour wall eating our chips before catching the afternoon bus. Harry's friend Doug was not nearly as boisterous or entertaining; which was probably just as well as neither of us felt like singing.

The next day we set off to explore some of the old forts that are dotted about on the cliffs above Arthur Bay. But it all felt so futile, so shallow; there was no purpose for being there, other than having a holiday, and it certainly didn't feel like that.

"But if we only take one rucksack, who's going to carry it?"

"We'll take it in turns."

"Oh yeah, I've heard that before! I'll end up carrying the bloody thing all day!"

"Bullshit! So we'll take two, see if I care."

"You don't have to get all shitty about it. We can take one if you want. I'm just telling you I'm not going to carry it all day."

"Who said you had to? Forget it, I'll take mine and you take yours! And I'm not getting all shitty!"

It was about our tenth day on the island that we climbed Mt Cook, or it might have been the twelfth; not much matters when not much matters. At least climbing the mountain was exhausting enough to leave no energy for arguments; but when we got back that evening tempers flared; burst into flames, more like. The frying pan I was supposed to have cleaned that morning before we left was covered in ants, as was our loaf of bread and the sugar. The jam jar was simply swarming with them — they were everywhere!

"Shit! Shit! Shit!" Glen exploded, flinging the frying pan out onto the sand. "You were supposed to wash the fucking thing!"

"So I forgot!"

"You're fucking useless!"

"Oh yeah, okay Mr Perfect! What does it matter anyway! I'll clean the fucking thing now!"

"Of course it matters, you stupid prick! Look at this!" and he picked up the bag of sugar, waving it in my face, ants scurrying up his arm, then he turned and hurled it into the trees behind our camp.

"What did you do that for? That's all we've got!"

"I don't give a stuff. I'm getting fucking sick of this, and you," and as he made to move off he bumped into me, so hard I stumbled and fell, smacking my elbow hard against some rocks.

"Jesus!" I yelled, grabbing my arm, then all I could feel was white hot anger. "Fuck you!" and I ran after him.

It wasn't so much a fistfight, although we did each land a few blows, more a rolling frantic wrestling match in the sand. One moment I was on top, next minute he was and we ripped each other's shirts. Glen cut his cheek on a sharp stick poking out of the sand and we ended up a hundred yards away from camp. Being quite a bit bigger than me, Glen always had an advantage, and gradually his size began to tell and when eventually he got me in a headlock there was little I could do but flail my arms and try and punch him in the stomach or kidneys. In the end I had to give in. We were both standing up, me bent double with my head tucked under his arm as I tried to push him towards the water — once there I thought I might be able to wriggle free — but he just dug his feet into the sand and closed his arm tighter and tighter around my throat until I could hardly breathe and was forced to cry out.

"You're breaking my neck!" He let me go more or less instantly, pushing me to the sand as he walked away, both of us gasping for breath.

By now it was dark and Glen went wandering off, disappearing down the beach; not that I cared where he was going. I went back to the camp and sat by the fire, rubbing my aching neck and sore elbow. I was still there half an hour later when Glen came back, looking as sheepish as I felt, blood running down his cheek.

Our camp was a mess, sand and ants were everywhere, but we cleaned it up together as best we could in the dark and then heated a couple of tins of sausages and beans and sat by the fire.

"Your face alright?"

"Yeah, it's not much. Your arm?"

"Yeah, it's nothing."

"Sorry."

"Yeah, so am I. I'll wash the frying pan" and I got up and went down to the water and washed all our implements. When I got back Glen was in bed, so I just put everything away and climbed in beside him.

"What are we going to do?" he asked ten minutes later, not hiding his despair.

"I don't know," and for half an hour or more we lay there in miserable silence.

"Why don't we go and see Harry tomorrow and ask about work," Glen suggested. "He might even have some work for us," he added hopefully.

"I doubt it."

"You doubt everything."

"No, I don't!"

"Yes, you do!"

"Oh, don't start again for Christ's sake!" and I turned on my side away from him.

It was easily the lowest we'd ever been, and both of us tossed and turned all night.

What were we doing in this fucking place! Later that night, although I didn't look at him, I was sure I heard Glen whispering a prayer.

We barely said a word the next morning until we got to Harry's smallholding, and as soon as we saw the place we knew there would be no point in mentioning work. We almost turned back, so dispirited were we. The bus was parked in the front yard like he'd said, but it was Bing, rushing up to the gate excitedly and obviously expecting us to come in that persuaded us. The only thing growing in the front yard, other than thick tufts of paspalum grass, was a pomegranate tree about twenty yards from the bus, and two goats were trying as hard as they could to reach the leaves on the lower branches, stopping to stare indignantly at us as we came through the gate. The block of land was about an acre and it was fenced off, but most of the wooden posts supporting the two strands of rusty barbed wire were leaning over, with long grass and weeds growing up around them. The fence didn't look like it could keep anything out, much less in. The house, or rather the three-roomed fibro shack, had also seen better days, with a rusty corrugated iron roof with wisps of thin blue smoke coming from the rickety brick and iron chimney at one end. Having decided we were no threat, the goats continued their efforts to get at the pomegranate branches as, accompanied by a still excited Bing, we stepped up onto the small front veranda. Beside the open front door was a single wicker chair with a much flattened and very grubby cushion on it. The chair looked like it had been placed there the day the shack was built and not been moved since.

"Anyone home?"

"Oi!" Harry's startled voice came from the darkness inside, and a moment later he appeared at the fly screen door, wearing old shorts and a moth-eaten singlet.

"Hello, boys! This is a nice surprise. We don't often get visitors. Just a tick, I'll get Edie" and he disappeared back inside. "We've got some visitors, love," we could hear him say loudly, and moments later he emerged pushing a wheelchair.

Straight away we could see there was something the matter with the woman other than not being able to walk. One arm sat limply in her lap, the fingers at funny angles, and one side of her mouth was more or less permanently half open and wet. She was quite a large lady, although she had obviously lost a lot of weight and her well-worn floral dress was now far too big for her. Stains of dribble and food were plain to see down the front of it, and the little clumps of wispy hair on her chin glistened with saliva. "This is Nick, and this is Glen," Harry introduced us, bending down so she could hear him and see who he was pointing at, and his wife gave a slow nod of her head but didn't say anything.

For a moment there was an uncomfortable silence, but Harry came to our aid.

"So what brings you here, boys?"

"Oh, we were just passing and thought we'd call in."

"Had a good look around, have youse? Lovely place, isn't it?"

"Yeah, we went up Mt Cook yesterday."

"Oh, yeah; lovely views up there, ain't there love," his voice rose as he bent down to his wife. "They've been up Cookie, love, we used to go up there a lot, didn't we?" and although her smile came out looking like a crooked grimace it was obvious from her eyes it was a genuine smile. "How about a mug of tea," he exclaimed, standing up. "Got time for a quick one, haven't you?"

"Sure," we shrugged, and he disappeared into the shack.

Again there was a heavy silence; what do you say to an old woman in a wheelchair, with a beard and dribble all over her front! Fortunately this time Edith Melling came to our rescue herself, and with her good hand pointed at the pomegranate tree, indicating she wanted to be wheeled over to it. Between us we tilted her chair back to get it down the step and wheeled her across the lumpy grass, the goats scampering out of the way. When we got underneath the tree she pointed at one of the fruits, as if trying to reach it herself.

"Shall I pick it?" Glen asked, and Mrs Melling nodded gently. Having picked one, she then nodded to another fruit and pointed at it, obviously wanting us to have one each. Then Harry emerged out onto the veranda carrying three enamel mugs of tea.

"Ah!" he smiled. "Shown you her tree already, has she, her pride and joy that, planted it herself sixteen years ago, didn't you love," and the three of us sat on the ground beside her in the shade of the tree and drank our tea, Harry giving his wife little sips from his mug from time to time. The quiet moment was shattered minutes later when from around the back somewhere came a loud, urgent squawking and shrieking. "That'll be Dave," Harry grinned, getting up. "Wants to go out, I reckon," and he stood up and bent down over his wife. "You okay for a bit, pet, I'll just go and see to Dave," and Edith gave a little nod. "Come round the back, fellas, and I'll introduce you."

Dave was an enormous sulphur crested white cockatoo, sitting on a perch in his cage and screaming his head off, his sulphur crest waving angrily about. "He gets a bit pissed off if I don't let him out straight away," Harry explained as he opened the cage door. "Don't you, mate?" and he went to scratch the bird on the chest, but Dave was not in the mood for play. He simply shrieked loudly, flapped his wings once and was gone, forcing us all to duck as he flew off to sit on the roof of the shack, where he sat fluffing his feathers, preening himself and glaring at us.

"I found him on the ground the day after Dave Sands died; the famous boxer, killed in a car crash in '52," Harry explained, seeing our blank looks. "He was just sitting there all limp like, and when I came up to him and he made no attempt to move I knew something was wrong. I never did find out what. I just brought him back here, put him on a sack in the kitchen and fed him warm milk and pomegranate seeds. It was touch and go for a few weeks, but like Dave Sands he's as tough as teak and he never gave in."

"What else does he eat?"

"Just about anything, but he has his specialties — Cornflakes, nuts, honey, cabbage, even meat sometimes."

"Cornflakes and cabbage!"

"Oh yeah, loves Cornflakes. You just can't give him too much of any one thing, that's all. Anyway, within a few months he was as right as rain and shouting the odds whenever he wanted something. I've got to understand his screams over the years. They're clever birds really. He knows exactly what he wants and when he wants it and look out if you don't give it to 'im! He'll scream the bloody place down."

"Does he talk?"

"Yeah, but usually only when he's in the cage. Sometimes in the late evenings he'll bump the gums to himself for half an hour or so, and he responds to certain words and phrases." Just then Dave squawked loudly and took off with a flourish, heading inland and disappearing into the trees.

"Goin' to visit his rellies, I reckon, or his girlfriend," Harry winked.

"Does he come back, then?"

"Oh yeah. I only shut the cage door to keep other creatures out. Just occasionally he's gone for a couple of days but he always comes back. He's not stupid. He knows where he can get a good feed and a comfortable bed and he'd kill for pomegranate seeds. Besides, I don't think the old bastard knows where else to go," he grinned.

Apart from two or three of the ubiquitous kapok trees and a wild fig tree, the main area of the backyard was given over to a very large vegetable garden, surprisingly well-tended compared to the rest of the place. It was completely enclosed in chicken wire, as was the chicken coop at the end of the plot. There were about a dozen chickens and a rooster, all of them having names, as Harry informed us. The rooster was called Humphrey, and the chickens were also named after movie stars, especially ones that had been in pictures he and his wife had seen together when they were younger. "It sort of reminds us of the good old days." He smiled. "When I go back to the house and tell Edie I've just fed Katherine Hepburn, or better still I show her eggs laid by Ingrid Bergman, you should see the smile light up her face."

"What happened to your wife?"

"Had a stroke about two years ago. Been getting a little bit better each day, but the Doc reckons she'll never fully recover."

"Do you look after her yourself?"

"More or less," he shrugged. "They wanted to put her in a hospital but I said no way — in sickness and in health I vowed. Our daughter comes over twice a week from the mainland, and once a week one of the nurses from the first aid station over at Arcadia calls in. And when I do the bus run, Norma, Doug's wife, rides over for an hour or so. But Edie's no trouble and I can look after her better than any hospital. If I do have to leave her on her own for a bit Dave stays with her, sits on the back of her chair and won't move until I get back. It's like he understands she's crook. I reckon he'd come and get me if something happened."

We went back to Edith still sitting under the tree and Harry showed us how to peel and eat a pomegranate. "It's the juice you're after," he explained, opening one with a penknife and letting us lick the juice off the blade. "I put it with scrambled egg, lovely. Isn't it, love!" He bent down to his wife, but she didn't respond. Her head was slumped on her chest, and with great care and tenderness Harry lifted it up and gently wiped her mouth and chin with his handkerchief. Then, letting her head fall slowly down to rest on her chest again, he stroked her hair and forehead. "Sleeps a lot," he whispered. "I'll just take her back inside." I had a lump in my throat.

We were just beginning to wonder whether we should leave or not when Harry came out and slumped into his wicker chair. "I've put her to bed. She gets a bit exhausted. I'll just sit here for a bit in case she calls out. She likes to know I'm still around until she goes to sleep." He smiled, but it couldn't hide his weariness or the strain he was obviously under. "Anyway boys, sit down, sit down." His chirpy nature didn't take long to return. It was obvious he wanted us to stay and talk, and we didn't really have anything better to do. "So what are your plans?" he asked, as we got settled on the veranda step, sitting with our backs leaning against the posts. Our hesitant shrugs and blank looks were answer enough. "No," he sighed sympathetically, "there ain't a lot to do for young fellas round here, is there."

"Is there any work at all over here?" Glen asked, and Harry shook his head.

"None that I know of son, I'm afraid. They've got big plans for the place, want to build a resort on Alma and a marina at Nelly Bay so I hear, but that's years away I reckon. Nobody comes here to work." He shrugged. "You want work, you need to go to the mainland. What do you do, anyway?" Then he realised what he'd said. "Not that I suppose you do anything yet, do you. How old are you?"

For ten minutes or so we talked about what we could or might be able to do, but it all sounded a bit bleak. Then Harry had an idea.

"You could head out west. I was talkin' to a bloke the other day, said they're cryin' out for workers in Mt Isa, thirty bob a day he says they pay for unskilled labourers," and Glen and I looked at each other, the first glimmer of hope lighting up our eyes. Mal Dixon had mentioned Mt Isa too; was it possible? Why not! The adrenalin was beginning to flow. Thirty bob a day!

Our growing excitement was interrupted a minute later when Doug arrived on an old motorcycle, opened the gate and came in, parking his bike next to Doris.

"Harry, boys," he waved, and climbed into the bus.

We waved back and Bing, who'd leapt up as soon as he saw him arrive, began barking excitedly, looking from the bus to Harry, as if pleading with him.

"Go on, then," Harry smiled, waving at the bus, and the dog was gone in a flash, leaping inside as Doug began reversing out of the gate. "He just loves riding round in Doris."

After the bus left I went over and closed the gate and was returning to the veranda when in a flutter of flashing white, yellow and sprawling feet, Dave came swooping down, landing deftly on the back of Harry's chair.

"Gidday old fella." Harry scratched his chest. "Had a good time?" and Dave stuck out his chest, demanding more scratches, beak open and crest erect with pleasure.

"Have a go," Harry offered, "you'll be his friend for life." We both gave Dave a scratch and were rewarded with little chirps of appreciation. "Now say the magic words," Harry grinned, and he turned his face and mouthed the words, "Pretty Polly" so Dave couldn't see or hear.

"Pretty Polly," Glen said.

"Get stuffed!" Dave screeched, and the three of us fell about laughing. Even Dave seemed to think it was funny.

When we got to the gates to leave, the goats were beginning to sidle back towards the pomegranate tree again. "Do they have names too?" Glen called out.

"Laurel and Hardy," Harry shouted. "Just as stupid and always together." And we all burst into laughter again and could just imagine Edith smiling her crooked smile of delight as he told her about them. "Well, *here's another nice mess you've gotten me into Stanley!*" Fifty yards down the track we turned back and waved. Harry was still sitting in his chair, Dave on his shoulder.

"Get stuffed!" screamed Dave.

* * *

That night Glen and I sat by the fire until the sun rose, talking about everything under it. Although we were excited at the prospect of going to Mt Isa, we were a bit cautious. After all, our two previous big ideas — cutting sugar cane in Ballina, and now coming here — hadn't exactly been raving successes. For the first time we seriously discussed what we were doing, and why; we talked about God, sex, money, our parents and our dreams and fears. When we finally went to bed I'm sure we both felt more like brothers than friends, it was like the night in the Mt Gravatt bus shelter, only this time there was real substance to our relationship.

I suppose the two subjects we spoke about most were our parents and what we wanted in the future. For my part, that was fairly easy. Despite my family history appearing far more traumatic than Glen's, on paper at least — parents divorce when children are very young, mother drags them away from their father halfway across the world, dumps them with her parents because she doesn't really want children and then buggers off to New Guinea — appearances don't always match the reality. My parents divorced because they just didn't get on any more; there was never any bitterness or rancour between them, at least not in front of my sister and I. Quite the contrary, in fact; each spoke of the other with great affection and respect. We also saw them both frequently after they divorced, and my stepmother was a loving, caring substitute. I lacked for nothing in the mothering department. I suppose my biggest problem was my father being so ill and dying. I loved him dearly and missed him terribly, and there was no doubt that had he still been alive, I would not have been sitting idly on this beach beside the fire under the moonlight. As for the future, I didn't really have any idea what I wanted to do or be, other than travelling and seeing things. I didn't want to be a fireman or a dentist. In fact I wasn't really interested in 'being' anything. It would be nice to have some money and one day have kids of my own, but other than that I didn't have any set ambitions.

Glen's upbringing, on the other hand, appeared on paper to be as close to the perfect, stable, well-off middle-class family as you could get. Both parents had good jobs and earned good money; they lived in a large house with a well-tended garden; went to church regularly and their children wanted for nothing. In truth, Glen's childhood had been about as close to hell as you could get. I'm sure these thoughts hadn't properly formed themselves in my young mind at the time, but I believe it was this difference in our upbringing that taught me not to judge a family situation — or any situation, come to that — by its appearance, either on paper or the neatness of the front garden.

Perhaps it was because of our very different backgrounds that Glen took life more seriously, was more focused and in many ways far more mature than I was; he'd had to grow up faster. Although he took me completely by surprise when I asked him what he wanted to do in the future.

"I'm going to join the Navy," he said emphatically.

"The Navy! Really! You never said that before!"

"You never asked. My dad wants me to join."

"Your dad! But I thought …"

"Oh, I don't like the arsehole, and I don't want to have anything more to do with him; when I get back I'm going to rent a room or get a flat or something. I'm not going home again. But when he was sober, he made sense sometimes. He says the Navy teaches you all sorts of useful things. You can get a trade, and when you get out employers want you because they know you've been well-trained. You get to travel for nothing, the pay and conditions are pretty good, and if you stay in for more than fifteen years you get a pension for the rest of your life."

"Fifteen years! Shit! That *is* the rest of your life!"

"You don't have to join up for fifteen, it's either six or nine, I think."

"Six or nine — that's half a lifetime! When is all this going to happen?" I asked him.

"After I'm seventeen in December, I've been thinking about it a lot lately, and getting here just made up my mind I suppose." He shrugged, then he looked quickly at me and added, "But I don't want to go home yet!" as if to reassure me he wasn't planning on leaving straight away. "I want to go back with some money in my pocket. I don't want to have to ask my dad for anything ever again."

"Aren't you frightened of him?"

"Not anymore" he shrugged. "Best thing I ever did was leave. He'll never hit me again." This he said with such calm certainty that I didn't really know what to say, and we both stared into the fire.

"But December is still a long way off." Glen broke the silence. "Let's just go out to Mt Isa and work for a few months, get some money and then make our way home. That's if you want to do that too," he added, with a little less certainty. "Or do you want to go off and find Carol?"

"Are you still shitty about her?"

"No. I was just pissed off that you fucked off like that!" Then he was silent for a moment and didn't look at me, as if what he was going to say was difficult. "One other thing, too, while we're at it."

"What?"

"I can just about cope with sneaking into hotels for a shower, but no more thieving!" Now he did look at me, the depth of feeling obvious in his eyes. I suppose I was a bit taken aback, and for a second I didn't say anything.

"I mean it," he said firmly. "Any more stealing and I'm going home! If we can't buy, borrow or beg it, we don't have it. I don't like doing it, and we'll only end up in trouble again." Curious how sometimes it is not until we are bluntly confronted with the consequences of our actions that we realise how sharply those actions can impact on others.

"No more thieving, promise," I said, looking him in the eye. "Let's go to Mt Isa!" and we stood up and spontaneously hugged each other.

The great thing about teenage angst and pessimism is that while it might descend like a violent storm when things don't go right, it can be blown away on the slightest breeze of optimism; thirty bob a day was an optimistic gale, never mind a breeze. By the time we fell asleep we'd not only earned two hundred pounds each, but spent quite a bit of it. Glen had gone home and rented a flat, telling his father he could stick his money, and his fists, up his arse; while I was the king of Theo's Milk Bar and Denise Phillips was pleading with me to take her dress off. Gee, cocks can be annoying things, especially when they're young. It's like they suffer from some sort of insecurity or inferiority complex and constantly have to let you know they're there.

We slept most of that day, and early the following morning held a ritual and satisfyingly violent demolition of our camp, although we kept the tarps and ropes to give to Harry. It would have been nice to take them with us, but they were far too heavy to take on the road. But we wouldn't have to rough it for long; we'd be in Mt Isa in a few days. "Goals and dreams are what get us out of bed in the mornings." We packed up and walked over to Harry's in time to catch the morning bus.

"Okey dokey Doris!" Harry climbed aboard. "Let's hit the road!" and Bing was beside himself with excitement, running back and forth up the aisle. We only picked up three other passengers on the trip but that made no difference to Harry, and as we came down into Picnic Bay we were all in full voice:

"... *here's what she said to me:*
Que sera sera ..."

THIRTEEN

The Flinders Highway

*B*ack in Townsville, the plan was to buy some clothes, stock up with enough food and cigarettes for four or five days, sleep the night up on Castle Hill, grab a shower in the hotel first thing in the morning, and then set off. First, we stopped at the taxi rank to see Mal, having told him we would look him up before we left the area, but he was on a job so we left a message and set off down Flinders Street to find a clothes shop. We needed new shirts, and our socks were like fishing nets and smelt almost as bad; and the soles of our shoes were beginning to wear out. In my case they were getting very tight too; funny how you don't really notice yourself growing. But new shoes were so expensive we decided ours would have to last until we got to Mt Isa. We hadn't spent much on the island — since the night at Kangaroo Point we had been much more careful with money — and Glen was still in charge, but now we each had an emergency ten shillings we kept stashed away. Not counting this, after buying the clothes and allotting one pound ten shillings for food and cigarettes, we still had about seven pounds left.

We emerged from the shop wearing our new shirts and set off back to find Mal, only for him to find us, pulling over quickly when he spotted us. We piled in and he drove off, turning into a side street to park and switching the engine off as he turned to us. "When did you get back?"

"This morning. We're going to Mt Isa."

If he was surprised by this he gave no indication, but there did seem to be something troubling him and he frowned slightly and picked up the copy of the *Townsville Bulletin* on the seat beside him. "Funny you should come today. I was just thinking about you. I'm afraid there's some sad news," and he handed us the paper. At the bottom of the front page was a photograph of Mrs Hayes, and underneath a sub-headline: 'Much Loved North Coast Identity Dies'. For a moment we were both speechless, and just stared down at her photograph.

The effect the news of Mrs Hayes' death had on us took us both by surprise, I think. We may have only known her for a few days, but they had been far more intense and stimulating days than we'd realised, especially for Glen. She was the first adult, other than his mother, that he'd really been able to relate to and, more than that, she was the first person he'd been close to who had died. For ten minutes we just sat in the taxi reading the article about her over and over again, tears never far away.

"I wonder what will happen to the Jessies?" Glen asked absently.

"Oh, they will be looked after," Mal assured us. "She had many friends who loved dogs as much as she did. They'll be fine." He smiled.

I am sure that had Mal known how upset it would make us, he wouldn't have shown us the paper so abruptly. "I'm sorry," he said. "She was a great lady. Look, why don't you come back to our place for awhile, have a feed and a comfortable night's sleep. You don't want to sleep up the hill tonight, do you!"

We ended up staying three days with Mal and Gillian Dixon, the great food, soft pillows and comfortable mattresses making it an easy decision. But they were also fantastic people and made us feel so welcome and at ease. Gillian Dixon was very calm and considerate. She even reminded us a bit of Mrs Hayes in that she wasn't the slightest bit judgemental, and both she and Mal were great listeners, showing a genuine interested in our plans. Any misgivings they may have had about them they managed to convey without sounding the least bit critical. Gillian helped us sort our gear out, getting rid of the last of the sand and ants, and we washed all our clothes.

Although neither of them made any attempt to dissuade us from going to Mt Isa, Mal was a little cautious. "I don't want to put you off, but it is quite tough out there, especially with the hot weather coming up in a month or so."

"Don't you think we should go, then?"

"Let me make some enquiries, see what the score is," he suggested. "I know someone who works in the mine office here." That night when he came back from work he had good news and bad news. The bad news was that from the Townsville office they would only employ people eighteen years and older. "It's just company policy; they can't be seen to be employing juveniles. The government doesn't like it. Besides, there is a much bigger pool of labour here so they can afford to be choosy."

"So what's the good news?"

"Well, speaking to a couple of other friends who have been out there recently, it seems that if you apply for work actually in Isa then they don't ask too many questions. The whole town is owned and run by the mine company," Mal explained. "Not just the mines, but the ancillary industries, even the shops are run by the company, and from what I hear they are so short staffed that even the most junior workers are getting twenty-five bob a day. I don't think you'll have any trouble getting a job," he smiled, and although he was obviously still a bit doubtful he didn't say any more. Even if he had, we probably wouldn't have listened; a minimum of twenty-five bob a day made more noise than any warning of how tough it might be. Early the next morning he drove us a few miles out of town and dropped us on the Flinders Highway. Mt Isa was five hundred miles away, due west.

* * *

One of my greatest idols is Mathew Flinders; he has to be the most amazing of all of Australia's many amazing explorers. Clever, inventive, a brilliant sailor and navigator, he was as imaginative as he was courageous. I love the story, very early on in his days in Australia, of him coming ashore on the south coast of New South Wales in his little boat *Tom Thumb*, only to be confronted by a group of agitated Aboriginals who must have been truly terrified seeing half a dozen white men emerge from the sea. To Flinders and his party, twenty to thirty Aboriginals waving spears and glaring at them from the tree line fifty yards away can't have been much fun either, but quick as a flash he realised he had to calm the situation down. Standing quietly by his boat at the water's edge, he told his men to lower their weapons and then slowly took out a pair of scissors from his bag and deliberately cut off some locks of his long, blond hair, letting them blow away in the wind. The effect was electrifying, and within minutes they were all sitting together on the beach, Flinders cutting the Aboriginals' hair as they marvelled at these strange, fair-skinned men and their even stranger tools.

I'm not one to hold a grudge, but the French are to be despised; not so much for the callous way they treated him, the months of solitary confinement and terrible diet from which he never recovered, but because he had such a brilliant mind and they knew it. At the time they captured him he was one of the most highly regarded navigators in the world, young as he was. Who knows what other discoveries and inventions the great man might have given the world had he lived. One thing's certain, he had already contributed far, far more to mankind than that jumped-up little toad of a general the French idolise. You just have to look at the number of mountains, rivers, streets and buildings named after him right around Australia to see that.

* * *

We got to Hughenden, well over a third of the way, in two days; not bad, considering. Our first lift, to Charters Towers, was with an older man and his wife, who as they approached us were having a heated discussion, obviously about whether to pick us up or not. When he stopped against her wishes she was furious, and as we settled down on the back seat you could literally taste the tension between them. For the first few miles he did try to make light conversation but it was hard going, his wife's heavy silence sinking his words almost as soon as they came out, and in the end he gave up and we were all silent. It's only about ninety miles from Townsville to Charters Towers, yet it seemed to take forever and the 1956 Hillman Minx is not a large car. By the time we got there it felt like we were in a Dinky toy, so oppressive was the atmosphere. We couldn't get out fast enough, we did turn to thank them and the man at least wished us good luck, but she refused even to look at us. Suit yourself!

Fortunately the scenery was fantastic. The Great Dividing Range certainly is something to behold; strange how you perceive things when you're young. I'd always imagined the Range as one long, thin ridge, at most only a few miles across, and that the mountains came back down on the western side as steeply and quickly as they went up on the eastern side. For well over a thousand miles since leaving Sydney we'd travelled parallel to this huge geographical feature, but you only really get a grasp of its size when you cross over it. I'd had no idea it was so wide — wider than many countries, in fact. Gee, Australia's a big place!

As with geographical features, architecture is not something for which teenage appreciation is highly tuned, but we couldn't help but be impressed with Charters Towers. I'm not sure what we'd expected it to be like; probably lots of shacks like the one Harry Mellings lived in, but whatever we'd imagined it wasn't the fabulous colonial and Victorian architecture of this once booming mining town. We had intended getting another lift that afternoon and maybe getting to Hughenden by nightfall, but we were so entranced we ended up walking right around the town, marvelling at the fantastic buildings. I think it was the fact that they were so sort of unexpected that made them stand out.

We found a park to sleep in, but we hadn't been prepared for how much colder it was compared to Magnetic Island. We lit a fire, and immediately the manager of the nearby truck stop diner came out and told us the police would jump on us for lighting a fire there. He was okay, and let us stay in the diner and then sleep on the floor after it closed at midnight. Which was just as well, because it was one of the coldest nights we'd experienced so far. Next morning we were having breakfast when two fairly rough-looking locals in their early twenties came in, obviously still suffering from the night before and shouting greetings to all and sundry. Their vehicle looked as wild as they did; a very battered 1957 long wheel base Land Rover, it had a massive bull bar on the front and four huge spotlights on the cab roof. The back had been cut away roughly and the seats taken out, turning the vehicle into a sort of home-made ute. They told us they were going to a large cattle station south of Hughenden to shoot 'roos, for which they were paid two shillings for every set of ears. They offered us a lift, but said we'd have to sit in the back. So what? We'd done that before.

Not like this we hadn't! Jesus, it was a terrible ride. It was like the Land Rover had square wheels. The road was supposed to be bitumen all the way to Mt Isa, but it was in terrible condition and very narrow; when a three trailer cattle road train came the other way we had to pull over and got covered in dust and grit. Then they stopped in Torrens Creek and said they were going to have a few beers and just left us sitting there. Why is it that some adults don't think it necessary to be polite and considerate towards teenagers! Little wonder we get bolshie! We hung around outside for a bit, but when a farmer came out and offered us a lift to Hughenden in the front of his Holden ute we accepted like a shot.

Hughenden was not the most inspiring of places. We'd come down off the Range by now, and the land was beginning to flatten out, the trees getting smaller, the vegetation sparser. It was late afternoon and we were getting a bit tired and hungry; it had been a short night and a long day. There didn't seem to be anywhere comfortable or private to sleep, so we walked out of town down the highway for a mile or so. At least we could have a fire out here. We cleared a place to sleep about fifty yards from the road under some small trees, lit a fire and were about to have a mug of tea when a police car, coming from Hughenden, stopped a hundred yards up the road from us.

For a moment nothing happened. Then a policeman got out of the driver's seat and went around to the passenger's side and opened the back door. Leaning in, he dragged an Aboriginal man out by the shirt and flung him against the side of the car. It was obvious the man was drunk as he could hardly stand up, and the policeman had to hold him up by his shirt. We couldn't quite hear what he was saying, but whatever it was it didn't sound, or look, too friendly. Then suddenly he stepped back a pace, and holding the Aborigine by the collar he hit him twice in the stomach, thumping blows that doubled him up. Then the policeman grabbed the Aborigine by the back of his belt and more or less chucked him into the scrub beside the road. "And fucking stay out!" This we did hear as he shouted it so loudly and angrily, and then after a quick look up and down the road, he kicked the prone man viciously in the groin.

"Jesus!" exclaimed Glen, instinctively rising, and just as instinctively I pulled him down.

"Don't let him see us!"

The policeman got back into the car and drove off, heading in our direction. We both lay as flat as we could, hoping he didn't see the wisps of smoke from our fire. He didn't, and as the car went past we stood up and looked back down the road to the Aboriginal, who was still lying where he'd fallen. We were about to set off to see if he was alright when suddenly the police car returned. We hadn't noticed that it had only gone a hundred yards or so up the road to turn around. As it came past us, gathering speed, there was no time to duck and the policeman spotted us.

Shit!

Immediately he slammed on the brakes and the car came to a screeching halt, then did a violent and unnecessarily spectacular u-turn in the middle of the road and came roaring back, coming to a halt in a cloud of dust. The sergeant got out, putting on his hat as he strode across to us.

"What are you two doing here!" he demanded.

All sorts of answers flashed through my mind, like "minding our own business," and "what does it look like, shithead!" but I settled for: "Having a cup of tea," although I couldn't help adding, "What's it look like?"

"Don't get smart, son. What's your name?"

"Nick."

"Nick fucking who!"

"Yeah! Alright, sergeant!" Why was it that these sorts of conversations always ended up like this?

"His name is Nick Thomas and I'm Glen Olsen," said Glen, stepping in before I screwed things up completely.

"What are you doing here?"

"Just having a cup of tea, like he said," Glen shrugged. "Why?"

"I'll ask the questions. Where have you come from?"

"Charters Towers this morning. We're going to Mt Isa."

For a moment the policeman stared hard at us, as if making up his mind about something. Then he stabbed his finger at us. "Right! You listen to me. This is my patch," and he waved his arm up and down the road. "From Hughenden right through to Cloncurry; my patch, you understand me?"

Not really, but we didn't say so.

"That means," he continued, "that anything that goes on along this stretch is my business! You get me?"

We still didn't have a clue what he was talking about, but Glen said, "Yes sergeant," anyway.

"Good," he said, dropping his finger. "So if I happen to go to Richmond or Julia Creek tomorrow or the next day and hear somebody's been tellin' stories, I'll know who it was tellin' 'em, won't I? Won't I!" he barked, making us blink.

"Yes, sergeant."

"Right. Now remember I can do you for vagrancy, loitering and for resisting arrest any time I want."

"Resisting arrest!" I exploded. "We haven't done anything!"

To my surprise the policeman just smiled and continued with studied reasonableness. "I just told you, son. Vagrancy and loitering are against the law. You two are breaking the law right now; break the law, you get arrested. Getting arrested sometimes makes people unhappy. Resisting arrest is one of the most common charges in the book, son. You can go to gaol for it. You with me?"

By now we were 'getting his drift', as Mr Archer might have said, and as it was obviously futile to say anything else we didn't. He left a few minutes later, warning us again of what he could do to us and telling us not to be in the area the following day. When we were sure he wasn't coming back we went down the road to see if the Aborigine was alright. It was starting to get dark but we could see he was still alive, breathing heavily.

"Are you okay?" Glen asked, bending over him. He stank of booze and dirty clothes, and at first we thought he was asleep. Then he waved his arm about and shouted, "Fuck off!" before mumbling something in an incomprehensible language, liberally laced with

English swear words. Do Aboriginals have swear words? We stood by him for a few minutes wondering what to do, but he seemed to be alright and he certainly wasn't dead, so Glen said, "Listen, mate, if you want a cup of tea and something to eat we're camped just up the road. Okay?" Again the man mumbled something unintelligible, but at least he didn't tell us to fuck off again. When we woke up next morning there was no sign of him.

We got to Richmond early the next morning, courtesy of a lift with a farmer and his wife who emerged from nowhere out of a gate not far from where the Aborigine had been lying. They were going into town shopping, and were as surprised to see us and learn where we'd come from as we were happy to get a lift so soon; we hadn't even packed up and they had to wait for us, which they did with good humour. We treated ourselves to a slap-up breakfast in Richmond — only another two hundred and fifty miles and we'd be there! We even began to contemplate making it that day, with a bit of luck. In the cafe we met an old bloke who, although he didn't say much about himself, wanted to know where we'd come from and where we were going.

His name was Charlie and he seemed okay, if a bit vacant. His clothes were a bit grubby and worn, but so were everybody's out here it seemed. The most notable thing about him was a large burn scar on the side of his head above his ear. He told us he could give us a lift, but was only going to the turn off to his property twenty-five miles west of the town.

"Oh, that's okay!" we told him confidently. "We're used to sitting by the side of the road!" For a moment he didn't say anything, and then surprised us a little by asking if we had any food and water. "Oh, yeah!" we assured him. "We've got everything!" "Hummm." He shrugged. "Okay, let's go."

Like his clothes, his 1952 Ford F1 pick-up had seen plenty of use but it sounded okay and we could at least sit up front with him. He dropped us off opposite an open gate, where a rutted track disappeared into the distance across the flat plains.

"How far do you go down there?" we asked, climbing down.

"Only about fifty miles," he shrugged. "See youse," and he went bumping off over the cattle grid and down the track. It was ten-thirty in the morning, and at twenty to eleven we could still see his dust. It wasn't really until that began to settle that we realised where we were.

If we'd thought we were alone and the only people in the world the day Mrs Hayes dropped us off, it was nothing compared to this. Since leaving Townsville we'd seen innumerable kangaroos, emus, brolgas, wedge-tailed eagles and galahs, vast blankets of them, swooping and turning in unison, grey-pink-grey-pink — aren't the birds of Australia just fantastic! There was wildlife all over the place! Now, suddenly, there didn't seem to be a creature alive anywhere. Flat, featureless land stretched for miles in all directions, still and deathly quiet, and nothing moved in the stunted undergrowth; even the ants seemed lethargic.

Two empty cattle road trains, quite close together, thundered by going east at about two o'clock, the drivers waving to us, but apart from that nothing came by. Then just after three o'clock, a car also heading east appeared on the horizon. It was travelling quite fast but it still took a few minutes to reach us; one thing about being out here, you could see a vehicle coming from miles away. We stood up to wave as it approached, and to our surprise the car stopped and a youngish man got out and quickly came across the road to us. Unusually, he was quite smartly dressed in shorts and long socks, shiny shoes and a crisp short-sleeved white shirt with button-down pockets.

"Gidday, boys," he smiled, and not hiding his surprise, asked: "What are you doing out here?"

When we told him, he shook his head slightly and sighed knowingly. "His name wasn't Charlie, by any chance, was it?"

"Yeah! Why?"

Again he shook his head. "Haven't got time to explain at the moment, I've got to get into Richmond, but I'll be back some time later tonight. It might not be for a few hours, but I will be back, and if you're still here I'll pick you up. You can come with me if you like, but you'll just have to hang around."

"No, it's okay, besides, we might get a lift."

"Sure," he smiled, "and if you do, jump in by all means, don't wait for me. But the road is pretty quiet on Sundays, so you might still be here when I come back. I take it you've got water and food?" When we assured him we had, he extended his hand and asked us our names. "I'm Dr Richards," then he raised his hand in apology. "Sorry, boys, I've got to go, but I'll be back," and running back to his car, he drove off rapidly.

Half an hour later we were sitting under one of the few scrubby bushes nearby that were large enough to give us some shade, when in the distance we heard a noise. "Listen, a truck!" said Glen.

"That's not a truck! That's a train!"

Since Charters Towers, the railway line had run more or less right next to the road; not that we'd seen a single train until now. As this one got closer it was obvious it wasn't a steam train, but one of the smart new diesel engines that were beginning to take over from steam. It was hauling several passenger carriages, behind which were a dozen or more freight cars of various make up. As it got nearer we walked over and leaned on the fence, waving with both arms at the driver. It was going quite fast and Glen held up our Mt Isa sign and we kept waving to the passengers, many of whom saw us and waved back. Suddenly we heard a squealing noise.

"It's stopping!" Glen shouted excitedly. "It's stopping! Quick, get our packs!" And we rushed back, picked up our bags and climbed over the fence. Running over to the line, we got there just as the guard's van pulled up, the guard standing in the doorway looking down at us.

"What's up, boys?"

"Nothing, we just saw you stopping. Any chance of a lift?"

"You what!"

"Well … we just …"

"You stopped a fucking passenger train for nothing!"

"We didn't stop it, we just waved …"

"Bullshit, the driver obviously thought you were in some sort of trouble. It's an offence to stop trains without reason, you know!"

"But we didn't stop it, we just waved … anyway, you've stopped now, so can we get on?"

"No you fucking can't," said the guard, and he leaned out and made a forward motion with his arm, like John Wayne setting out with his troop from the fort. In the distance we could see the driver had climbed down from the engine and was standing beside it looking back towards us, as were many of the passengers, their heads poking out of windows to see what the problem was. At the guard's signal the driver waved back and climbed up into the engine, and the train began to inch away.

"But that's ridiculous! You've stopped!"

"Yeah, and now we're going again, and I'll be reporting you in Julia Creek!" And he stayed in the doorway looking back at us until the train was far enough away that we couldn't jump on or anything.

Shit! Shit! Shit! How fucking stupid can you get! But we could only stand there, almost in tears, watching the train disappear down the track. Moments later things got even worse when a small truck came past on the road going in our direction, and despite our frantic waving its driver didn't see us. Jesus, life can be so unfair sometimes!

By nine o'clock that night, life seemed even more unfair. The doctor hadn't returned, but because we'd expected him at any minute we hadn't eaten. When hunger got the better of us, we had to scramble about in the dark, heating up some tins and hunting about for bigger pieces of firewood as it had suddenly turned really cold. "How can it be so hot in the day and so bloody cold at night?" Glen protested, putting on another pair of socks. At half past eleven we had to accept the fact that the doctor probably wasn't going to come until the morning, so we put an old sleeper we'd found on the fire, wrapped ourselves in our duffle coats and lay down.

I thought it was a dream when I heard the doctor's voice calling. "Hey, boys! Nick. Glen! You there?" And bleary-eyed, we looked into his torchlight. "Sorry I'm late," he apologised as we got going. "I was held up, so I had a bit of a kip before I left. Got to be bright-eyed and bushy tailed for my surgery in the morning." After we were settled and on our way, we told him our story, leaving out a few things; and then he told us all about Charlie Stebbing.

Charlie didn't own any property at all, it seemed, but lived in an old drover's shack that a local station owner let him use. "These days he's a bit of a bum, but he was born and bred out here and in his younger days he was highly sought after as a stockman and drover. He knows the land like the back of his hand, even the Aboriginals respect him," the doctor told us. "Then about eight years ago, he and his wife were involved in a bad accident just west of here. His wife was killed, and Charlie suffered terrible burns. He never really recovered, and a few years later he had a complete nervous break-down. The other car was driven by a man from Melbourne, and since his breakdown Charlie has had it in for interstate people, especially Victorians. Not only does he blame them all for his problems, but he thinks they're soft and stupid and don't understand the ways of out-back Queensland life, which is true sometimes. His usual trick, if he happens to see a Victorian number plate coming towards him out here, is to wave them down and tell them the road ahead is shut and they'll have to turn back. Most famously, though, a couple of years ago he came across a travelling salesman from Melbourne who had broken down between Hughenden and Richmond. He was heading for Mt Isa with a boot full of smart Van Heusen shirts, of all things. Unfortunately for him, the first vehicle to come by was Charlie and he took an instant dislike to the man and his 'poofter' shirts." The doctor grinned.

"What happened?"

"A bit like you, really. Charlie told the salesman he was only going a few miles up the road, but could drop him at a bus stop, which would take him to Richmond."

"A bus stop!"

"Sounds stupid, I know, but it seems the bloke believed him. Anyway, Charlie knew of an old drover's hut on the side of the road about four or five miles away, and he dropped the bloke off there. Unfortunately, by the time the bloke got back to his car three or four hours later, the shirts had all been stolen. Of course they picked Charlie up, but he just denied any knowledge of them. However, over the next few months a lot of Aboriginals were seen wearing smart new shirts," he smiled.

"But we're not Victorians."

"No, but you are from Sydney, which is almost as bad. Oh, the old bugger might be as mad as a cut snake, but he isn't evil. That's why he asked if you had water. He'll check later today to see if you're still there; if you had been, he'd have given you a lift back to Richmond. Charlie thinks inconveniencing people teaches them a lesson."

"But how could he have known we wouldn't get a lift, that we'd be stuck there all day?"

"He didn't, but he knew there'd be very little traffic about on a Sunday. Even if you'd only sat there for a few hours, it would have satisfied him."

As they say about every cloud, there was one positive outcome of our extended stay, had we got an earlier lift or been allowed onto the train in the afternoon we would not have arrived in Julia Creek at such a perfect time. It was ten to five in the morning and we hadn't had a shower since leaving Townsville, so we said our farewells to the good doctor and set off down the nice quiet street to find a nice quiet hotel with nice hot showers; easy as tip-toeing up the stairs.

FOURTEEN

Julia Creek

Everything was going just fine. We made it up to the bathroom without seeing a soul, had a shower, washed our underpants and shirts, wrapping them as ever in our towels before setting off back down the corridor; no need for burglar alarms when you have creaking floorboards. But we were getting the hang of this caper and we weren't too bothered. In fact, I was so relaxed I was just thinking there must have been only one set of plans for all these old country hotels, so similar in layout were they, when suddenly one of the bedroom doors at the end of the corridor nearest the stairs opened and a large man came out, wearing nothing but underpants and a towel draped over his shoulders. He had an enormous belly and was yawning and scratching his crotch as he came towards us. There was nothing else to do but try to brazen it out, and for a second I thought we'd succeeded as initially he didn't seem to notice us at all. But as we drew level he stopped abruptly, as if suddenly realising we were there.

"What room are you two in?"

"Fourteen," I said, as confidently as I could.

"Fourteen my arse!" he growled, and his hand shot out and grabbed me around the neck under the chin with such force that my head was flung back and smashed into the wall, causing me to drop my rucksack and towel, underpants spilling out.

How was I to know there were only nine rooms!

"You cunts have been in the fucking showers!" he yelled, as if he couldn't believe it was possible, and twice more in his fury he banged my head against the wall and I think I might have come close to passing out. I vaguely remember Glen pulling the man's arm to make him loosen his grip on my neck, as I was also frantically trying to do, arms flailing. Then a woman with blue curlers in her hair suddenly appeared at the man's shoulder, shouting something, and another man in pyjamas arrived, grabbing Glen and wrestling him to the floor.

The next thing I recall with any certainty was both of us being frogmarched down the stairs and into the bar by three or four younger men who had heard the commotion. They made us sit on chairs at the back of the bar and stood above us, daring us to make a run for it. Within minutes the bar was half full of people in various stages of dress or undress, two of them women in dressing gowns, one of them being the lady with the blue curlers. Then the man who'd originally grabbed me came into the bar, now wearing a pair of shorts and a blue singlet.

"Right!" he barked to one of the younger men. "Go and get Ted Masters. I'm goin' to crucify these little pricks!"

"We only had a shower," said Glen.

"You shut your mouth!" snapped blue singlet, then he did a double take and glared at Glen. "Wait a minute! Are you a fucking Pom? You fucking are, aren't you! Well, that just fucking caps it," he exploded, and he stepped forward and grabbed Glen by his shirt, virtually lifting him out of the seat with one hand while he raised the other one as if he was going to give him a hard backhander. "I'm going to …"

"Leave it, Reg !" ordered the lady in blue curlers, grabbing his arm. "Let Ted deal with them." For a second I thought he wasn't going to take any notice, but eventually he lowered his hand. Cursing, he shoved Glen back down into the chair. Then he looked at his watch.

"Right, everybody, excitement's over." And he turned to us. "If either one of you so much as moves I'll beat the shit out of both of you, understand!" Then he ushered everybody out and locked us in the bar and there we sat, not game to move, with Reg or one of the other men coming to check on us every now and then.

We'd never been so relieved to see a policeman as when Constable Ted Masters arrived a couple of hours later and came into the bar accompanied by Reg, although it was short-lived relief as after asking our names it suddenly dawned on him and he pointed at us.

"You're the two kids who stopped the train yesterday, aren't you?"

"We didn't stop it! We just waved and *it* stopped."

"So I suppose you're going to tell me you didn't break in here, either!"

"But we didn't! The door was open. All we did was have a shower!"

"Bullshit!" snapped Reg. "I want 'em charged, Ted. Breaking, entering, trespass — I don't give a shit what it is. They just can't get away with it!" The constable was quite young and obviously not very experienced, and we could see he felt almost as intimidated by the landlord as we were.

"Yeah, okay Reg, calm down!"

"Fucking calm down!" he exploded, and sighing slightly, Constable Masters held up his hands to deflect Reg's anger and turned to us.

"Okay, you two. Go outside and get into the back of the police car, and don't try any funny business."

"But what about our gear?"

"I said, go outside and get in the back of the police car — now!"

Driving us to the police station, the constable was deep in thought and didn't say a word. Even though it wasn't far, by the time we got there we were champing at the bit.

"So, what's going to happen to us?" I blurted out as we pulled up.

"I don't know yet," he frowned, obviously not completely happy about the situation.

"Sergeant King will be back in a few days. Until then you will have to stay in the cells."

"But we only had a shower!"

"You were trespassing, and the landlord has every right to prosecute you; now I need to take down some details," and he sat us down in his office and made a note of just about everything there was to know about us: addresses, phone numbers, parents' names, where we lived, how old we were, where we'd come from, where our parents were now, where we'd been living and how we had earned a living for the last few months. He wasn't angry or intimidating or anything, just breathtakingly pedantic. We found out later we were the first people he'd processed before locking them up, so he was going to do it right.

All our instincts told us to say as little as possible, so we didn't mention Gympie or Yeppoon, but the questions all seemed so mundane and nothing to do with our present situation that it didn't seem to matter that much. Also, after our experience in Yeppoon we were definitely not going to tell another pack of lies. Eventually the constable was happy and made us sign and date the piece of paper he'd written it all down on alongside his signature, then he stood up and ushered us outside to the cells in the backyard.

"But we're hungry! We haven't had any breakfast!"

"I'll try and sort you something out later," he said and he shut the door.

What do they call it when something happens that has happened before?

Living in small towns in the middle of nowhere, where everybody knows everybody else's business, might be one of the drawbacks for the residents of out-back towns, or maybe it isn't; for us, it was a godsend. Within a few hours just about everybody in the town had heard about the two Pommie teenagers sitting in the cells who'd had a shower in the pub. As promised, the constable returned an hour or so after locking us up with two plates of sausages, fried tomatoes, beans and toast and two mugs of tea. An hour later he came back with our rucksacks, which he allowed us to keep in the cell, so when we heard the door being unlocked later that afternoon we just assumed it was him again. It was, but standing next him, much to our relief, was Dr Richards.

At first the constable was not too keen on the doctor's idea that we be released into his custody. "I don't know, Doc, I mean they stopped the train and they were trespassing. Reg wants to pursue the matter, and when I rang Sergeant King he told me I had to hold them until he gets back in a few days."

"A few days! You can't hold them that long without charging them, Ted! Besides, they're minors. Look, I'll have a word with Reg. In the meantime they can stay in the old nurse's quarters behind the hospital. I'll guarantee they won't go anywhere until this is all sorted."

Obviously relieved to be rid of the responsibility, Constable Masters agreed, warning us before we left of the consequences of running away.

The hospital was just a small wooden house of four or five rooms and attached to the back was an extra small room. It was an unlined weatherboard with a sink, a double bunk, a small wooden table, a couple of chairs and a window that looked out over the overgrown back garden. "Might be a bit musty. Nobody's lived in here for awhile," Dr Richards said as he opened the window. "But it will be more comfortable than the cell, I reckon." He sat down and sighed. "Maybe you'd better tell me your side of the story?"

Twenty minutes later he left, telling us it might be best if we kept a low profile while he went and had a word with the landlord of the hotel. Just outside our little room, in the back garden of the hospital, he showed us an old fireplace where we could cook and he told us we could use the bathroom in the hospital. We didn't see him again until the following morning, and then it was all in a bit of a hurry as he had patients to see. "Okay, I've spoken to Reg. He's alright really, a bit gruff maybe, that's all, but he doesn't think you should get away with it scot-free so what I suggested is maybe you could do some work for him. How about it?"

"Sure."

"Okay, do you want to come with me now and I'll take you over to him?"

To our surprise, Reg seemed to have calmed down considerably; not that he was about to embrace us or anything! But he was at least reasonably amenable, so we didn't feel too bad when the doctor left us with him. Our job was to paint a rust-proofing undercoat on the roof of the hotel. The roof had recently been repaired and several new sheets of iron had been laid along the front, and after the undercoat was finished, which Reg had been going to do that day himself, proper painters were going to come and paint the entire building.

"You don't have to be too pretty about it," Reg told us. "Just make sure you cover the whole roof, and try and keep it out of the gutters, okay?" And he handed us each a large pail of rusty red paint and an eight-inch brush. Positioned on the street corner, the hotel was L-shaped, meaning the roof area was broken up and fairly accessible so we weren't too phased by the task, although it wasn't until we got to the base of the ladder that Glen informed me he didn't like heights.

"Just don't look down." I dismissed his concerns and we took our shirts off. The ladder was positioned around the back of the hotel where the roof was not as high as it was on the front street side.

Our plan was to do the back side of each leg of the L first, and then come back along the front side; starting at the top of the ridge and working our way down to the gutter in strips, like mowing a lawn. The pitch of the roof was not great so it was fairly easy to crawl about, placing our weight on the rows of nails holding the sheets of iron in place. As neatness wasn't a priority we were able to go quite fast, and within two hours we'd finished the back of the roof. By this time heat was becoming the biggest problem. It may not have been a particularly hot day by Julia Creek standards — eighty two degrees Fahrenheit we learned later — but by midday just touching the iron with our hands was painful enough, especially the shiny new sheets. Kneeling on it or holding on for any length of time was almost impossible.

Because of this, most of our grip came from squatting sideways, one leg slightly lower than the other like a wedge. With hindsight we should have come down and waited until it got cooler, or started again before it got too hot the next morning; something the landlord should probably have insisted upon as well. To squat in the middle of an iron roof, in the middle of the day, in the middle of Queensland, even in the middle of August, is not the smartest thing to do. No doubt the landlord saw it as part of our punishment. However, we were getting it done and so we pressed resolutely on. Although Glen had gradually become more at ease, he was emphatic that if we went down he was not going to come back up again.

This meant I had to go down and replenish both our tins of paint. When I got back after the second re-fill I could see Glen was very anxious, being left up there alone with nothing to do but look down had not been easy for him.

"Are you alright?"

"No not really, come on let's just get on with it!" he snapped, as if embarrassed I'd seen his discomfort.

I handed him his bucket of paint and together we clambered over the ridge of the roof onto the street side, using our brushes and tins to lean on. Whether it was because he looked down, or because the new sheets of tin were not only much hotter but more slippery, I don't know; all I do know is that he suddenly yelped loudly and his feet were whipped from beneath him as if he'd been tackled by Johnny Raper. He crashed down, frantically grabbing the ridge with both hands to stop himself sliding off. His tin of paint thudding down beside him, some sloshing out but miraculously the tin stayed upright and I watched, mesmerised, as it slid slowly down the roof on its bottom, certain at any moment it was going to hit one of the nail heads and topple over. But it didn't. Instead it came to rest in the gutter, tilted over very slowly and stayed there, paint pouring out in gentle gulps into the gutter and down the front of the hotel.

Shit!

By the time I could get down to right it, getting covered in paint in the process, red paint was everywhere. It was running along the gutter, down the front posts which supported the veranda, and dripped onto the footpath below — as luck would have it right outside the front door of the hotel. The wind was catching drips and flecking the door as well.

"What in the blazes is going on!" a familiar voice bellowed.

I turned to abuse Glen, and only then did I hear his whimpers and realise he hadn't moved. He was lying flat on his stomach, hands gripping the ridge of the roof for dear life.

When I got to him I reached out and grabbed the ridge to hang on myself, only to cut my finger on a corner of the tin, my blood now joining the red paint. "Come on!" I urged. "We've got to get down."

"I can't let go! I can't let go!" Glen cried out, and nothing I did or said would convince him to let go.

In the end it took about half an hour to get him down. The fire brigade was called and two men had to more or less prise his hands free, which they did with great care and concern. "You're okay, son, you're okay now." By the time we finally reached the ground, even Reg was almost concerned for him … almost!

"For Christ's sake, what have I done to deserve those two?" I heard him shouting to his wife, as the fireman helped us onto the truck to take us back to the hospital. It was only when we reached the ground that we realised Glen was quite badly burnt. His fingers and hands where he'd clung onto the hot tin ridge were very red, and there were three angry red stripes matching the corrugations of the roof running down his chest and stomach. It was only like bad sunburn and hadn't broken the skin or anything, but it was pretty painful and the nurse at the hospital rubbed some soothing cream into the burns. The cut on my finger was not that bad either, but the doctor still thought I should have a tetanus injection.

The next day, early in the morning, Sergeant King turned up at the hospital. I suppose both Glen and I had secretly been hoping he wouldn't be the same sergeant we'd seen kicking the Abo, but we weren't all that surprised to see it was, and when he came bursting into our room our hearts sank. He was followed by a nurse who was, obviously, unsure of what to do.

"I thought it must be you two! Right, get your gear together and come with me!"

Not again!

We were making our way out through the hospital to the police car parked in the street when Doctor Richards pulled up outside, stethoscope around his neck.

"Just a minute, Sergeant; what's going on?"

"This is police business, Doc. I'd prefer it if you didn't interfere."

"I didn't think it was police business any more. No charges have been laid."

"Look, Doctor, these two are vagrants. I've already caught them loitering. They illegally stopped a train, and they've trespassed on private property. Also I'm doing a bit of digging and waiting for a report from the Townsville police."

"But you just can't go round locking them up while you 'do a bit of digging!'" the doctor exclaimed.

"It's called suspicion, Doc. If I suspect criminal activity, I can arrest who I like."

"Criminal activity! What are you talking about?"

"You've got your job and I've got mine, Doctor," and he made to leave, motioning for us to lead the way.

"Yes, and my job, Sergeant, is to look after my patients, and these two are my patients, and I say that medically they are not fit to be held in gaol, quite apart from it being a complete nonsense!"

By now another nurse and a patient had come out onto the little veranda and the sergeant was forced to consider his position, the veins in his neck standing proud as he fought to control his anger. But he didn't say anything. He just slammed his hat on and headed for his car, shouting back: "If they abscond I'll hold you responsible, Doctor!"

That evening the doctor joined us by the fire and for an hour or so we discussed our situation. "I had another run-in with Sergeant King this afternoon," he told us. "It would seem he has it in for you two for some reason. You wouldn't know why that is, would you?" He raised his eyebrows and Glen and I looked at each other and shrugged.

"We saw him punch and kick an Aboriginal the other day, just outside Hughenden, and he knows we saw him, but don't tell him we said so! He warned us not to say anything."

"I'll bet he did!" The doctor pursed his lips knowingly. "I thought there must be something. I'm afraid such behaviour is endemic in some sections of society out here. Things are changing slowly, and a lot of people are beginning to challenge the way we treat Aboriginals, but it is a slow process." He sighed, as much in frustration as annoyance, then he waved his hands as if to get rid of the subject. "That apart, is the sergeant likely to find out anything about you in Townsville? I mean, have you been in any other trouble? Anything at all, for your own sakes you need to tell me."

So we told him the full story of our trip and our plans for the immediate future, leaving nothing out, and afterwards he smiled slightly.

"Quite an adventure, but I shouldn't think there is anything the sergeant can use against you, even if he is able to find out about Gympie. By the sound of the constable in Yeppoon I doubt he would even have reported you officially, so I wouldn't worry about that. As for working in Mt Isa, I suspect that will be much tougher than you imagine, but it's the business with Sergeant King and the Aboriginal that is potentially the biggest problem."

"Why?"

"I'm not sure yet. I'll see you tomorrow night," and he left, deep in thought.

The next night when he came back he didn't look too happy. "As I suspected, Sergeant King is pursuing the matter, although he has accepted there is nothing to arrest you for with regards to the hotel. But he has rung your mother," he looked at Glen. "No doubt laying it on thick! So I suggest you give her a ring," and then he turned to me, grimacing slightly. "He has also contacted Epping police. It seems they have your fingerprints on file. You didn't tell me that!"

"But that was ages ago! I didn't do anything. I was never charged or anything!"

"Maybe, but you should have told me about the fingerprints. Now I think we are going to have to move fairly quickly."

"What do you mean?"

"The sergeant is angling for you either to be sent home as soon as possible or be placed in a young offenders' institute because you're homeless minors. If he makes enough noise about that he may well get his way. He is like a terrier with a wet rag when he gets going and he will not give in easily. He is claiming you are too young and don't have the skills to work in Mt Isa, you have no experience of the conditions out here, you have nowhere to live and no relatives nearby. Of course there is no mention of Aboriginals, but I have no doubt what you witnessed is the driving force behind his actions. But he will say he is doing it for your own safety and the safety of the community, because he doesn't think you can survive out here, or look after yourselves; at least not without getting into trouble or being a nuisance. They are powerful arguments, especially in light of you having had your fingerprints taken. The police usually only do that when they charge somebody." Then he sighed. "Even if you weren't charged, I'm afraid Sergeant King will paint the worst possible picture and I am sure the authorities will consider his evidence."

Once more all our plans and dreams seemed to be crumbling before our eyes. The galling thing was that this time it wasn't really our fault. Circumstances had conspired against us, and suddenly a rush of anger consumed me. "I hate being young! Everybody thinks they can push us around! We haven't done anything wrong! What's the matter with the bastard! Why can't he leave us alone? We don't give a stuff that he beat up an Abo. We're not going to dob the prick in or anything!" I was close to tears and Dr Richards put his hand on my shoulder sympathetically, but I was on a roll. "We *can* look after ourselves and we *can* survive sleeping rough. We've been doing it for three months already, for Christ's sake! And apart from that one time in Gympie we've worked hard for our keep. So we had a shower! Big deal, we'll pay for the fucking thing if it matters that much!"

"All we want to do is earn some money!" Glen joined in, matching my desperation. "That's why we've come out here. I can't go home with no money, and I won't go home with no money just because we saw some bastard beat someone up!"

The doctor was wise enough to know when silence was the best option, and for a moment he looked from one to the other of us, as if making up his mind about something. Then he completely surprised us by smiling. "Don't get too upset, boys. Where there's a will, there's a way. Personally, I have no doubt you can take care of yourselves and you could easily find work in Mt Isa, tough as it will be. My concern is that even if Sergeant King is unsuccessful in sending you home now, he will, I am certain, make life very difficult for you. Vagrancy is an ambiguous law. He could arrest you for it the moment you walk out of here, and every time he caught you sleeping rough! He does that a few times and you become repeat offenders. Couple that with being homeless minors, and you could end up in a young offenders' institute, a place to be avoided I can tell you. The best thing we can do, I think, is get you out of his reach as quickly as possible, and I just might be able to help there."

We were silent for a moment as we digested this, and then he continued. "It doesn't apply to all of them by any means, but some of the police out here are what you might call old school, and the treatment of Aboriginals is becoming a really sensitive issue. Sergeant King is one of those fiercely opposed to any change in the status quo, and unfortunately he still wields a lot of power. He won't rest until you two are out of the way, one way or another. If it wasn't for him, I'd say go ahead, see if you can make a go of it in Mt Isa and I admire your spirit, but ..." and he held out his hands.

"So, why don't we just tell the authorities what we saw?" said Glen. "Maybe then he will leave us alone."

"If only it were that easy," the doctor shrugged. "No. I don't think that's a good idea. It will be just your word against his and the police will close ranks, which won't help the Aboriginals, and it certainly won't help you at all."

"So, he just gets away with it, like that prick at Yeppoon!" and the doctor smiled sympathetically.

"I understand your frustration, boys. Really I do, and I'm impressed by your determination. But as I said, I may be able to help; I just need a few days to sort it out. In the meantime I want you to stay here, or at least within the hospital grounds. Speaking of which ..." He got up and surveyed the garden. "You could do a bit of weeding and clearing out here if you want to earn your keep. I have to go to Richmond for a surgery tomorrow, but I'll be back the next day and then I'll try and sort something out. Just promise me you won't leave these premises. I doubt the sergeant will come here again, but if he catches you outside he may well arrest you."

We promised.

We spent the two days hacking down the weeds and clearing the little garden behind the hospital, but it was three days before Dr Richards came back and he was genuinely impressed with our work.

"That's brilliant, boys! I've never seen it looking so good! I'll pay you for this."

"You don't have to ..." but he waved us away.

"Of course I do. Besides, I have funds available for upkeep and so on. Now then, I have some good news for you."

Dr Richards originally came from Wagga Wagga in New South Wales and he still had many contacts down that way, one of them being his younger brother, John. His brother had bought a cherry orchard near Young recently. "He's gone out on a limb a bit," the doctor grimaced. "Borrowed heavily to get started, but he is hoping for a bumper crop. It's been a good growing winter for cherries so far, apparently. Anyway, come early October he will be looking for two people to stay in the pickers' sheds on the orchard to keep the birds away from the ripening fruit — crows mainly. For this he will feed you and pay you each two pounds a week. Then towards the end of October he will start picking. It will probably take three or four weeks and then you can earn anything up to eight, even ten pounds a week, depending on how hard you are prepared to work. However, he has said that if you do the bird scarecrow job first he will guarantee you six pounds a week come picking time."

"But it's only August! What do we do now?"

"I'm coming to that. John is friends with the owner of an orange orchard in Leeton, which isn't that far away from Young, and he has arranged for you to work there first, picking oranges for three weeks or so. He can't say how much you'll earn. Again it will depend on how hard you work, but he says the average is at least five pounds a week. By my reckoning, in two months you could earn at least forty pounds each fairly easily. And remember, you will be fed and given somewhere to sleep on both jobs so it won't cost you anything. What do you say?"

Although for a moment neither of us said anything, I could almost hear Glen's brain churning the figures over in his head: forty pounds! Say two pounds a week to rent a room, two pounds a week to eat, I could live on that for ten weeks! "Sounds brilliant!" he beamed.

"But how do we get down there? It's taken us over three months to get up here!"

"Ah!" the doctor tapped his nose. "While I was in the police station the other day, Constable Masters received a phone call from a removal company who'd just moved a family from Dubbo to Mt Isa and were hunting about for a load to take back. In fact, it was hearing that call that gave me the idea to talk to my brother. So, after I rang him and organised the work, I rang the removal company and they are happy to give you a lift down there. You have to meet them at the roadhouse in Cloncurry in two days time. Three or four days to get down there, then it's only a hundred and fifty miles from Dubbo to Young. You can do that in half a day with a bit of luck!"

"But won't we get into trouble if we leave? The sergeant warned us not to go anywhere." For a moment the doctor was silent, as if choosing his words. "Life is not quite the same out here as it is in cities. The weather, the isolation, the distances, it can get pretty tough. Occasionally it is necessary for us to make up our own rules. Sergeant King often makes his up as he goes along. I'm just making up a few of my own." He smiled. "I'll take care of the sergeant. I'm sure once he knows you have left the area completely he will let the matter drop. Besides," he smiled again, this time with just a hint of mischievousness, "I held an Aboriginal clinic in Richmond the other day and I heard something about one of them being beaten up. Of course the man concerned won't make a complaint or say anything, but next time I'm in the police station I'll let it slip that I've heard a rumour." You just don't expect nice, decent doctors to be so devious, do you?

FIFTEEN

J & J Bourke & Co.

*J*im and Joe Bourke were as outback in nature as they were in name; languid, wry and laconic. Joe was several years older, obviously the boss, and more reserved, but they were remarkably similar. Both were tall and slim, had reddish hair, freckles and walked with the same distinctive gait common to men who've sat in a saddle as often as a chair. They also dressed exactly the same — fleecy-lined check shirts, heavy boots and thick grey trousers held up with rope belts.

They were the proprietors of J & J Bourke Removalists, their removal truck being a 1957 Ford Thames Trader with the back extending out over the cab like a big box, and it was up there, in a space six or seven feet wide, four feet deep and three feet high, on a nice supply of soft blankets, that we sat, slept, ate and played endless games of hearts. On each side a one-foot high sliding window provided fresh air and a reasonable view as we rolled and bounced through the vast, dusty nothingness, rarely going faster than fifty miles an hour and on the many rough sections of road often no more than twenty to twenty-five miles an hour. From Cloncurry to Dubbo via Winton, Longreach, Blackall, St George, Moree and Walgett — Jesus, it was a long way!

Born and bred on their father's sheep station near Walgett in Northern New South Wales, Jim and Joe Bourke had been too young for the war, and their father and older brother were exempt as they had to run the farm; so unlike the vast majority of men of that era, their family had not been affected by the war too much. Knowing their elder brother would take over the station when he was gone, their father insisted the two younger boys learn another trade, and from a very early age had encouraged them to repair and maintain all the farm equipment. By the time they were in their late teens, Joe and Jim Bourke could dismantle a truck or rebuild a tractor with their eyes closed. When their father died a few years after the war they began their removal business in an old Ford half truck, originally staying in Walgett, mainly moving goods about. But there wasn't much work, so a few years later they moved to the larger town of Dubbo where they could access the lucrative Sydney market. Now, while still only small, they were one of the most respected and reliable removal firms in Central Western New South Wales. Joe was married, and his wife ran the office from their home in Dubbo and took bookings while they were away.

All this we learned from Doctor Richards as he drove us from Julia Creek early in the morning. "They have a very good reputation and I've told them all about you," he grinned, "so they know what to expect." It was just gone seven o'clock when we pulled into the road house truck park just outside Cloncurry where the brothers were waiting. Their big, blue, rectangular removal van was easy to spot with their name emblazoned in big red letters down each side. After introductions all round, the doctor shook our hands warmly and wished us good luck. It was a fairly emotional farewell. He had been very good to us, but he waved our somewhat self-conscious thanks away. "It's a pleasure, boys; been nice to meet you. Just get down there and earn some money," he grinned. "And give my regards to my brother and his wife."

Inside the roadhouse we had a quick breakfast while the brothers gave us an even quicker briefing. "Empty trucks don't make money," Joe told us, adding that once they got going they would not stop too often. Taking it in turns to drive, they would sometimes do two four-hour shifts each before stopping for a sleep. "Usually we only stop long enough to have a piss and change positions. So I suggest you have a piss too whenever we do stop." He smiled.

"Yeah," Jim chimed in. "We've got bladders like camels, but if you get desperate just belt on the roof. One of us should be awake!"

"There's a jerry can of water strapped inside you can use, but we will stop once a day for a good feed," Joe assured us, ignoring his brother, "oh, and make sure you stub your cigarettes out properly. Start a fire in the back and you might be stuffed. That's about it. As Jim says, you got a problem just belt on the roof or yell out the window." That was it. After we'd eaten and gone to the toilet, we climbed into the back of the truck and scrambled up to our loft room. Joe shut the double doors and we were off, locked inside our big box of a home — only one thousand two hundred and fifty miles to go!

We drove for eight, relatively incident-free hours before we stopped for ten minutes not far from Winton. The only event of any note was encountering a huge herd of cattle we came upon strewn across the road south of Kynuna. It took us nearly an hour to get past them. There was so much dust we had to close the windows and it got a bit stuffy. Once we climbed down to stretch our legs in the cavernous main bay, which was more or less empty. The brothers had managed to secure a few items for the return trip, some crates they had to deliver in Longreach and an old Norton motorcycle to drop off in Moree. Other than that, there were a few wooden boxes of food and equipment and their rolled-up swags to sit on, but the truck bounced and lurched about so much that it was almost impossible to stay on our feet, or our seat.

It is truly disconcerting being in the back of a truck in the semi-dark when you can't see or brace yourselves for bumps and bends, and we got an idea of how frightening it must be for cattle and sheep to be transported like that. No wonder they crammed them in so tightly. Consequently, most of the time we stayed up on our plat-form above the cab. On long, straight stretches we were able to sit up fairly comfortably and play cards, but much of the time we just lay on our stomachs, staring out of our respective windows for hours at a time. When we did stop by the side of the road it was only for a quick brew of tea and a piss.

"Everything okay?" Joe flung open the doors and we climbed down. It was like being let out of gaol. From one of their boxes, Jim pulled out a primus stove and within minutes we were all sipping sweet black tea and eating gingernut biscuits. Joe spent most of the break walking slowly round the truck, kicking tyres and looking under-neath while Jim sat on the back and rolled cigarettes, which he did with great speed and expertise, placing them in an old tobacco tin when they were finished. By the time we set off again, he had thirty or forty ready to go.

"Should last us an hour or so," he winked, and began packing up the primus stove.

"Okay," said Joe, chucking the dregs of his tea away, "let's get goin'. We'll pull up for the night about fifty miles the other side of Winton. Ought to be hungry by then, eh?"

It was dark when we passed through Winton so we didn't see much, not that I think there was much to see, and within minutes we were out on the open road again. Hunger began to gnaw. It must have been about an hour later I suppose, and then everything hap-pened so fast it was over almost before it began. For some time we'd been going quite fast, obviously down a good section of road, so the sudden braking was completely unexpected and we were flung forwards, then there was a loud bang and the truck shuddered and lurched violently, sending us both flying upwards and sideways; Glen crying out when his head hit the roof. It was pitch black. We had no idea which way was up or down and for a second I thought the truck had rolled over. Then a voice called up through the window.

"You okay?"

"Yeah! What happened, for Christ's sake!"

"We hit a 'roo! Hang on, I'll let youse out," then the doors opened and Joe was standing there with a torch. "Bit of a rude awakening, eh!" he said, calm as you like. "Might as well come down. We'll stop here for the night now." We followed him round to the front of the truck where we found Jim examining the damage. There was a large dent in the mud guard but fortunately the headlamps had been protected by the bull bars which were covered in blood and fur. One leg of the kangaroo was wedged under the front axle and Jim knelt down and reached in, dragging it out by its foot.

"Big bugger," he said, disparagingly flinging the leg to the side. "Reckon he's dead?"

"No need for a second opinion." Joe nodded his head sagely as he removed a large blood-soaked piece of fur from the bull bar, although it was impossible to tell which part of the kangaroo this was, or even that it was, or had been, a kangaroo. "Didn't see him 'til it was too late." He shrugged, as much to himself as anybody.

"He can't have been payin' too much attention neither!" grunted Jim, as he crawled underneath the vehicle to check there wasn't more of the creature caught up somewhere. They were both so calm and matter-of-fact, it was as if nothing extraordinary had happened at all. But despite their droll nonchalance, I think they knew just how close we'd come to having a nasty accident.

They seemed completely unruffled, but Glen and I were certainly shaken up. Noticing this, Joe gave Jim a nod and took us by the arm. "Come on. Let's light a fire and get some tucker on," and while he helped us collect wood and start a fire, Jim positioned the truck off the side of the road so the headlights illuminated our campsite. By the time he joined us we had a roaring blaze going, but best of all he brought with him one of the wooden boxes from the back of the truck, the contents of which cheered us up no end. To begin with there was a large esky, and inside it on the top was a tray full of steaks, sausages and bacon. Beneath, in the ice, was half a dozen bottles of Resch's DA beer. Also in the box were kerosene lamps, plates, saucepans, frying pans and other cooking equipment. This was the way to camp! Amazing what a bottle of beer, a nice hot fire and a big plate of sausages and beans can do for shock.

After dinner Glen and I boiled some water and washed up. Since our fight on the beach we had agreed to do this together every night after eating, no matter what, and now we just did it automatically. Neither brother said anything, but we saw the little look of surprise they gave each other. While we did this they retrieved their swags from the back of the truck and began spreading them out by the fire. "You can sleep in the truck if you want," Joe told us, but the fire was nice and warm. Besides, we would be locked in there again the next day for twelve hours or more, so we got our gear out and made up our beds beside theirs. Then Jim got up and went to the truck to turn off the lights. He returned with a guitar which he kept in the cab, and for a while he sat strumming away although no particular tune. It soon became obvious he couldn't play the thing very well. He just knew about six different chords, changing keys from time to time to suit his offering.

"*I woke quite early one fine day, the earth lay cool and still*
When suddenly a parrot perched upon my window sill.
He began to trill and chatter, his greetings to the day
A song to make our earth-born troubles simply slip away.
He sang of far-off places, of laughter and of fun,
It seemed his very chatter brought up the morning sun.
I stirred beneath the covers and crept slowly out of bed
gently closed the window and crushed his bloody head.
Somebody should have told 'im, or given 'im a warning,
I can't stand fucking parrots and I'm not real good in the morning"

Maybe it was in relief, I don't know. All I do know is Glen and I laughed like we had never laughed before until tears streamed down our cheeks.

"It ain't that bloody funny," Joe admonished, but he couldn't stop grinning either. Laughter is like money. The more there is, the more it makes.

"*Bloke goes to the doctor, says, doc, I've broken my arm in three places!*
Doctor says, well don't go to those places any more!"

"How about the wild rover," Joe grunted, pulling his head under his blanket, no doubt having heard it all before a hundred times. There was a pause while Jim strummed the guitar, searching for the right chords; then he began to sing in a haunting, gravelly, semi-baritone voice, flavoured with just a hint of the Irish lilt of his ancestors.

"Oh, I've played the wild rover this many a year,
And I've spent all my money on whisky and beer.
But now I'm returning with gold in great store,
Determined to play the wild rover no more.

After searchin' for months I'd found me a seam,
As thick as four fingers, a prospector's dream.
Enough for my mother and father to see,
The wild rover days were over for me.
But on the way home to a shanty I went
And told the landlady my money was spent.
When I asked her for credit, she answered me "Nay,
Such custom as yours I can get every day!"

So I drew from my pocket some gold nuggets bright
And the landlady's eyes opened wide with delight;
And she said, "I have whisky and wines of the best,
Those words I've just spoken were done so in jest."

So I rolled out my swag and filled up my pot;
Relating tall tales and not thinking a lot.
And in a whirl seven days, or it might have been eight
Were gone in the haze of the inebriate.

There was Kitty and Betsy and Margaret and Blue,
And three or four more that belonged to our crew;
We'd sit up till midnight and make the place roar
'Til the gold in my pocket was in there no more.

Now I'm a pauper, forced to repent,
On a cold bed of straw I lie down to lament,
I'd squandered my fortune, not once but twice,
The wild rover paying the wild rover's price.

So I'll go home to my parents and confess what I've done
And ask them to pardon their prodigal son,
And if they will do so, as so often before.
I'll promise I'll play the wild rover no more."

Warm fire, full tummies, black sky ablaze with stars; we fell asleep with smiles of delight on our lips. What close, nasty accident?

Next morning the brothers were up by four o'clock and we were woken to the sound of eggs and bacon being fried. Joe made us all egg and bacon sandwiches for lunch and before the sun was up we were on our way. We pulled into Longreach at about eight o'clock in the morning, where we helped them unload the crates at a factory on the outskirts of town. Then Joe said, "How about a comfy shit and a hot shower?" We parked not far from the main street and walked to the hotel carrying our towels and toothbrushes. "Stopped here on the way up," Jim informed us as we went in. "Landlord said we could use the bathroom on our way back if we wanted. Best I check though, eh! Don't want to end up in gaol, do we?" And both he and Joe chortled heartily. Oh, very funny! But there was no doubt it was more relaxing having a shower without looking over our shoulder at every noise.

"Room fourteen my arse!"

By ten o'clock we were on the road again, Barcaldine, Blackall and Tambo going by without incident, and it was just getting dark when we stopped a few miles from Augathella. Jim opened the passenger door, and by standing up in the cab he could lean out and talk to us, more or less through our window. "How youse doin', getting pissed off yet?" he grinned. "Joe wants to get down to the Warrego Highway tonight if we can, 'bout another sixty mile. Reckon you can handle that?"

"Do we have a choice?"

"Not really," he grinned again. "Beer and T-bone steaks for dinner, though, should be worth waiting for," and we set off again.

They certainly were worth waiting for, and once again we fell asleep under the stars beside the fire, entertained by Jim and his guitar in his own inimitable way.

"What's grey and got a trunk?

"An elephant!"

"No! A mouse going on holidays!"

Then we sang a rousing rendition of a song even us city boys had heard of, even if we didn't know or understand some of the words, but clinking beer bottles and thumping an esky made up for our moments of silence. Even Joe joined in.

"… and glory if he gets her, won't he make the ringer go!
Click go the shears, boys, click, click, click,
Wide is his blow and his hands move quick …"

After this we settled down as Jim slowed the pace, gently strumming his guitar.

"Our gran taught us this one," he smiled.

"Two old ladies, we sit down to tea,
I'm eighty-four and she's eighty-three.
I hate her and she hates me, but we're the only ones left now you see.

We meet every Wednesday at half past three
I go to her, then she comes to me.
I bore her and she bores me, but we're the only ones left now you see.

She boasts of a party at number three
When Fred kissed her instead of me
But I wear his ring, so it's plain to see why I hate her and she hates me.

Never trust your best friend, so the rest say
And I don't trust her, not to this day.
But the rest are gone, so we'll pour some tea, for we're the only ones
left now you see."

Then he stood up, tall and erect, and gave a little drum roll on the back of the guitar; the national anthem at the end of the show.

"Australians all let us rejoice, for we are young and white.
The yellow hordes are on their way, but we know we are right.
Though we can see, undoubtedly, our neighbours are all Asian
We'll sing and dance and wave the flag because we are Caucasian."

Early the next morning we arrived in Mitchell, only to discover the road they wanted to take to St George was cut by floods and we would have to go the long way round through Roma. We were over halfway there when we had the blowout. It was not quite as dramatic as hitting the kangaroo, but it still frightened the life out of us. It wasn't a loud bang ... more a pop like a rifle shot, but the truck lurched precariously and we could sense Joe struggling to control it for a second or two. The burst tyre was on the inside wheel of the nearside double wheels at the back, making it slightly more complicated to replace. "Could have been worse, I guess," Joe sighed. "Yeah," Jim added cheerfully. "Front tyre goes, you've got no steering at all!" and he knelt down, examining the damage, stripping off a piece of the split rubber. "Right," Joe stood up, getting all businesslike. "You two, cup of tea while we fix this."

Watching the two of them work together was amazing. Without communicating at all they went about their tasks independently yet perfectly coordinated, as if they'd done it a hundred times before. No jobs were replicated, and they never got in each other's way. While one got the jacks out, the other got the spanners and tools. One loosened the nuts, while the other retrieved the spare wheels from under the truck; Jim punctuating the process with his little asides as he worked.

"I reckon we'll use the round wheel today ..."

"Why wouldn't the spanner go out with the nuts? Because they were all such tight bastards!"

"Knock, knock!"

"Who's there?"

"Amos!"

"Amos who!"

"A mosquito!"

Despite their efficiency, it still took them nearly two hours to change the wheel. Just jacking and chocking the truck up level and secure took half an hour.

In the meantime, Glen and I had taken the primus stove out of their food box and began making tea. As we dug in amongst their tins of food we saw the tin of apricots, and immediately agreed we should make our hosts a little treat. Over the weeks, and especially on Magnetic Island, we had experimented with dampers, not only with the consistency of the dough and the heat of the fire but with the ingredients. We discovered they tasted a lot better with a bit of salt sprinkled into the dough, sugar too sometimes, even a dollop of Carnation milk; then, instead of twisting the dough round a stick and losing or burning half of it in the fire, we began making lots of little dampers, like thick pancakes, and frying them slowly in the fat of tinned corned beef, or preferably bacon fat when we had any. Then one day, more or less by accident, Glen poured some coconut juice into the dough instead of water, and the result was really nice. It got us thinking about what else we could put in them, and the only thing remotely suitable we had in our stash at the time was a tin of apricots. Emptied onto a plate and chopped up finely, we poured that into the dough and stirred it thoroughly, binding the mixture together before patting them out into little flat cakes and frying them. Bingo! Eat your heart out, Mrs Beeton! They were terrific, or at least we thought so.

The ones we made that day may not have had any coconut juice in them, but they were just as nice and the look on Jim's face when he ate one was priceless.

"Well, bugger me!" he exclaimed. "These are beaut! What do you call 'em?"

"Don't know. Apricot cakes, I guess."

The blowout happened about half a mile outside a small village and the truck was stopped just in front of the sign. "That's what you should call 'em, I reckon." He nodded at the sign. Muckadilla cakes they were. We buried the empty apricot tin beneath that sign — it might still be there!

In Moree, after we delivered the motorbike, Joe gave us an hour to stock up on food and cigarettes and we were anxious to find out if they were still giving out vouchers in New South Wales. They were, but by the time we left the police station we were beginning to wonder if it was a legal requirement to hand out welfare in a patronising manner. Still, I guess if it were dispensed with dignity and no questions asked we'd all be on it, wouldn't we? When we got back to the truck the brothers were waiting for us.

"Okay?" Joe asked, and we waved our vouchers victoriously.

"So you didn't meet anybody you liked better than yourself, then," Jim stated.

"Sorry?"

"Our granddad used to reckon that if you went out and didn't meet anybody you liked better than yourself, then that was a result. Although he didn't say if it was a good or bad result; that was up to you," he grinned.

By now it was the thought of spending the night under the stars listening to Jim that fortified us as much as anything during the long hours on the road, so we were a little disappointed to hear he was going to stop off in Walgett that night to see his girlfriend. As it turned out, we were still royally entertained. We got there at about seven o'clock, and having dropped Jim off in the town, Joe parked up on the banks of the river next to a barbecue pit. Within an hour Jim returned with his girlfriend and five or six of his young mates, and over the next hour or so dozens of cars and trucks arrived as word spread that the brothers were in town for the night. Eventually there must have been about fifty people there, mostly young men getting wilder and louder. Glen and I joined in for the first few hours and had a few bottles of beer each, listening to them tell stories, abuse each other and catch up on the gossip. Then Jim and his girlfriend left and Joe came over to us and suggested it might be an idea if we slept in the truck. "Could get a bit rough out here soon." He had to shout to be heard over the noise. "You can watch all the action from up there," he suggested.

He was right. By midnight most of them were paralytic, shouting and yelling. They played mindless games like seeing who could climb highest up a large gum tree. Bottles were smashed and tempers flared, two blokes had a wrestle and fell into the river and there were two fistfights that Joe allowed to go on long enough for the participants to land a few blows before he intervened; and we thought only people our age behaved like that! The police arrived at one stage, but when they saw it was Joe in charge they went away, satisfied he could handle things.

In the end the party wore itself out as parties do, and the next thing we knew Joe was bashing on the side of the truck to wake us. Yawning copiously, we emerged to find hundreds of bottles strewn about and half a dozen young men flaked out beside the fire, Joe going from one to the other retrieving his blankets. "Come on, get up, I'm outta here!" Groaning and holding their heads, they rose and went stumbling off to their cars. "Can't handle it, you shouldn't drink," he called after them, grinning. After a quick breakfast we helped him clean up the area before we left, dumping the bottles into two old forty-four gallon drums. Jim was staying on in Walgett for a few days, so we were able to cram in the front with Joe for the remainder of the trip and we arrived in Dubbo late that afternoon, four days after leaving Cloncurry.

Joe invited us to stay at his place for the night. Cathy, his wife, was more than welcoming. She cooked a fantastic meal and made us smoked ham and tomato sandwiches for our lunch, and gave us a loaf of her lovely home-made bread. The next morning Joe drove us out to the Newell Highway at the southern end of town, and we shook hands. In some ways it was almost a relief that Jim wasn't there; saying goodbye to nice people didn't get any easier, especially when we knew we would probably never see them again. Although we were both certain of one thing; if we didn't get to ride in the back of another removal truck for fifty years, it would be too soon.

SIXTEEN

William Forsyth Remington Fellows

*B*y midday we were eating Cathy's sandwiches by the side of the road, three miles south of Peak Hill, having been dropped there by a farmer at the turn off to his property. I'm not sure why exactly, but both of us felt quite elated and buoyed; it was as if somehow we were starting out on our trip all over again. Young had become our Magnetic Island and here we were, already only a hundred miles or so from it. Although there were some dark clouds on the horizon it was a lovely day, with a gentle breeze, peaceful and calm and a brilliant blue sky. The scenery added to our feelings of wellbeing and we were not in the slightest bothered there was no traffic. Gum trees, cockatoos, Merino sheep, and rolling hills of brown pasture all being uniquely Australia, sort of makes you want to walk through it. So, we set off with a jaunty stride.

"Where the blue gums are blowing, the Murrumbidgee's flowing, beneath a sunny sky."

Two hours later the dark clouds on the horizon had become black angry clouds above our heads, split asunder by bright lightning flashes. The gentle breeze had suddenly picked up to gale-like proportions, and we were about to get 'a wet fish and no bottoms', as my grandmother used to say. Ten minutes before, we'd passed a large three-sided barn in a field, so we raced back down the road. We were too late; five hundred yards from the barn the rain began pelting down like steel rods, so hard it hurt our heads, and scrambling over the fence we sloshed across the field and burst into the old wooden building in a rush of sopping wet, panting excitement, shouting to be heard over the thunderous din on the corrugated iron roof.

"Wow! Talk about rain!"

"I'm fucking drenched!"

"Shit! The bread's all soaked through!"

"Everything's bloody soaked through!"

Funny how very loud noise sometimes acts like a stimulant, creating a sort of gripping excited tension, which doesn't really exist but still leaves you feeling buggered when it stops.

"Let's light a fire!" Glen yelled. "I'm freezing!"

"What with?"

"There must be something in here!"

"Right, you look for wood and I'll find a place to sleep before it gets too dark!" And we set off in different directions with urgent fervour.

The old barn was cavernous, at least a hundred feet long and about twenty feet high, with a ten-foot wide open-sided loft running around two sides, supported on rough wooden poles. There were a couple of old hay carts and ploughing implements strewn about, with harnesses and other bits of equipment hanging on the posts, and in the corner, under the stairs leading up to the loft, were several bales of hay.

"I've found somewhere!" I shouted, running over to test the hay. It was bone dry and reasonably fresh, and I bounced up and down on it for a moment. "Yeah! Fantastic!" Meanwhile, Glen had found a back door and gone outside.

"Out here!" he yelled. "There's a fire and everything!" And he came rushing excitedly back into the barn. "Come and see. It looks like somebody lives here!"

"That's because somebody does live here! Now will you two stop shouting!"

"Jesus! Who said that?"

"I did!" And looking up, we saw a dishevelled man with a matted grey beard looking down at us. He was sitting on the loft floor, his legs dangling over the edge, the heels of his socks completely worn through.

"For Christ's sake! You scared the shit out of us!"

"And you woke *me* up!"

"Sorry ... we didn't ... I mean ... do you really live here?" By now both of us were shivering with the cold, and with a wave of his hand he dismissed our apologies and motioned to the back of the shed. "Go and dry yourselves, you're making my floor wet; go on then! You won't get dry staring up at me, will you?"

A sloping corrugated iron roof attached to the wall and supported at the front by half a dozen rough poles ran right along the back of the barn. Although open to the elements it was remarkably dry underneath despite the ferocity of the downpour, which was now beginning to ease. Halfway along there was a large semi-circular fireplace made of stones, with three or four logs burning brightly and a billy full of steaming water standing on a metal plate over one corner. Next to the fire was a rusty camp oven hanging from a metal tripod, and beside it several large logs were obviously used as seats. A kerosene lamp hung from the roof and a rough wooden shelf was nailed to the wall, and on the shelf were an enamel plate, mug, knife, fork, spoon, some tea and sugar, and various tins of food. There was even a piece of rope to hang our clothes on strung between two of the roof beams. At the far end was a water tank.

"Crikey!" exclaimed Glen. "He's got everything out here."

"Yes; and I know exactly what's there, too!" The man's voice came from the other side of the wall.

"Can we light the lamp and hang our clothes on the rope?" I called out.

"That's what they're there for, my boy, and while you're at it you can make us all a cup of tea, two sugars and a dollop of Carnation in mine, and fill the billy up afterwards. I'll be out in a tick."

We'd changed our clothes, hung up our wet ones, put a couple of tins of food on the metal plate to warm up and made three mugs of tea by the time he came out to join us.

"Ah! Tea! Very civilised." He was now wearing an old worn cardigan and slippers, and as he sat down it was impossible not to notice the telltale whiff of stagnant sweat and dirty clothes. In fact he was almost as scruffy and smelly as Jerky Joe, with a similar paucity of teeth. His hair was as matted as his beard, and his fingernails must have been at least half an inch long.

"Now then," he smiled, getting settled on a log. "I suppose introductions are the order of the day. I'm William, and you are … ?"

"Nick, Glen. Do you really live here?"

"Do you mind if I ask you first how old you are?"

"Thank you," he nodded when we told him. "I suppose I could ask what you are doing out here? But that would be prying, and I have no wish to pry."

"Are you English?" Glen asked.

"Unlike yourself obviously." But the rebuke was gentle, and he smiled as he said it. "Yes dear boy, I am a Pom, or at least that is where I was conceived and born, but I don't claim allegiance to any one nation. I am a citizen of the world. Like a migratory bird, nationality means nothing to me. But do I detect just a touch of Burnley in your voice?"

"Blackburn."

"Ah, yes, close though, close. Right ho! Youth before beauty!"

"Sorry?"

"You tell me all about yourselves, then I'll tell you about myself."

We ate while telling him our tale, and after we'd made up our beds on the straw bales we sat around the fire and listened with growing amazement to the story of William Forsythe Remington Fellows.

"Very grand name, isn't it? The Remington bit is from my mother's side. She had something to do with the American Remingtons. Which is where the joke originated, I believe — 'My mother was a Remington and my father was a Colt 45.' He grinned.

"But don't be misled. Behind my illustrious name lies a very mediocre human being indeed, I'm afraid. And to think my family had such plans for me." He sighed heavily.

"I'm from the Shropshire arm of the Fellows clan, you understand … never did take kindly to failure, that lot. Expensive public school and university educated Fellows are not supposed to end up here." He waved his arms about in explanation. "Of course, the war sort of upset one's prospects a little, but in all honesty I have only myself to blame for my circumstances," and he smiled broadly again, exposing all seven of his black and brown teeth. "So I have no complaints."

"How long have you lived here?"

"You mean Australia, or this barn?

"Well, both."

"I came to Australia in 1947 …"

"That's when I came here!" I said.

"Well, we will at least always have that in common, won't we," and it was difficult to tell if he was being sarcastic or friendly.

"After the war people were sort of wandering aimlessly all over the place in England, across Europe in fact, and the longer one had been in the army the more aimless one's wanderings seemed to be." He grimaced. "I suppose after I was discharged I just got caught up in that swirl of humanity. Somehow I ended up in Melbourne working as a bank teller, but I hated it … absolutely hated it. Then one day I read a book called *Walden*, and I haven't looked back since. As for this barn, I've been coming here now for about eleven years."

"Eleven years!"

"Yes, I can't believe it myself sometimes"

"What do you mean, 'coming here'?" Glen asked

"Ah, very observant," he raised his finger in recognition. "This is one of several homes I have dotted about the country. Oh, I don't own any of them, of course, but the people who do own them are very accommodating and I've got to know them over the years, or rather they've come to accept me." He smiled.

"How do you live? Are you on unemployment benefits?"

"I most certainly am not!" he said emphatically. "I take nothing from any state, except their air and water, and no nation can claim ownership of those."

"But how do you get your food and stuff?"

"Oh, I do a bit of work here and there for my keep; simple house maintenance, pulling fences, helping at shearing and harvest time and so on. I also have a few traps," and he pointed to a variety of vicious-looking rabbit traps and crayfish baskets hanging on the wall. "But I'm a bit like a nomadic South American Indian and I try not to denude any one place, leave some goodwill behind to sustain me next time I pass by, if you get me. In fact I'll be leaving here soon; Hay, I think, will be my next abode. I haven't been out there for awhile."

"How many places do you have?"

"Oh, about a dozen; three or four in Queensland, five or six more here in New South Wales and a few in Victoria."

"But what about all your stuff? Have you got a car?"

"Good heavens no, dear boy!" he reared back. "Wouldn't be seen dead in one. I do carry a few bits and pieces with me, mainly my library, but over the years I've accumulated sets of furniture in each place, such as it is," he pointed to the camp oven. "These I leave behind; not that much of it really belongs to me, more they are communal things. This place is often used overnight by drovers and the like, and the few items I do own are usually still here when I return. My belongings are not exactly sought after items."

"You have a library!" Glen exclaimed, rather than asked.

"Find it hard to believe that someone like me might read, do you?" he asked, feigned indignity exposed by the twinkle in his eye.

"Well … no, I just …"

"Never assume, boy! Never assume!" Then he chuckled to himself. "But it's quite understandable. I'm not exactly the image of a well-read, erudite chap, am I?"

"I'm sorry, I didn't mean …"

"Stop apologising, boy. You don't mean it and I don't need it. Do you read yourself?"

"Well, yes," said Glen. "But not so much lately. It's hard when you're always on the …"

"Rubbish, boy, rubbish! A man should always have a good book by him." Then he suddenly got up and went and stood outside, staring up at the still overcast black sky for a moment. "Hmm, I'm late for my medicine. I'll just pop up to the mezzanine lounge and get it," and he disappeared into the barn and we could hear him climbing the loft steps. "Put another log on the fire, will you," he called out.

When he returned he was carrying a bottle Glen and I instantly recognised as port, and a small leather bag, a bit like one of those old doctor's bags only softer. "My library," he said, placing the bag down next to Glen. "Have a look through them if you want."

"How did you know what time it was? There aren't any stars or anything tonight." He touched his nose conspiratorially. "Internal clocks, my boy, very handy things. We've all got one. It's just a matter of learning how to use it. Let me see, I'd say it's about nine forty-five," and he looked at Glen as he checked his watch.

"It's nine fifty!" said Glen, amazed.

"Damn, must remember to wind mine up," he grinned. "Care to join me?" He offered us the bottle. "One of my many weaknesses, I fear."

"No thanks. We got really sick drinking some of that a few months ago."

"Very wise. Not good for the young liver. Not good at all," and he held the bottle up to his mouth, swallowing great gulps for what seemed ages. "Ahhhh!" he exclaimed, letting the bottle down. "Very nice, although I suspect it is as bad for the older liver as the young." He grinned. "See anything you like?"

Glen had been taking some of the books out of the bag, placing them on a log as he looked at them.

"I've never heard of most of them."

"No, I suppose not. They're not exactly your Roy of the Rovers stuff."

"You've got a Bible!" said Glen, unable to contain his astonishment as he took it out of the bag, and this time William laughed outright.

"Ah, the unbridled innocence of youth!" and he took another long swig from his bottle.

"Do you believe in God, then?" Glen asked, and William put his bottle down and looked him in the eye for a few moments, as if making up his mind whether the question had been asked flippantly or from genuine interest.

"No," he said, firmly but calmly. "Perhaps more correctly, I should say I don't believe in religion, although I do believe in prayer and faith."

Our bemused expressions made him smile briefly.

"Why do I have a Bible then, you want to know; faith in what, you ask?"

"Well ... I just ..."

"That's okay," he raised his hand. "It's a fair enough question. I have the Bible for two reasons. First, because there are some very interesting stories in it, and we all like interesting stories, true or not. But I also have it to remind me how dangerous the church is, and how damaging religion has been for society."

Sensing our confusion, he had another quick drink. "It is a bit confusing, isn't it?" he said. "But God is confusing. Or rather, we have made him confusing."

"So, who do you pray to?" Glen asked.

236

"I don't know; and it doesn't matter. To me, God is who you confide in privately, who you talk to when you're down or you just want to get something off your chest. It makes no difference if he exists or not. It's the act of prayer that's the comfort. He might listen to you or he might not; that's not the point. The point is that we all need and want to express our troubles from time to time, talking about them out loud in the privacy of our own minds. I believe prayer is essentially that; a personal, private affair between a man and his inner self, his conscience if you like. The trouble is, two thousand years ago the church came along and hijacked that personal, private affair and called it religion. Now religions — all religions — are nothing more than huge clubs, playing on that human need for a spiritual connection or faith; contact with our inner self, I like to call it; and they have turned what should be a private affair into huge public affairs. Vast, corrupt, undemocratic clubs making up rules and laws as they go along to suit their own agenda, and spouting endless dogma with threats of damnation or worse for those who don't join them. The churches of religions are like middle men, feeding off our insecurity and fears. It's in their interest to scare the shit out of us, tell us we're all sinners and we'll go to hell if we don't join the club and repent. Oh, I am quite sure there are many honourable and well-meaning people within churches, but religions don't care about the spiritual wellbeing of individual men and women. They only care how many members they have."

Then, surprising us both, he chuckled to himself and grinned at us. "Of course my views on the subject didn't exactly endear myself to the family and I was always lumped in with that other black sheep, Uncle Mortimer, who'd seen first hand the carnage and stupidity of mankind during the First World war. Somehow he managed to survive and not long after his return the entire family trooped off to church as usual, sitting in our own special pews. The vicar at the time was fond of giving fire and brimstone sermons. "Repent ye sinners for the devil awaits!" and so on. He used to frighten the life out of me. Anyway on this Sunday the vicar was about half way through his sermon, fist shaking with passion, when Uncle Morty suddenly stood up and shouted "Rubbish! Heaven or hell! To me it doesn't matter, I've got good mates in the former and family in the latter!" and he strode from the church. I was only a very small boy at the time but I thought it was the funniest thing I had ever heard. The rest of family, however, were mortified and I don't think they ever forgave him!"

Although we all laughed at this it was difficult to know what to say to this outburst, and after our giggles subsided we were silent for a minute or two, staring into the fire. Neither of us had ever heard anybody talk quite so bluntly against religion before. Of course, like all kids we had heated debates about the subject in the milk bar from time to time, but I think basically most of us just accepted that God existed; after all, he had been around for thousands of years, so who were we to challenge it? Of the two of us, I suppose I was the more ambivalent; my father had not been a religious man, and although I know he did have fairly strong feelings on the subject he never spoke to us either for or against religion. Glen was much more disturbed. His mother was a regular church-goer and he himself had attended Sunday School on a regular basis, and although he didn't know it, on more than one occasion on our trip I had seen him, or at least heard him, praying. Now I could see him struggling to come to terms with William's words.

"But you can't prove there isn't a God," he said.

"Very true, my boy, I can't, just like nobody can prove there is. But I don't know that it's up to me to prove or disprove anything. I'm not trying to influence others, I don't have sets of rules how people should live and behave, and more importantly I don't foist those rules on society, demanding they be obeyed. I don't lecture people about sex, tell them what to eat or when to pray. Surely it is they;

those clubs who put such demands upon us; that have to do the proving. Or do we just blindly accept their laws, their demands?" Saying this, he picked up one of the books. "D. H. Lawrence," he said and waved it at us before leafing through it. "He knew a thing or two about human nature. Yes, here we are. *'And people who talk about faith, faith in anything, usually want to convince or force somebody to agree with them, as if there was safety in numbers, even for faith.'* And as he put the book down he smiled at us.

"Throughout history, mankind has had such a need, such a yearning for belief that we have become suckers for it and can be persuaded to believe almost any nonsense if it makes us feel better, happier, safer. But there is light at the end of the tunnel. Few people today believe in the unbelievable and often violent religions of the past, the Greek goddesses, the Egyptian priests or the countless Norse Gods, seemingly one appointed for every act of nature or human behaviour they couldn't understand. The current fashion is to have only one God, responsible for everything, and although I don't believe in it, I have no idea if it is true or not. What I am sure about is that the religions that claim to speak on his behalf and that pressure us through our ignorance, fear or guilt to join their clubs, will eventually become as irrelevant as the God of thunder. Nonsense never lasts."

Then he took another drink of port and smiled gently at Glen. "I'm sorry if I've shocked or offended you, dear boy. It was not my intention. They are only my opinions, my beliefs, and I can be just as wrong as anybody else, which is why I will not carry on this conversation. If I were to try and persuade you further to accept my views I would be no better than the religions I criticise for doing the same thing. I too have no proof, no evidence to support my assertions, so why should I expect you to believe me. No! Each man must make up his own mind about such things and there I suggest we let the matter lie. Port and religion don't usually mix." He smiled as he took another long draught.

We were all silent for several minutes, and then Glen said, "What I don't understand," he shook his head, "is what someone like you ... I mean ... why ... ?"

"Why is someone like me, so well educated, so well dressed and so well groomed, living out his days like this? Is that what you mean?"

"Well, yes."

"Cowardice is the answer, dear boy. Pure, simple cowardice. I can't face or cope with society, so I hide myself away, sustained in my bitterness by port and Thoreau."

"Thoreau?"

"A nineteenth century American author," and he picked up another book. "*Walden*; this is my Bible. It might not be quite your cup of tea just at present, but when you get a bit older you should read him one day. Everybody should read Thoreau one day. In fact, if as many people read Thoreau as read the Bible, the world would be a much nicer place, I fancy."

"Do you have any family in Australia?"

"No." He shook his head, but didn't elaborate and just stared into the fire. Whether it was the port or not we couldn't tell, but his mood seemed to change suddenly and for a moment we thought we might have annoyed him and we looked at each other. "No, no family," he said flatly, still staring into the fire. "In fact, I've never been particularly interested in sex, strangely enough. I think when that part of me was being installed in the womb I must have been asleep. I would have made a good priest I think, not that they would ever have ordained a sacrilegious bastard like myself!" and he laughed uproariously, then just as quickly became very sombre again. "But I mustn't get started on that again, no, not that again. Now then, boys, I'd like to be alone if you don't mind. You're probably tired anyway after your journey, and if you're heading off early tomorrow you'll need your sleep. All I ask is that your departure in the morning is not quite as loud as your arrival this evening!" And he took another long swig at the port bottle and didn't even look at us as we left.

When we woke in the morning we could hear him snoring in the loft above, and beside us on the straw was the book *Walden*. On the inside cover, he'd written: "To Glen and Nick, in memory of three ships that passed one night." And it was signed: "William Forsythe Remington Fellows."

Two days later we arrived in Young and went straight to the police station to get the address of John Richards.

SEVENTEEN

God Save the Queen! Davey Crockett, and John and Emma Richards

*T*he conflicting attitude of Australians towards Poms in the 1950s was very confusing for a child. Of course sport had always been a source of passionate rivalry; Mr Archer had made sure I was well schooled in that! But there was more to it than just fierce competition. On the one hand was the country's enthusiastic, almost sycophantic relationship with the King or Queen of England, more fervent than in England itself in many respects. Prime Minister Robert Menzies, who seemed to have the job on a permanent basis, was an ardent royalist and every government office, every school hall, every police station, post office, municipal office, community centre, even railway station waiting rooms had a portrait of His Majesty, and woe betide anybody who didn't show respect to it. When George VI died, the ABC played dirge music on the wireless for hours at a time and the mood was so sombre and heavy it felt like the end of the earth or something. Then in 1954 the country came to virtual standstill for the Royal Tour, and hordes of us school kids were herded into I think it was the Sydney sports ground to see the Queen. It took two hours to get there, two hours to get herded, two hours standing there and two hours to get home, and all I saw was the top of her hat as the Land Rover went past; my vision completely obscured by Mrs Muir's bum and the little flag on a stick bloody Cynthia Dempsey kept waving in my face.

On the other hand, in stark contrast to all this dutiful respect, was the seething anger and resentment many Australians had for the English after the war. At school and selling papers in the pub I was frequently abused, called a Pommie bastard and worse, as if I was personally responsible for the disaster of Gallipoli, the fall of Singapore or the collapse of wool prices; yet the Queen, who also just happened to be a Pom, was revered like a God! Of course, other nationalities and migrants, Italians for example, were routinely insulted and abused, far worse than Poms usually. I remember our butcher wouldn't serve 'dagos'. He wouldn't even allow them into the shop! And it really wasn't very long ago. Then of course there were the poofters; boy! You didn't want to mention you were one of them in the Epping public bar! Gay Mardi Gras? Forget it; only the very, very brave 'came out' in 1961 Australia. Jack Cooper and his ilk positively despised them.

Despite all that, without doubt those who suffered the worst were Australia's very own original people. Surely if anybody had the right to call themselves 'fair dinkum Aussies', it was them. But 'abos' and 'gins' were not only cruelly insulted and vilified, but completely disenfranchised. They couldn't vote, couldn't buy land, couldn't enter politics or public houses and were hounded out of the centre of towns and cities by the police, often by public demand. In the 1950s, racial intolerance and abuse was almost a way of life; everybody was guilty of it, which wasn't surprising given it was Australian government policy after all! But few western countries were free of such bigotry in those days, and certainly the Poms had nothing to be self-righteous about.

For some reason I was never too bothered by verbal abuse. I might not have been very good in a punch-up, but from an early age I realised that returning insulting abuse with even more insulting abuse was far more effective and hurtful than a smack in the mouth. It meant, of course, that I got the odd smack in the mouth myself occasionally for my troubles, although I always felt it was a bit of a victory if they had to resort to violence. But it has always been fairly easy for smug Pommie bastards to get under the skin of sensitive Aussies. Just asking what 'cultured' meant usually did the trick, although there were plenty who thought you were talking about oysters.

I suppose I can claim, with a modest amount of shame, to have contributed to the change in the social fabric of Australia in the 1950s. After all, it was because of thieving little arseholes like me that rules, laws and regulations were enacted and people became more cynical, less trusting and obsessed with security; locks, burglar alarms and insurance. Although in my defence, on this day Davy Crockett and Cassandra Roberts were as much to blame.

The car was parked in Epping's High Street, with the passenger side window fully wound down and there, sitting on the passenger seat, was a big fat purse, covered in colourful beads. It was Saturday morning and I was heading for the pictures early, knowing the queue would be long; for in two hours the premier of the film of the century was about to be screened. No Saturday matinee had ever been as important as this! "*Davy! Davy Crockett, king of the wild frontier. Born on a mountain top in Tennessee … something or other … you ever did see.*" It cost nine pence to get in, which I had from my paper round, plus sixpence for a Fanta and a bag of chocolate bullets at interval. What I didn't have was the hat, which, to my despair, I saw almost everybody in the queue did have; Eric and Dave, Brian Seymour and Ronnie Watson; even Cassandra Roberts had a hat! A girl! Oh, the humiliation! How could I possibly stand in a queue, already snaking up the street, if she had a Davy Crockett hat and I didn't!

Being *the* fashion accessory of the decade, Martin's, the gentlemen's outfitters at the top of the street, had cunningly ordered in dozens of them to coincide with the film, retailing them for three shillings and sixpence and even staying open late on Saturday especially for the event. There was I, desperate for a hat; there was the purse, shouting 'open me!' There were the hats in Martin's window, shouting 'buy me!' But most of all there was Cassandra Roberts, shouting 'look at me!' Wrong, immoral, disgusting, disgraceful as it might be, there is a certain spine-tingling excitement about stealing four shillings from a purse in broad daylight in front of dozens of people. See, I wasn't all bad! I rarely took more than I needed.

I wore my Davy Crockett hat with great pride and pushed into the queue in front of Cassandra. Inside, four or five of us be-hatted eleven-year-old 'Davys' sat in a row, and were so busy being loud and obnoxious that we didn't notice the anthem begin. Suddenly I was clipped around the ears and my hat was ripped off by a man behind me. "Take your hats off and stand up!" he hissed, prodding the others stiffly in the back. "Show some respect, you little bastards!" And he caught up with the song with vigour and passion. "*Long live our noble Queen!*" I recognised him from the pub, an ex-digger. He was a mate of Jack Cooper's, and just as bitter and angry when it came to Poms. If that wasn't confusing and ironic enough, the following weekend I wore my hat to the milk bar and left it sitting in a booth while I played the pinball machine. When I went back half an hour later it had gone. Somebody had pinched it. Utter bastards! Was there no decency left in the world!

* * *

Constable Tyler of the Young police more than restored our faith in policemen. "'Course you can, boys," he smiled when we asked if we could have a voucher. "Understand how these things work, do you?"

"Yeah, we know we've got to get work after this but that's why we're here. We have a job to go to in a few weeks."

"Good on yer; who would that be with, then?" And when we told him, he beamed with pleasure.

"Johnny Richards! Well, bugger me!"

"You know him?"

"Know him? Went to school with him. Bonza bloke is Johnny. Does he know you're here?"

"No. We need to find out where he lives. We're supposed to call in and meet him."

"I can do better than that," the constable said. "I can take you out there! Come on," and he grabbed his hat. Why couldn't they all be like that!

Fifteen minutes later we drove into the front yard of John and Emma Richards' small farm. Playing on the veranda of the weatherboard cottage was a boy of about four years old. He was hiding behind a large firewood basket, firing his toy rifle at us as we came up the steps. Most notably he was wearing a Davy Crockett hat and instantly I was transported back to that Saturday matinee; not all that long before perhaps, but, whatever your age, a third of your life always seems a long time ago.

I think both Glen and I fell in love with Emma Richards the moment we first saw her. Twenty-six, tall and elegant, she was truly beautiful, with a wonderful smile, gentle eyes and easy manner. She was three months pregnant with her second child, and had that complexion and air of serenity that so often accompanies that condition early on. "Hello, boys," she greeted us brightly, coming out onto the veranda. She waved at Constable Tyler as he hooted his farewell and headed back to town. "We've been expecting you. John's out at the orchard. I'll take you out there later. How about a cup of tea first? Have you eaten? Robbie, Robbie, come and meet these two nice boys."

Replete with ham and pickle sandwiches and lovely fruitcake, Emma drove us the four or five miles to the orchard in a very battered 1947 Ford half ton pick-up. We squeezed into the front with her, Robbie sitting on our laps and Morgan, their black and white sheepdog, panting happily in the back. On the way she explained that they didn't live on the orchard as there was no house there. "We're leasing the farm at the moment, but we hope to build a house on the orchard after this crop," and then she swore softly under her breath as the gears crunched. "This is my dad's. He lent it to us so I would have a vehicle while John was at the orchard. I'm still getting used to it," and she did a very professional and smooth double shuffle to engage the gear and grinned triumphantly. "But I'm learning!"

"Woof" agreed Morgan from the back.

John Richards was a sort of male equivalent of his wife (although he wasn't pregnant) — the same age, he was tall and striking with the air of someone at ease with himself and the world. Just inside the front gates of the orchard were two weatherboard sheds with iron roofs and dirt floors, and we found him inside one, his head buried in a tractor engine. He shook our hands warmly, after picking up Robbie who rushed over to him.

"Good to see you, boys," he grinned. "Have a good trip down?"

"Well ... it was entertaining." He smiled at that.

"Yeah, I can imagine. The back of removal vans aren't the smoothest, but they're great blokes, the Bourke brothers, aren't they?"

"You know them!"

"Oh yeah. Emma's brother went to school with them."

Although both Glen and I were surprised by this, we probably shouldn't have been. Since leaving the throngs of Sydney we'd been all too aware how sparsely populated the countryside was, and frequently came across people who knew, or at least knew of, other people, hundreds, even thousands of miles away. "The back of beyond," the documentary filmmaker John Hyer had so vividly described the outback. The residents of Julia Creek might have scoffed at the idea of Young being called 'outback'. After all, it was only a hundred miles or so from Sydney, where people were flat out knowing their neighbours, much less anyone ten miles away! Even so the phenomenon of country people all seeming to 'know' each other was a stark illustration that despite its enormous size, Australia was really a very small place.

"Right," John said, putting his son down and briefly touching his wife's stomach and smiling at her. "I guess you want to know the score."

Probably eighty percent of the orchard was still in bloom, lovely little white flowers tinged with pink. There were roughly seven hundred trees, John told us; neat, straight rows disappearing over the undulating land, only to reappear in the distance. The grass strips down the middle of each row were neatly mown, and the earth at the base of each tree was freshly turned and free of weeds. "They're looking good," said John, stopping by a tree with no blooms, tiny little fruits just beginning to emerge. "We had a good, cold winter; cherry trees love cold winters. I reckon some of these will be ready to pick by the end of October, love," he addressed his wife.

"Bit earlier than you thought, then," she smiled.

For half an hour we strolled through the orchard, Morgan and Robbie running about while Emma picked blossoms, cleverly entwining them around a length of paspalum grass to make a sort of Roman crown. "There are two major problems for early season cherries," John explained. "The weather, of course, but we can't do anything about that. The biggest headache, though, is birds, especially crows! In a few more weeks the fruit will be starting to get plump enough to interest them. Then they'll arrive in their squadrons." He grimaced. "That's where you come in."

"What I'll want you to do is stay out here in the sheds and walk around the orchard several times a day to scare them away. Sounds easy, eh, but believe me, crows are the most cunning creatures on earth so you're going to have to be on your toes. Some of the orchards nearby use carbon guns that go off at set intervals, but I'm not so keen on them, the birds get used to them. Nothing beats unpredictable human intervention, especially when you've got a shotgun," he grinned. "But as I say, that won't be for a few weeks. Meantime, how do you feel about going down to Leeton to pick oranges? I know the owner. He has a bit of a reputation as a slave driver but his bark's worse than his bite. He pays good money, and says you've got a job if you want it. I can take you down there, but you'll have to make your own way back here. Three or four weeks down there, then come back here and work for me for five or six weeks. What do you say?"

We stayed the night with them, sleeping on cushions on the floor of Robbie's little room, a situation he found hugely exciting. As soon as his mother said goodnight and shut the door he was out of bed and jumping all over us, and all-in wrestling became the order of the day. "For heaven's sake, boys!" his mother burst back into the room. "Stop it! Get back into bed, young man," and she tucked Robbie in again, scowling at us, but she was smiling as she left. We giggled ourselves to sleep. Early the next morning John drove us the one hundred miles or so down to Leeton. We went straight out to the orchard, which was about eleven miles from town, with a large, brightly painted orange sign greeting us at the gates.

"*Welcome to Golambino Bros Orchards. The finest oranges in the world from the finest orchards in the world.*"

"They have a healthy opinion of themselves," John smiled.

Half an hour later, having introduced us and chatted for a bit, John shook hands all round and set off back to Young, the case of oranges he'd received as a gift on the seat beside him. "See you in four weeks, boys."

EIGHTEEN

The Golambino Bros.

The Golambino brothers had arrived in Australia with their families in 1950. In total they numbered eleven: the two brothers, their wives, and seven children between them. A distant cousin had migrated in the 1930s and settled in Leeton, where he started growing oranges. So it was that only a few days after getting off the ship in Pyrmont, both Golambino families ended up in the town. Within five years they were successfully farming two orange orchards of their own, side by side. "We own the businesses, but we don't own the land," Pietro, the twenty-six-year-old second son of Giovanni Golambino explained as he showed us where we would sleep. "But we will in a few years," he added proudly. "Here you go," and he opened the door of the small weatherboard shed. It was about fifteen foot square with a rough wooden floor, two windows on each side and half a dozen canvas stretchers that looked like they'd come out of a hospital or somewhere; spaced out, three on each side. Beside each stretcher was a plain wooden stool and a small, two-foot high old wooden fruit box to use as a cupboard and table. "You're the first to arrive," he said, "so you can grab any cot you want. Come up to the house later and get a pillow and a blanket," and he left us to it.

There were six or seven sheds, two of them partitioned off into three small rooms for married couples, and over the next few days they filled with workers. We were joined by four men in our hut, considerably older than us; two were friends from Melbourne who told us they came up to Leeton every year, although it was the first time they'd worked on this orchard. The other two were newly arrived Italian migrants who'd been sent out to the farm by the police. At the back of the main house, about a hundred yards away, there was a shower block and two chemical toilets. The showers consisted of canvas bags with shower roses attached, which when filled with water were hauled up over wooden poles with a rope and pulleys. There was hot water, but you had to fetch it in buckets from outside the kitchen, which was eighty yards away. Most pickers couldn't be bothered, so cold showers were the order of the day, ensuring nobody stayed in there too long!

An equal distance on the other side of the house were two large sheds where the packing, sorting and dispatching was done. The sheds were used by both the brothers as the two orchards produced different sorts of oranges, an early and a late variety, meaning they were picked at different times and the brothers could share equipment like sheds, tractors, wooden bins and ladders, and workers too. All this we learned from Pietro over the few days we were there before picking began. He'd sort of taken us under his wing and shown us about the orchard, which was beautifully maintained, as was the whole place, in fact; Golambino Bros orchards were obviously as highly organised and well-managed as the sign outside suggested, a situation made perfectly clear to us the afternoon before picking started.

"Okay! Welcome everybody. I am Giovanni Golambino, this Mrs Golambino, these my daughters Gina and Rosina, and my sons Dario and Pietro. Over there my brother Roberto and his wife, also Mrs Golambino," he grinned. "Next my nieces Giorgina, Sonia and Carlotta. All work here; now you come work here too, so we welcome you. *Tutti benvenuti*, as we say in Italy," and he beamed with pleasure and opened his arms wide as if to embrace each of us. He was a short, squat man, and even standing on the second rung of an

'A' frame ladder many of the pickers were as tall as him. Wearing a pair of worn, baggy overalls, his family and his brother's family were lined up on the ground on either side. Standing in a gaggle in front of them, just outside the main packing shed, were about twenty workers, all summoned to hear the boss, Glen and I among them.

"Right!" he shouted to regain attention, pleasantries plainly over. "Golambino Brothers like everything be simple. First: simple plan; must have plan, no plan, much confusione; so dis di plan. Tomorrow we start pick six o'clock." Then he held up his hand, ticking off fingers as he spoke. "Eight o'clock breakfast; ten o'clock smoko; twelve o'clock lunch; three o'clock smoko; five o'clock finish; six o'clock dinner.

Every day same plan; simple plan; easy understand plan. Yes!" A few murmured their consent, but we were all a little subdued by his Mussolini-like manner. "Excellente!" He smiled briefly before continuing. "Next: simple aim; to finish picking in twelve weeks, first this farm, then my brother's. Yes!" And he waved his arm vaguely in the direction of the trees growing on the hillsides in the distance. This time nobody said anything, as it was obvious he was not asking our opinion on these matters and he went on quickly. "Last: simple hard work. We pay good; give good bed; good food; Sunday off. You give us simple hard work. Yes!" And he held out his arms again, this time with a "What could be simpler!" expression and smile. Then he stopped smiling, and added, "You donna like-a dis plan, you donna like-a dis aim, you donna like-a di hard work! Answer also simple! We donna like-a-you stay here!" and he climbed down from the ladder, simple lecture over.

His plans may have been simple, but he seemed to have one for just about every aspect of life on the farm, not just working but living and eating as well, none of which were debatable options. You either did everything like Mr Golambino wanted or you left. I suppose because we were nearer childhood than adulthood, this control of our lives and the fairly rigid regime didn't bother Glen and I too much; we were accustomed to being told what to do. If anything, it was reassuring; you always knew where you stood, what you had to do and how you had to do it. Stick to his conditions, and Mr Golambino was a reasonably kind and considerate boss. Stray from them, or attempt to do things in your own way, and he was a "bad tempered arsehole", as one of the pickers called him when he quit.

The day's picking began at six am sharp. Mr Golambino was pacing up and down in the orchard long before the few people who turned up late more than once showed up to face his wrath. Three times late and he fired you. No matter that you were paid by the weight you picked and not by the hour; if you didn't work as hard as he thought you should, he let you know. On our second day, Pietro had taken us out into the orchard and shown us how to pick the oranges and place them in the canvas bags that hung around our necks. He demonstrated how to position the wide-based, 'A' frame wooden ladders, sort of burying the tripod leg in the tree between the branches for stability. The ladders were ten to twelve feet tall, and standing at the top with a heavy bag of oranges swaying around your neck could be quite hairy if they were not correctly positioned. We were each given a pair of tough canvas gloves, to which Mrs Golambino and her daughters had attached old shirt sleeves, enabling us to cover our arms up to our elbows. The branches, leaves and twigs of orange trees can be deceptively sharp and spiky sometimes. Each picker had his own wooden bin, and the bins were towed out on a trailer by Pietro or his brother each morning and parked between the rows of trees. It was Pietro's job to keep an eye on these bins, and as they filled up he brought out another empty one and took the full one away. Each picker had his own colour, usually just a daub of paint on the end of his bin; mine was yellow and Glen's was brown. Back in the picker's shed the contents were weighed and a note of the colour taken and ticked off against our names. This job was the responsibility of Mr Golambino's oldest daughter Gina, who was also the paymaster and tally clerk. In fact each member of the respective families had responsibility for various tasks while the two brothers sort of oversaw the whole process, constantly moving about from orchard to shed, checking the quality of the fruit, exhorting people to work harder or faster and berating those who didn't.

It was also a 'plan' that each tree had to be completely picked clean before moving on to the next, and to facilitate this Mr Goloambino liked the pickers to work in pairs, allotting each pair a set of trees to pick each day. This suited Glen and I well enough but for some, paired with a stranger they didn't get on with, it was not so readily accepted. But like it or not the system worked. With just two pickers concentrating on one tree, people didn't get in each other's way, and more importantly it prevented the smart arses from rushing off and picking only the easier fruit reached from the ground. The whole procedure, in fact life on the orchard in general during harvesting time, was run like a military operation. It was not popular with everybody, maybe, but it meant the orchard was harvested with speed and efficiency, tree by tree, row by row.

When you are first confronted with an orange orchard, or any orchard for that matter — hundreds of trees, literally dripping with fruit and stretching for hundreds of yards down well manicured rows — the task appears enormous. Psychologically it makes you feel you have to hurry, otherwise you will never get it done. At least that's how it made Glen and I feel. Add to this the teenage boy's inability to do anything without turning it into a competition, and it meant we set off at a manic pace. Virtually ripping the oranges from the trees, rushing up and down our ladders and running to empty our bags into our bins, each determined to empty more bags in an hour than the other. This caused much amusement amongst the other works and the Golambinos, not that we noticed, so intent were we on our competition. But well before breakfast on the first day Mr Golambino was hollering at us. "Santi numi, boys! Slow down! Slow down! No good rip fruit off! Must twist, like this. Twist, put; twist, put; twist, put!" And he proceeded to pick more oranges in two minutes than we had in five, with not one twig or leaf getting into the bag. "Clean bag, good bag," he winked. By knock-off time that afternoon we'd got the hang of things, and although we were as fast as most of the others, we had slowed down considerably, not that we had a choice. It looks so easy to pick oranges, and in many ways it was; it was certainly easier than cutting sugar cane! But climbing up and down a ladder twenty or thirty times a day with fifty pounds of fruit swinging round your neck slows down even the most manic worker.

If the harvesting was organised like a military operation, so was the preparation and serving of meals. The two Mrs Golambinos were responsible for food, with the help of two women who lived nearby. Right along the front of the house ran a wide veranda, and at one end a serving hatch had been cut through into the kitchen like a big window. All meals were served through this hatch, with the workers queuing up back along the veranda. On the ground below the veranda was a large paved patio area, covered with an iron roof supported on posts, and under this were several rough wooden tables and benches. Most of the workers ate there, although some of the married couples took their meals back to their huts; a stack of tin plate lids were piled up on the serving hatch next to the plates specifically for this purpose. Like the stretchers we slept on, these lids, and the plates, mugs, knives and forks all had a small crest on them, and looked like they had come from a hospital as well. Beside the hatch on the veranda was a wet garbage drum, and on the other side a big tub of hot, soapy water, and we were asked — ordered, actually — to scrape all our leftovers into the drum and then leave the plates and knives and forks soaking in the tub. Not doing so, or leaving your dirty plates on the bench unscraped, elicited a fierce earful from one or other of the Mrs Golambinos, sometimes both of them at once!

Breakfast consisted of Cornflakes and lovely fresh creamy milk, delivered to the orchard every morning in quart churns by the dairy farm up the road. Sausages, beans and scrambled eggs followed with toast and, of course, orange juice. Lunches were nearly always salads, with cold ham or chicken and freshly baked bread, and dinners were nearly always stews or spaghetti with meatballs or fried lamb chops, with lovely tomato and basil sauces. The exception was Friday, which was fish pie night. The most eagerly awaited meal, however, was Sunday lunch. For every other meal the Golambino family ate inside in their dining room, but on Sunday, after the family returned from church, the tables on the patio were festooned with colourful tablecloths and a wonderful spread was laid out. Cold meats left over from the week, salads, lovely bread and always a pudding of some sort with custard. On Sunday night cheese and biscuits and an array of little cakes were left on the serving hatch for us to help ourselves. There might have been plenty of complaints about Mr Golambino's rules and abrupt manner, but we didn't hear one about the food. It was fantastic! Although we did have to pay for it, a set amount being withheld from our wages each week for food and lodgings, with Mr Golambino assuring us it was only enough to cover costs.

On Friday and Saturday nights the men of the family would bring out chairs and sit on the veranda, filling a large ice chest with beer, and all the workers were invited to join them if they wished, Mr Golambino selling the beer for what he had paid for it. There was no limit to how many bottles a worker could have, but it was made abundantly plain that any more than three was excessive and at nine o'clock sharp the 'bar' was shut. A few of the workers had vehicles and at the weekends they would go into town, some coming back the worse for wear, but anyone who turned up for work still drunk, or late because of a hangover, only did so once.

Of all the 'plans', though, the one that caused the most friction was Mr Golambino's insistence that all pickers had to work in the sheds one day each week. Workers in the sheds were paid by the hour, which was considerably less than you could earn picking; if you worked hard, that was. But the main thing people objected too was Giorgina Golambino, who was in total control of the packing shed, along with her sister Sonia.

Like everything else, the sorting and packing process was done with great efficiency, freshly picked fruit going in one end and coming out the other in labelled boxes, ready to be loaded onto trucks. Having weighed each bin on arrival from the orchard, the oranges were tipped out onto a large wooden platform where they were roughly sorted, green or damaged fruit being taken out, along with any leaves or twigs. They were then sent down a wooden encased conveyor of rollers into a rectangular tank of water where they were washed, waxed and moved along the tank by two workers with large wooden hoe-like tools. It was their job to make sure all the oranges were completely submerged, and then to coax them onto another conveyor belt at the end of the tank which took them down to the final sorting platform. From this platform there were two conveyors leading to the packing area about thirty feet away; one for 'premium' fruit, the other for 'standard'. These two belts fanned out in a V shape and it was there, in the middle of the V, deftly and quickly deciding which oranges went down which belt, that Giorgina Golambino stood for most of the day, shouting instructions over the noise of the clattering rollers and abusing the entire shed if any leaves or bad fruit ended up on her table.

At the end of these two belts were small bays with eight-inch high wooden sides where the oranges finally came to rest. Next to each bay was a table, and beside it a stack of wooden boxes made of four-inch wide thin wooden slats with separate lids. Beside these was a large banding tool, which crimped flat steel bands around the boxes when filled. It was at the end of the 'standard' fruit belt that Glen and I worked whenever we were in the shed. We swapped jobs about, either packing the oranges — always forty-eight to a box, three layers of twelve in three rows of four, separated by two layers of six in two rows of three — or putting the lids on the boxes, banding them and sticking on a label. This done, the boxes were sent down yet another roller belt to the truck loading bay at the end of the shed where Dario Golambino was in charge of organising orders and dispatches, loading and doing local deliveries in the brothers' one ton truck. Sydney, Melbourne and other interstate orders were picked up during the week by trucks sent from the respective shops or markets.

The standard fruit was fairly easy to pack as it was done without any wrapping. The premium fruit, however, was individually wrapped in a small piece of wax paper with the Golambino logo on it. Although there were far fewer of these, they took much longer to pack as it had to be done with great care; a box of Golambino 'premium' oranges retailed for much more than a standard box, no doubt the reason why Sonia Golambino was in charge of this area. Fortunately she was much easier to work with than her sister.

I don't know how old Giorgina Golambino was; thirty, thirty-five maybe, but unlike her two younger sisters she was not particularly attractive, being plump and square-faced. She looked a bit like her father, perhaps the reason she was so short tempered! Once the process in the shed started it was relentless, like an orange sea, and at each stage you had to work fast and constantly. Stop even for a few moments to have a cigarette, and oranges would begin to pile up, spilling over the sides of the belts or sorting areas, one of Giorgina Golambino's many pet hates. Having had a run-in with her about something, two men flatly refused to work in the packing shed again after their first day, saying they were losing money and that they'd signed on to "Pick, not bloody pack and get abused!" They were sacked on the spot, accompanied by much anger and shouting from both sides. Mr Golambino's control over every aspect of his workers' lives was total, and in public at least, he backed his family member in every dispute. "Dis my house! My orchard! You want work here, you do like I say!" The turnover of staff was fairly frequent.

No departure was more dramatic than that of Jack, who arrived at the orchard a week or ten days after us. He was about thirty, I suppose, and kept himself very much to himself. We never even knew his last name, much less where he came from, but he seemed likeable enough. Good-looking, he was fit and strong and worked hard, but from the outset it was obvious Mr Golambino didn't like him. Initially we thought it was because Jack had insisted on working on his own. "I don't work with nobody," he stated flatly. "I'll pull me weight, pick one tree at a time, you'll see the results, I just do it on me own." Being short two or three pickers at the time, Mr Golambino reluctantly agreed, and by the end of the first day when Jack had picked half a bin more than everybody else with not a leaf or twig in sight, he couldn't really argue. Even so, after a few days it became obvious both the brothers were watching the newcomer's every move with suspicion.

Then one evening Glen and I were returning to our hut from the showers, taking a short-cut around the back of the hut next to ours, which happened to be Jack's. As we came around the corner there he was, locked in a passionate embrace with Carlotta Golambino, pressing her hard up against the wall, her dress riding high up one thigh. We tried to pull back but she spotted us and desperately broke away, gasping with shock and pulling her dress down as she ran off. At eighteen, Carlotta was the youngest of the family and suddenly Jack didn't look so friendly. "You two keep your mouths shut, you hear."

We never saw them together again, although over the next few days we noticed the little smiles Carlotta gave whenever the two were in sight of each other. The Golambinos obviously noticed this too, and if it looked like Jack and Carlotta might be left alone together one or other of the brothers would suddenly appear. One Friday evening, after Jack had been there about a week, several of us pickers were sitting on the veranda after dinner drinking beer with Pietro, Dario and Giovanni; Roberto Golambino and Jack not amongst us. Suddenly from the direction of the packing shed came a great roar of anger, and Roberto came around the corner pushing his daughter Carlotta in front of him. He yelled at her in Italian and pointed to the house and instantly Carlotta wheeled round, stamping her foot in fury and shouting back at him in Italian, obviously incensed at what her father had said. Then Jack appeared around the corner behind them.

"Leave her alone for Christ's sake! She is bloody eighteen!"

"Don't you talk me bloody!" Roberto Golambino shouted, advancing towards him. "You finish here! Go! Now! Five minutes I no want see you here no more!"

"We just had a kiss!" Jack exclaimed, holding out his hands as if pleading with all of us witnesses up on the veranda "She kissed me t..."

"I no hear this!" shouted Roberto. "Fuck you! You go now!" and Jack turned, shaking his head.

"Ah, fuck you too! Stupid dago!" This last he grunted, more or less to himself as he turned to go, but Roberto Golambino heard it and almost had an epileptic fit.

"What you say!" he screamed and immediately he turned on his heel, went storming past a now sobbing Carlotta and ran up the veranda steps two at a time, shouting over and over again, "You no call me that! You no call me that! Nobody call Golambino that!" and he disappeared into the house.

By now Giovanni had come down from the veranda and was standing in front of Jack. "You hear him," he said. "You finish here now."

"But he didn't do anything, Zio!" cried Carlotta and her uncle turned, put his arm around her and spoke gently in Italian for a moment, causing her to turn and run up the steps, clearly distressed; just as she was about to go inside her father came bursting out onto the veranda brandishing a shotgun and pointing it at Jack.

"No, Papa, no!" Carlotta cried.

"You call me dago now! You call me dago now!" yelled Roberto, charging down the stairs.

"Jesus!" Jack exclaimed, backing away. "You're fucking mad!"

"I no fucking … ! I give you fucking … !" and he lifted the shotgun to his shoulder. By now all the women had come out onto the veranda, their hands over their mouths in horror, Roberto's wife shouting hysterically. Then Pietro ran down the stairs and grabbed the shotgun barrel, lifting it in the air. "Not like this, Zio, not like this!" After a brief struggle and cursing in Italian, his uncle let him take the gun.

"You go now," Giovanni turned to Jack. "Gina!" he called over his shoulder. "Get his money ready. He go front gate! I pay him there!" And still shaking his head, Jack went off in the darkness to get his gear. By the time Giovanni went to pay him tempers had calmed a bit; Roberto Golambino was even sitting quietly sipping a beer. Pietro broke the shotgun to unload it, then he looked at his uncle with surprise. "It isn't loaded!" Roberto Giovanni shrugged his shoulders and smiled. "Si. But he don't know dis."

Amazing how time flicks by when you are fully occupied and worn out each day. On Magnetic Island the days had taken weeks to pass. Now, they took hours. At night during the week there wasn't much to do after dinner, but most of us were in bed well before nine o'clock anyway. The four others in our hut were not exactly riveting personalities, and although we played draughts and cards with them occasionally we never really got to know them very well. The two men from Melbourne kept themselves very much to themselves and the two Italians, although slightly more lively and amusing, spoke very little English. I suppose the best thing that happened was that for the first time in my life I began to read things other than *Blinky Bill* and *The Famous Five*. Sonia Golambino had a fairly extensive library and was always reading, and she began lending us books. It was she who introduced me to Jane Austin and A. J. Cronin, Daphne du Maurier and Hemingway. It was a revelation, and some days I couldn't wait for night to come so I could get back to those books. Glen also read avidly, although he always had done so, and we both tried to come to grips with *Walden*. Glen at least finished it, but I couldn't understand half of it. Thoreau sounded like a bit of a weirdo to me. But I would go back to him years later, as William Fellows had suggested.

Of course the best thing about the orchard was that we were paid each week, our first regular income! After food and lodgings had been taken out and some income tax withheld — we were assured we would get this back but we never did. Nobody ever told us how, but even if they had we would probably not have understood the procedure; makes you wonder just how much tax departments have made out of the ignorant or uneducated over the years. We ended up earning a little under seven pounds a week; not quite as much as we had hoped, but still not bad, and as we weren't buying anything except cigarettes it soon mounted up. We were paid on Fridays and knocked off an hour early for the event, queuing up along the veranda to receive our little brown envelopes through the serving hatch. Before Gina Golambino handed the money over we had to sign for it in a large ledger, and for some this was the hardest, or at least the most stressful part of the job.

On our travels — notably at Butts sugar plantation and the Proserpine Show — we had come across a few people who had difficulty reading and writing, but we hadn't really taken much notice. Now it was the sheer number of illiterate workers on the orchard that brought home to us not just how common this problem was, but how difficult, even traumatic life can be for those who can't read or write. Of the thirty or so pickers working on Golambino's orchard while we were there, at least seven could not sign their names or read. I suppose it was because I had just discovered the magic of reading myself that it made me more aware of this, but if the pickers on Golambino's Orchard were a cross-section of the seasonal workers' population, how many other illiterate people were there! One man, receiving his first pay envelope, had not realised he would have to sign for it, and when he arrived at the hatch and Gina placed the ledger in front of him he was so humiliated and embarrassed it was equally humiliating and embarrassing to watch. He left the veranda more distressed than Carlotta Golambino, and we never saw him again. We didn't see much of Carlotta for several days after her little incident, either. Pietro told us she wouldn't come out of her room.

A few evenings after this we were sitting on the veranda when one of the men, drinking beer out of his mug, asked what the crest was, and Pietro and his father chuckled to themselves. "They're from Cowra prison," Pietro said. "Dad's cousin and a few other friends were interned there during the war. The prison shut down in 1945, but before they were released all the internees had to help move and stack the prison equipment into a storeroom. Stretchers, blankets, chairs, plates, all sorts of stuff." He smiled. "A year or so later, when dad's cousin was starting up his orchard on the other side of town, he needed equipment for the pickers' huts so he and some of the other internees went back to the prison. Nothing had been moved. The shed was still stuffed with gear, so they just helped themselves — three truck loads, they took! Even the small stools you have in your huts came from there!'"

"Only fair payback," interrupted his father, grinning broadly. "They put us gaol, we take their plates!"

Halfway through the fourth week, Mr Golambino asked if we'd

mind staying on for another week. Due to the large turnover of staff, which was almost entirely of his own doing, picking had not progressed as fast as he'd anticipated, and he told us he didn't want to lose two such good and experienced workers so close to the end.

"But we're supposed to go back to Mr Richards' orchard tomorrow."

"Si, si, but I ring him okay, if okay him, okay you? I pay you bonus maybe," he added with a wink. Flattery *and* more money. Once we learned John Richards didn't mind, we were easy to persuade.

True to his word there was a two pound bonus in our pay packet at the end of that week, and early the next day we set off back to Young with Dario, who was more or less going via there on his way to Forbes to make a delivery. We left Golambinos with pockets bulging and cheeks covered in lipstick from the two Mrs Golambinos. All the men shook our hands warmly, and Sonia gave us a box of paperback books. Even Giorgina Golambino stopped work for a minute to come out and wave goodbye. Life on Golambino's orchards might have been strictly regimented, and we'd had to work hard, but it had been the best time of our trip so far in many ways.

NINETEEN

The cherry orchard, and Danny and Ronnie

*D*ario dropped us off outside the Richards' farm at about ten o'clock, and after lunch we set off for the orchard; John was anxious we should start our bird-scaring job immediately. We knew from Doctor Richards that we weren't going to be paid much to do this, so our biggest concern was food and whether we would be entitled to vouchers if we were officially working. We now had a reasonable bankroll behind us, and Glen in particular was anxious to keep it. We needn't have worried, though; before we set out, John sat us down and made sure we fully understood the financial arrangements. For the first few weeks he could only afford to pay us two pounds a week, as his brother had said, but he would buy our food and he showed us a box he had made up for our first week. It was full of assorted tins, flour, sugar, tea, eggs, bread and various other goodies, the like of which we would never have got with one voucher. "It won't cost you a penny to live out there. You just tell me what you need each week, and I'll bring it out," he smiled. "When we start picking I will guarantee you six pounds a week each, happy with that?"

"Sure."

"I'll stay out there with you tonight" he continued, "just to get you settled and show you a few things." Then he and Emma kissed and hugged and he ruffled Robbie's hair, telling him to be a good boy, and we were off, piled into his Dodge pick-up, Morgan barking joyously in the back with our swags. As we clambered in we noticed a special rack on the floor under our seats. Housed in it was one of the tools of the trade we were about to embark on, a shiny double-barrelled shotgun, and on the shelf behind our heads were several boxes of cartridges; Glen and I grinned at each other with boyish delight.

"Davy. Davy Crockett. King of the wild frontier!"

Nature is indeed a remarkable thing. The difference in the orchard in just five weeks was amazing. There was not a flower to be seen, all the trees were now covered in dark green leaves, their branches heavy with clusters of fruit. As we pulled up in front of the sheds it was obvious that the trees were not the only things to have changed. In the smaller of the two sheds John had partitioned off a section, laid a rough wooden floor and built three simple wooden bunk beds, each bearing a thin mattress and pillow, two sets of them still wrapped in the paper in which they'd come. The bottom bunk of the third bed had obviously been recently used, and John explained he'd been sleeping at the orchard for the last few days as the crows were becoming a real nuisance. Should we have come back the week before, we wondered, but he waved our concerns away.

"No, no, it's fine. They've only just started to get bad."

"Are we the only pickers, then?" I asked, looking around for more beds.

"No," he chuckled. "When we get going there will be thirty or forty, but as this will be one of the first orchards in the area to be harvested there are plenty of local pickers available so I've promised them the work. Most of them are friends, really; relatives, neighbours, old school mates, the football team. It's my first crop, so I reckon a lot of them are just coming to see if I know what I'm doing, although no doubt they'll want paying too," he grinned.

At the end of the shed beside the water tank he'd erected a simple shower system, and out the front, attached to the wall, he'd built a small lean-to under which was half a forty-four gallon drum on bricks that we could use as a fire; he'd even supplied an old camp oven. "Belonged to my grandfather," John told us, spreading out the triangle of metal legs and hanging the oven from it. "Only thing I haven't got round to yet is a dunny, but I'm going to dig one out the back before picking starts. Meantime you'll have to make your own arrangements. All I ask is that you do it a hundred yards away and cover it up."

The larger shed had also been reorganised, with a large sorting and packing area constructed; and in one corner, stacked to the roof, hundreds of open-topped cardboard boxes with *Richard's Cherries Young* proudly emblazoned down each side. "Now then," John clapped his hands together, "let's get you sorted. First some shotgun lessons, and then I'll show you how to drive that," and he pointed at the old Ford tractor parked on the other side of the shed. Our smug looks gave it away, but the impromptu test drive we each made confirmed it and he was truly surprised. "Didn't know you city blokes could spell tractor, never mind drive one," he teased. "So!" He held up the shotgun. "Let's see how good you are with this, then."

Fifty yards behind the sheds John's land ended, and a barbed wire fence marked the border with his neighbour. Over this fence was pasture land, stretching up the hill to several acres of natural bush and gum trees five hundred yards away. "Come on, let's go and find us a couple of bunnies. Best way to learn to shoot is to shoot something," he told us. Although it was his neighbour's land, John said he didn't mind if we went up there to get firewood. "He won't mind if we shoot a few rabbits, either, bloody nuisance they are! Pretty good tucker, too, although a shotgun is not the best way to kill them if you're going to eat them, too many pellets," he grimaced.

As we walked up the hill he showed us how to hold the gun safely when it was loaded, and how important it was to carry it correctly. "They can be dangerous things if you're not careful. You need to treat them with respect. Two pieces of advice: always remember it is a double-barrelled gun, so after you've fired one shot there is still another cartridge loaded, unless you pull both triggers at once that is, which isn't advisable," he smiled. "Secondly, whenever you are out and about in the orchard, the one carrying the gun needs to know where the other one is at all times! Might sound unnecessary to say, but in the heat of the moment when people are out hunting in groups you'd be surprised how many accidents there are!"

About ten yards from the bush he knelt down, indicating we should join him, and pointed to the dozens of little holes running along the edge of the tree line. "One is bound to come out in a minute if we're quiet." Keeping a watchful eye on the holes, he went through the loading and unloading procedure and showed us how to tuck the gun firmly into our shoulders. "Here we go," he whispered, taking the gun back and pointing to a rabbit cautiously emerging from a hole, nose twitching, ears cocked. Slowly he bought the gun up to his shoulder, and when the rabbit came right out of its hole and was standing erect he calmly blew its head off. Then he handed me the gun and we settled down to wait.

As we sat there, I was struck by how multi-talented country people were. Carpenter, plumber, mechanic, farmer, hunter, dunny digger *and* cherry orchardist — the ingenuity and skill of country farmers has to be seen to be appreciated, and they did it all as if it was the most natural thing in the world. When I mentioned this to him, he was very pragmatic.

"Case of have to," he shrugged. "If I had to call a tradesman out every time I had a problem, I'd be broke!"

Despite John's warning about the 'kick', I would have been knocked over with the first shot if I'd been standing up, I'm sure. I thought I must have missed the rabbit by a mile, so violently did the barrel jerk upwards. But when the smoke cleared, there was another dead rabbit, splattered everywhere. In the end we came back down the hill with four of them. Back at the sheds he showed us how easy they were to skin; it just peeled off like a banana. Then he showed us how to cook them over the fire, using one leg of the camp oven tripod as a skewer. He was right, there were so many pellets it took us ages to pick them out, but we weren't so keen on the taste. It was tender enough, but it was very strong, and by the time we'd finished one both Glen and I had decided we didn't like rabbit meat much.

If crows don't have a sixth, seventh, eighth, even a ninth sense, then I'm a kindergarten teacher! They seem to know exactly what you are going to do seconds before you do it. Just as you pulled the trigger, certain you had the bird plum in the middle of the sights, it would dart off, going in a completely different direction to the pellets, which blew harmlessly away. Even in flocks of nine or ten, as they often were, we still missed; it was as if they could actually see the pellets coming and dodged them in flight. It was several hours the next day before we managed to down the first bird, and even then it was more a glancing blow than a direct kill. It fell to the ground, one wing badly damaged, but it was still alive and we had to break its neck.

Cunning as they may have been, by the end of the first week we had killed about forty crows and noticeably disrupted their movements. Each day we went out into the orchard at least five or six times, especially just after dawn and an hour before dusk, when they seemed to be most active. And it wasn't just crows, either; there were flocks of white cockatoos some days, magpies too, but the crows were easily the biggest problem. The more canny they got, the more crafty we got. Sometimes we went out well before dawn so we could be at the bottom end of the orchard to surprise them as they arrived with the sun. Sometimes we walked together, other times we split up, coming from different directions, running and shouting. We took the tractor out most days, taking it in turns to drive while the other one stood on the back, blasting away. We were Hopalong Cassidy and The Lone Ranger chasing the Indians. Boy, did we have fun!

John came out two or three days a week to do odd jobs about

the orchard and we helped him dig the dunny. He was impressed with our growing pile of crow head trophies, but raised his eyebrows a little at the number of cartridges we'd used to get them! Emma, Robbie and Morgan usually came with him, Emma bringing us little home-made goodies, and every Thursday John brought a box of food and paid us our two pounds. Our beds were more comfortable than the Golambino's stretchers, although we missed their meals and the company, Friday nights and Sunday lunches especially. But John and Emma looked after us royally and our time on the cherry orchard flashed by, and, of course, we stuffed ourselves with cherries! Cherries for breakfast, cherries for lunch, cherry dampers, stewed cherries, cherries fried with tinned corned beef; by the end of the second week our shit was purple. Most nights after dinner we'd sit by the fire going over the day's events and reading books under the kerosene lamp, sometimes until gone midnight before we fell asleep, excited by the prospect of the next day's adventures.

One Friday, after we'd been there about three weeks, John came out accompanied by an older man and together they went out into the orchard, closely examining and tasting the fruit. We learned later that he was one of the most respected and experienced cherry orchardists in the area, and John had asked him to come and advise him about when to start picking. For some time John had been concerned about this as he'd secured two large orders, each of several hundred cases, with the stipulation being the cherries had to be ready to eat then and there. As he would be one of the first orchards harvested that year, he was reasonably confident he could sell most of the crop; early season cherries were much in demand, and besides, the orders were so large he couldn't afford to lose them so they more or less dictated when he could start. We followed them around the orchard, the old man stopping every now and then to feel and taste the fruit. After only ten minutes he stopped and turned to John. "I reckon these cherries are about as ready to pick as I've seen! You could start right now if you wanted, but they should be perfect by Monday. No later than that, though, they'll be falling off the tree otherwise!" he warned. You could almost see the conflicting emotions of anticipation, excitement and relief ripple through John's body. At last, all that work, all that loving care, all that worry and debt, at last he could harvest the fruits of his labour, and he and Emma hugged each other with delight as the old man drove off.

That evening, about an hour after John and Emma left, we were sitting by the fire when a smart 1955 two tone blue FJ Holden special sedan, the one with the horizontal grille, turned into the gates in a cloud of dust. It had Victorian number plates, and the two young blokes in it must have seen us sitting there, but instead of stopping they drove around the back of the sheds, as if they were about to head off over the fields or something. More than a bit surprised, we jumped up and ran round the back just as the two were alighting from the car.

"Come right in!"

"Sorry, mate, just thought I might as well park out of the way," the driver said, smiling. "Hi. I'm Darren. This is me cousin Ronnie. We heard there might be some work here?" And as he moved towards us, hand outstretched, his limp was obvious.

"Well … I don't know. Mr Richards is going to start picking on Monday but you'll have to see him first. You just missed him. If you came from Young you must have passed him on the way — green Dodge pick-up …"

"No, we came from the other way," Darren cut in quickly, looking around. "Reckon he'd mind if we stopped here for the night? We got swags and tucker." There didn't seem to be any reason why not, and besides, who were we to say yes or no, so they went back to their car and pulled out their gear.

"Where have you come from?" Glen asked Ronnie, who so far hadn't said a word.

"Mildur ..."

"He means Parkes," interrupted Darren, smiling. "Today we came from Parkes."

"Oh yeah," agreed Ronnie, "Parkes, today we came from Parkes," and he burst into a high-pitched sort of giggle, punctuated by little snorts. As we walked back around to the fire Glen and I exchanged quizzical looks.

And quizzical was the word to describe the cousins. In fact there were three strange things about them. The first and most obvious was that at nineteen, Darren was three years older, yet he was almost half the size; his withered right leg and thick-soled boot causing him not so much to limp as lurch, his foot flicking out sideways with each step he took. The second strange thing, which although just as obvious, took a moment to sink in, was their clothes. Here they were, our age — in fact, Ronnie was younger than Glen — yet they were dressed like middle-aged working men, a sort of cross between Mr Butt and the Bourke Brothers; thick grey trousers held up with braces, check shirts and heavy boots with string for laces. The third strange thing about them, or at least about Ronnie, became more than apparent over the next few days.

We'd shown them where they could lay out their swags beside our bunks, and when they opened them we could immediately smell the distinctive odour of stale sweat and filthy clothes. Not only did they dress like middle-aged working men, they smelt like them, too! It was a situation made even more noticeable because they were so young. Did we smell like that? I wondered.

"You blokes eaten yet?" Darren asked as we went back out to the fire. "We ain't, we're starvin', ain't we, Ronnie?" and he pulled out two tins of baked beans from his bag, punched a hole in them with his opener and placed them on the metal plate.

"Yeah," agreed Ronnie, "We ain't eaten yet."

"Have you ever picked cherries before?" Glen asked him.

"Dunno," he grunted, immediately looking at Darren.

"No, we ain't never done that. Picked asparagus, though," and he picked up the tins of beans, which could only have been lukewarm, opened them and gave one to Ronnie, who instantly began manically shovelling beans into his mouth, sauce running down his chin and onto his shirt.

"Take it easy, boy! Take it easy!" Darren admonished him gently, and put his hand on his shoulder. "Ain't nobody gonna' take it off ya!"

"Haaa, ha, ha, haa," Ronnie shrieked, spoon suspended in midair as he glanced nervously at his cousin for a second, as if to check how seriously he was being told off. Realising it was only a gentle rebuke, he set off spooning in the beans as fast as ever, in between each mouthful somehow managing to snort, "Yeah! Can't take 'em off me, can't take 'em off me!"

The looks Glen and I gave each other now were more than quizzical!

For the hour or so we sat by the fire that night, Ronnie hardly said a word unless prompted, and even then Darren nearly always interrupted and answered for him; most of the time he just sat staring into the fire, occasionally giggling to himself. When Glen got up to go to the toilet and kicked over some tins of food we had stacked beside the fire he jumped up, pointing and shouting out. "Yer knocked 'em over! Yer knocked 'em over!"

"Okay, Ronnie. Okay," Darren put his hand on his shoulder "It ain't nuthin'," then he smiled at us, shrugging his shoulders. "He gets a bit excited sometimes, don't you, Ronnie boy?" and he gently pushed him back down.

"Yeah," Ronnie chortled. "I get ixtited!"

Jesus!

That night, after we'd all settled down, Glen and I got up on the pretext of going to the toilet and once outside we put all our money into an old jam jar and buried it next to the water tank.

The next day was Sunday and John and Emma arrived early in the morning, with half a dozen other vehicles following them over the next few hours. In all about twenty people eventually turned up, friends and old school mates of theirs who were going to help with the picking. Then Emma's father and uncle arrived mid-morning, in a large truck stacked with twenty or more ten-foot ladders and a similar number of wooden bins and canvas picker's bags. There were a dozen twelve-foot trestle tables, two large metal drums and various other pieces of equipment necessary for the harvest, and most of the day was spent unloading the truck and organising the packing shed. With some effort, the large metal drums were manhandled into the shed where they were filled with water to wash the cherries, and the trestle tables were set up in rows, empty cartons piled up on each one ready to be filled. By late afternoon all was ready and someone cracked open a few bottles of champagne; toasts and salutations were given all round. The four of us were invited to join them, but after filling our glasses we went back and sat by our fireplace, feeling a bit out of place somehow. John had been a little surprised by the presence of Darren and Ronnie; not that he said anything, but we could tell he was a little annoyed. However, he was not the sort to stay annoyed for long, and the party-like atmosphere and anticipation of the harvest soon overcame any irritation he may have felt.

I suppose it was about 1am when the wind woke us up. John and his friends had left about eight, waving cheerily, horns hooting, the next day's tasks on everybody's mind. Because of the early start we'd gone to bed soon after, leaving the shed door open as it was a sticky, humid night. The wind slamming the door shut woke us, but quickly realising what it was we just turned over and went back to sleep. Within an hour we were woken again, this time by the clang of one of our saucepans crashing into the water tank. We got up and went out into the lean to; it was pitch black, the wind now a ferocious gale, and our shed rattled so much we were worried it might get blown away. Then for twenty minutes or so it rained, as hard as it had the day in William Fellow's barn, if anything it was even harder, stair rods of rain. The noise was incredible and suddenly Ronnie went berserk, running out into the yard in his underpants, yelling and whooping!

"We don't get much rain where we come from," Darren explained.

"Where's that, then," Glen shouted, smiling at Ronnie's manic dancing.

"Oh, out west a bit." He waved." Ronnie! Ronnie boy! Get back in here, you'll catch a cold." Fifteen minutes later the rain had eased and Ronnie was shivering by the fire just as John's pick-up came splashing into the yard. It was only when he leapt out and ran into the orchard, leaving the engine running, the lights on and the door open, that the seriousness of the situation hit us and we quickly followed him. We didn't need to go far; the beam of John's torch told the story. The ground, for as far as we could see, was covered in a carpet of cherries.

An hour after dawn the full impact of the storm became clear, and it was obviously nothing less than a disaster. Tree after tree had been almost completely stripped of fruit, hundreds of thousands of plump ripe cherries lying, at best bruised, on the ground, the crows having a feast. John estimated that over seventy-five percent of the crop had been lost, yet he remained remarkably calm and philosophical, blaming himself. "I guess I waited too long," he shrugged. "I should have started picking last week." But all the calmness in the world couldn't hide the fact that he was completely shattered. We were never to know the full extent of the financial cost of the storm, but it must have been significant as we overheard a conversation with John and his father-in-law about insurance. It seemed John's only insurance had been with the Farmer's Union, enough to cover only about a tenth of the losses. John and Emma were now not only broke, but heavily in debt; there were not two people alive who deserved that less.

The next day more than one hundred people turned up at the orchard unannounced, and for two days they worked from dawn to dusk, helping to salvage as much fruit as possible and refusing any payment. Friends, relatives, John's entire football team and residents of Young whom he hardly knew but who'd heard what had happened came to help, Constable Tyler among them. It was amazing, and John and Emma were visibly moved and buoyed by the gesture. We stayed at the orchard for two more days, helping where we could, but it was obvious we were no longer needed. John was very apologetic and gave us each five pounds, money he could ill afford we were sure, but he insisted we take it. Apart from Mrs Hayes dying, the day we left Young was probably one of the saddest days of our trip. Both John and Emma put a brave face on things, but as we drove out of the yard they stood rather forlornly, arms around each other, waving farewell, Robbie running around excitedly after Morgan, oblivious of their anguish.

* * *

Over those last two days at the orchard, Darren and Ronnie had kept a very low profile. Early each morning they walked off up the hill at the back and didn't come back until it was almost dark. I suppose this wasn't surprising; they didn't know John and he didn't know anything about them, nor had he offered them a job. Not that we'd learned much about them ourselves; whenever we tried to find out, Darren was very non-committal, even evasive. Apart from Ronnie's slip about Mildura, Victoria hadn't been mentioned again, or anywhere else for that matter. In contrast they knew quite a bit about us, especially about Glen joining the Navy. Since we'd arrived at the orchard, barely a day went by when he didn't talk about it. In a few more weeks he would turn seventeen, and as the money piled up in our jam jar so joining the Navy became a distinct possibility, not just a dream. We may not have saved quite as much as we'd hoped, but we had over thirty-five pounds each, more than enough, he reasoned.

In contrast, I had no plans at all. It was now mid-November and we'd been on the road for over six months. I suppose I would happily have carried on if he'd wanted to, and I began thinking vaguely about doing so on my own, but on our last night at the orchard Darren and Ronnie sort of made it inevitable that we would head for home. As we settled by the fire, Darren suddenly announced, "Hey, if youse is going back to Sydney, we could give youse a lift! We ain't never been to Sydney, we ain't never seen the sea neither, have we, Ronnie? Can you see the sea from Sydney?"

That was about it, really, and as I didn't have any other plan I joined in the virtually impossible task of trying to answer Ronnie's simple question: "How big is sea?"

Sydney here we come.

Learning of our plans, John gave us a map, pointing out that the quickest route to Sydney was through Crookwell to Goulburn and up the Hume Highway, but when we mentioned this to Darren he became quite agitated.

"No! No! I don't want to go that way. We're going through Forbes and Bathurst!"

As it was no skin off our noses which way we went we didn't argue the point, not that any amount of arguing would have changed his mind, so adamant was he. Thus it was that we set off for Sydney via Forbes and Bathurst, with Darren driving, me next to him in the front and Glen and Ronnie in the back.

The previous night it had been noticeable that Darren's limp had suddenly become much worse. "I reckon I walked too far today," he winced, taking off his thick boot. As a child he'd had polio and his right leg was not much thicker than my arm, the foot bent out at a strange angle. We'd only gone about ten miles when he pulled over, saying he couldn't drive any more as it hurt. I was behind the wheel like a shot — I'd never driven a car before! I'd also never driven one with a column gear shift, and the first few miles were a bit hairy as I had to look down at the gear lever each time, causing us to swerve about erratically. Eventually I got the hang of things and we sped through the open countryside with what I imagined was casual non-chalance, one hand on the steering wheel, the other arm leaning on the open window, fingers tapping the roof. Fortunately there was hardly any traffic, and although it was a dirt road it was in good condition so we made good time. At one stage I was doing nearly ninety miles an hour, a trail of red dust swirling about behind us. *Whoopee!*

For some time Ronnie had been getting more and more upset, complaining about the heat and shouting out ever louder, "Too hot! Too hot!" The sun was streaming in his side of the car, so to shut him up Glen offered to swap places with him. In moving across, Ronnie's foot hit the back of my head and I ducked, quickly glancing back to see what it was. When I looked back at the road we were halfway up the mound of gravel piled up in the middle, suddenly I couldn't control the steering wheel and Darren was shouting: "Slow down, for fuck's sake!"

Although it is all a bit of a blur, I remember stabbing on the brakes, far too violently for the situation, no doubt; then the steering wheel was more or less ripped out of my grasp and the car skewed sideways and just took off. The next thing I remember was being upside down, thick dust and the strong smell of petrol wafting through the car. For a few seconds, apart from the ticking sound of a hot engine cooling down, there was a bewildered silence, each of us overwhelmed with relief to discover we were still alive. Then wisps of blue smoke started coming from the engine, and Darren galvanised us all when he yelled out: "Get out, Ronnie boy! Get out! The engine's on fire!"

Amazingly, apart from a scratch on Darren's arm and a bump on Glen's head we were all okay, although I will never know how, and having scrambled out we stood in a dazed confusion in the middle of the road. The car was a complete mess, lying on its roof with the bonnet embedded in the bottom of the ditch, the back high in the air, wheels still turning lazily. Then, at virtually the same moment, Glen and I looked at each other in horror. Our money! Most of it was in Glen's bag in the boot.

Shit!

With no thought to the smoke now pouring from the engine, we ran together and ripped open the boot lid. Fortunately, because the rear of the car was upside down and sticking up, our bags simply fell out and we dragged them back into the middle of the road, where we sat, catching our breath. It had all happened so fast, it was difficult to grasp that it had happened at all.

For several minutes we watched and waited for the flames to appear, but none came; in fact if anything, the smoke seemed to be getting thinner. Perhaps it wasn't on fire after all! We got to our feet and began dusting ourselves off when a loud *whoosh*, and a rush of air almost knocked us over again. In seconds the car was engulfed in flames, the ferocity making us back hastily away, worried the thing might explode. But it didn't. There were just a few *pops* and *bangs*, a pall of thick black smoke billowing into the air. Moments later, to our astonishment, Darren picked up his gear, thrust Ronnie's bag into his arms and yelled, "Come on, boy! We gotta get outta here!" And together they scrambled over the fence and set off as fast as Darren could hobble, across the field towards thick bush a hundred yards away; they were out of sight almost before we realised they'd gone. "Jesus!" Glen exclaimed. "Where are they going?"

We knew we couldn't be that far from Forbes, so after recovering from Darren and Ronnie disappearing so abruptly, we set off up the road. Half an hour later the police car came into sight, and never had we been so relieved to see one. We should have known better.

"You two know anything about the vehicle back there?" The

constable asked, getting out and putting his hat on, his mate staying inside talking on the radio.

"Yes, it flipped over."

"So we noticed. Your car, is it?"

"No, it belongs to the two other blokes we were with."

"Which two other blokes?" He looked around.

"Well ... they pissed off as soon as it burst into flames."

"I see. And where did they go?"

"We don't know, they just pissed off, into the bush," I waved. Then the policeman's mate got out of the car and the two of them conversed briefly.

"Okay, get in the car," the first one said, his tone setting off alarm bells.

"Why? Where are we going?"

"Never mind that, just get in the car!"

Not again!

At the police station they put us in separate cells, and I sat in mine for over an hour before a plain-clothes policeman with another uniformed officer came into the cell.

"Why am I in here? Where's my friend?"

"Okay, son. Just calm down," said plain-clothes.

"But we haven't done anything!"

"So you think writing off a stolen car and leaving the scene is nothing, do you?"

"Stolen! We didn't know it was stolen! It was just an accident. We didn't *leave* the scene, we just went to get help. We would have reported it!"

"Hmm," murmured plain-clothes, clearly not impressed. "You said there were two others ..."

"Yeah, Darren and Ronnie. They're cousins. It was their car, we just ..."

"Right," plain-clothes interrupted me. "I want you to give your details to this officer and explain exactly what happened," and he got up and left the cell.

Shit!

In the end it was fairly easy to prove who we were; a quick phone call to John and Emma confirmed our story and we were released, although we had to remain in the area and I was given a stern warning about driving without a licence and the consequences if I was caught doing so again. Country police were very relaxed about that sort of thing in those days. The worst thing was they'd informed Glen's mother and my sister of the situation, and as being caught in a stolen car didn't sound too good, Glen in particular knew he would have some explaining to do. Two days later, just to make sure we went home, the police drove us to Parkes and put us on the first train to Sydney, warning us of dire consequences if we didn't turn up. The last thing they wanted were two homeless Pommie teenagers hanging around their patch! Not that their desire to see the back of us ran to paying our fare!

As for Darren and Ronnie, we never saw them again. Where they'd gone, even where they'd come from, remained a mystery to us; although they were such a distinctive pair, it was doubtful they would have avoided capture for too long. The police did tell us that the car had been stolen from a caravan park in Goulburn the same day the cousins arrived at the orchard; the perfect place to hide for a few days while the initial hunt for them took place. It also explained why Darren had been so adamant he wasn't going to Sydney in that direction. The long train ride home gave us time to reflect on all this, and both of us knew we had been seriously lucky; one, both or all of us could have been badly injured or killed in that car.

TWENTY

Sons and mothers

"*L*ook back, just don't stare," your grandmother will have advised you, and it is strange how odd everything seems when you first get home after a long time away. Structurally, nothing may have altered, yet somehow nothing is familiar. This was especially so in Theo's milk bar, where a new set of fifteen and sixteen-year-olds had taken up residence, hogging the pinball machine and jukebox; they all seemed so young and silly. Theo himself still ran the place, but Denise Phillips and her lovely legs had moved away; at least she hadn't gone on a world cruise with him! And remember Cassandra Roberts, she of the Davy Crockett hat? Pregnant with Ronnie Wilson's child; they were both younger than me! Fancy having a baby at that age. I wouldn't know what to do with the thing! Predictably perhaps, Barry Wiley was still about, a brand new wide-eyed audience for him to impress with his sexual exploits. And to think I was once in awe of the bloke, dickhead! I went home.

Fortunately, for the first few days after we got back Glen stayed at my place. Had he not been there, I am not sure what I would have done. Nothing is quite as depressing as coming home to an empty house. He'd gone to see his mum the day after we got back while his dad was at work. When he came back it was obvious it had been a fairly emotional visit, but despite his mother's pleas he was determined never again to sleep under the same roof as his father. A week later, on his seventeenth birthday, he began the process of joining the Navy and within ten days he was gone. I'm sure had we known then that we would never see each other again, our parting would have been far more difficult. As it was, it felt like he was just going out to get the milk. We shook hands, even hugged each other briefly, but a quick handshake and a "See ya mate, take care of yourself," didn't really do justice to our relationship, how close we'd become, the people we'd met and the experiences we'd had.

Christmas and New Year came and went, and gradually my money began to run out, but it was difficult to motivate myself. I felt somehow lost, as if my life was in limbo, and I'd sit on the veranda until the early hours, singing loudly to a radio — as loudly as Mrs Henderson next door could cope with. I knew my stepmother was returning in a few weeks and that I would have to get some sort of job then, but I didn't really make any effort to find one. I spent most days in the local snooker hall, and a few nights a week some of the old crowd started playing cards again at my place, but it was never the same as before and I certainly didn't make any money out of it. Then one evening about five o'clock I was sitting on the front veranda listening to the radio when it hit me.

"... ah but, two hours of pushing broom
Buys an eight by twelve four bit room
I'm a man of means by no means ..."

Of course! That's it! Monto! I'll go to Monto! Work and Carol, what could be better than that! I even thought about leaving right then, but I knew I had to get sorted first. I wasn't about to set off as unprepared as Glen and I had originally been. What I could do, though, was begin to pack, so I went into my bedroom, happier and more buoyant than I'd felt since we got back. Then from out in the street came a loud and prolonged hoot. I went to the front door to find a smart Ford Customline parked outside the gate, engine running. A bloke I didn't recognise was driving, but inside were Johnny

Mickelton, Ronnie Wilson and three or four other blokes I vaguely knew, waving manically at me. At first I thought they wanted to play cards, so I yelled out that I couldn't that night, but Johnny stuck his head out the window, shouting: "No, we're going up to Terrigal Beach, surf club's putting on a barbie. Come on. It'll be great!" To this day I do not know why I went with them.

We'd just flashed across the Hawkesbury River Bridge, beer bottles frothing, Bobby Darren blaring: *"Splish splash, I was taking a bath, on about a Saturday ..."* when the police siren sounded and the motorbike pulled alongside, the cop motioning for us to pull over. "Gidday, boys. In a bit of a hurry, are we?" He asked cheerfully enough, then he poked his head through the window and ran his eyes over the seven of us.

"Bit crowded in here, isn't it. Whose car is this?" The silence was as incriminating as it was deafening. Oh no! For Christ's sake, no!

One of the central pillars of western democratic law is that a person is held to be "Innocent until proven guilty." However, when a motorbike traffic cop stops a speeding Ford Customline crammed with seven teenage boys, all of whom are drinking, none of whom have a licence and some of whom have, at best, implausible reasons for being in the vehicle, and a few of whom have skeletons in their police cupboards; then that tenet goes straight out the window and that wonderful line from an American television cop show springs to mind. "You boys is in a whole heap'a trouble, 'cause I is the sheriff of Boon county!"

This in turn creates a situation of logistical complexity and mind-boggling confusion. First, two police cars are despatched to the scene to collect the suspects, with an extra policeman going along to drive the Ford Customline; then, in convoy, they depart for the police station where each of the suspects is placed in a separate room and questioned, even interrogated, long into the night. During the course of which, alerted to their son's predicament, parents and other relatives begin to arrive, some accompanied by family solicitors; until, by

2am, there is a gaggle of people milling about in the foyer, all wringing their hands with anguish and proclaiming their son's innocence. Despite the best of intentions, nothing is quite so embarrassing for a teenage boy, innocent or not, than a hand wringing parent. Fortunately I was spared this ignominy — for the time being, that was.

Of course, unbeknown to all but one of the rest of us, the car had been stolen by the driver, whose name I didn't even know! It turned out he was a serial vehicle thief and got his kicks from pinching cars, especially big, expensive ones, and then showing off to his peers by giving them lifts in it. Rarely did he keep the vehicle for more than a few hours, stealing a car in Parramatta and taking it to Bondi, where he would dump it only to steal another one and take it somewhere else. He was smart enough never to steal or leave a car near his home, and on this occasion he'd stolen the Customline from a used car lot in Maroubra, specifically to take to Gosford where he planned to dump it. Five of us that night may not have had the slightest knowledge of any of this, but saying so was easy; proving it was not!

Eventually us 'innocent' ones were released, although in my case, due to my 'skeletons' I was warned not to go anywhere in case they wanted to question me further. Which was why, a few days later, I was still at home, Monto but a distant dream, when the phone rang. I'd had no idea she was coming, much less was in town. "Hello. Nicholas? It's your mother. I'm booked into a twin room in such and such a hotel in Milson's Point. Come over and stay for awhile." It was not so much an invitation as a summons, but I hadn't seen her for awhile so I set off, slightly anxious but happily enough. In the end I stayed with her for about a week, and by the end my life had changed forever.

* * *

When a mother ups and leaves her husband and young children for no discernible reason, relatives and friends are shocked and amazed.

When she does so just after a traumatic war, then society itself is not only shocked and amazed but unforgiving and vindictive. A woman walking out on her husband was one thing, but that she could so callously leave her children as well was almost inconceivable in war-torn 1945 England. Hadn't millions just sacrificed themselves to make the world a better place for children? Wasn't motherly love one of the most instinctive and cherished qualities of a woman? What was the selfish cow thinking of; had she no sense of responsibility, no shame, no heart! Even animals didn't leave their young in vulnerable times!

This was the dilemma that confronted my mother, made even worse because the reason she left *was* primarily selfish and she knew it. There was no dreadful husband, no poverty, no lack of love or support; she just wanted to be free of the encumbrances of a husband and children. In 1947, having reluctantly accepted their separation was permanent, my father agreed she could take us children to Australia to live with her parents and he would come out later once their affairs in England had been settled. So it was we arrived in Queensland that year, and she dropped her bombshell on her parents. I have many letters my father and mother wrote to each other during that time, and although reasonably polite, each trying to understand the other's point of view, they ooze with the torment of the situation. Shortly before my mother died in 1978 she did explain how traumatic a period it had been, especially the dreadful night in 1947 shortly after we arrived when she first told her parents of her plans to go to New Guinea and asked them to look after us until our father came out. My grandmother, a lovely, kind and thoughtful woman, was slightly more sympathetic than my grandfather; well, a lot more actually, but she too had great difficulty understanding how any woman could ever leave her children, never mind *want* to leave them. My grandfather barely spoke to my mother ever again.

Given the clamour of outrage and the terrible burden of guilt and anguish involved, it is difficult to imagine any woman of the time ever making such a decision, much less carrying it through. Yet my mother did, and regardless of the rights and wrongs or how selfish it may or may not have been, one thing is certain. It must have taken a deal of courage and determination. When she heard that my father had married my stepmother she was greatly relieved, knowing that now at least the children would be well cared for. It no doubt came as a bit of a shock, therefore, to find ten years later, having been kept up-to-date of my goings-on by my sister, that she was required to sort out her son. Fortunately — or perhaps unfortunately for me — she bought her formidable determination with her.

At the time she was struggling to make ends meet, running a native trade store up in the wilds of the Southern Highlands of New Guinea. On top of that, the journey from there to Sydney in 1961 was still a fairly arduous one. Thirty nail-biting minutes from Wau to Lae in a single-engined Pilatus Porter was a hair-raising trip at the best of times. On an overcast day you just had to pray that the clouds the pilot couldn't avoid didn't contain a rocky mountain! "Land on a billiard table, take off on a cricket pitch," was the plane's boast, and in the rugged and precipitous mountains of New Guinea it often needed to! After that, an hour in a twin engine DC3 Dakota from Lae to Port Moresby sounds a doddle by comparison; after all, that sturdy reliable workhorse had won the war in the Pacific twenty years earlier. Maybe, but sitting in a DC3 at ten thousand feet is about as comfortable as riding a three-legged camel in Antarctica! Next, after a two-hour wait in Moresby, came the stretch to Brisbane via a one-hour refuelling stop in Townsville, this time in an iconic three-tailed Lockheed Constellation. It might have looked a wonderful plane, but it wasn't the swiftest, needing every minute of the six hours flying time. Yet still the trip wasn't finished, with another two-hour wait in Brisbane and a three-hour flight to Sydney. Couple all this with the fact that she felt partly responsible for the reason she had to undertake this journey in the first place, and you have a mother not best pleased with things when she arrives, making her even more determined not to leave until she had sorted things out. Not that she was angry, or anything, just filled with dogged resolve to straighten me out once and for all.

The first twenty-four hours were the most difficult, with a no-holds-barred, often fractious mother-and-son heart-to-heart. I can't remember everything we talked about, or maybe I choose not to, as she did most of the talking. The majority of it being of the "Look at yourself. Wasting your life. Associating with the wrong people," variety.

"How about starting an apprenticeship?" she suggested in the dining room that first night. "Butchery or carpentry, get yourself a skill."

"But I don't want to be a butcher or a carpenter!"

"Well, what do you want to be? A car thief? A prisoner? Because that's what you will end up being if you keep going as you are!"

"But I didn't steal the bloody car!"

"No, but you were in it with boys who did steal it! Being caught in a stolen car once in your life may be forgivable, but twice in two months! It's just another sign of where you are heading, Nicholas!"

Like a cornered rat, my only defence was attack. "Well, maybe I wouldn't be like this if you hadn't pissed off and left us!"

For a moment she looked at me and I thought she was going to be angry, but instead she sighed and nodded her head. "Perhaps" she said graciously. "But I don't apologise for leaving. It might have been worse for all of us if I'd stayed. I just don't think I was cut out to be a mother. Your father was a wonderful, kind man, but we had just fallen out of love, or rather, I had fallen out of love with him. He was twelve years older than me and I was very young when we married, both in years and maturity. It's no excuse and I hope one day you will understand, but I needed to get away, to find out who I really was."

Looking back, I can see my big mistake was mentioning that Glen had joined the Navy. We'd gone for a walk around the harbour early one morning and were sitting on a seat under the bridge, watching the ferries go by, when she enquired after him and instantly I could see her eyes light up, making me leap up.

"No! No way! I am not joining the Navy!"

"Why not? Sounds like a wonderful solution to me. It's well paid and you get to travel the world. You want to travel, don't you?"

"Yes, but not like that! Nine years you have to join up for! Bugger that!"

"What about the Army then? You only have to join that for three years. Look!" she turned to me, the bit now obviously well between the teeth. "Many of us find ourselves drifting in our lives sometimes. It was like that for me with your father. I just had to break that cycle. It wasn't easy, but it was the best thing I've ever done. Joining the Army could be the same for you. It will help you in so many ways, give you time to mature. In the meantime you'll get paid, be well fed, have somewhere to live, they will teach you all sorts of skills and you will still only be twenty-one when you get out! Regardless of who or what is to blame for the situation you find yourself in, you have got to start taking control of your life, Nicholas, and *now* is the time to start!"

Her persistence coupled with my own feelings of being 'lost' meant I didn't stand a chance, really; and so it was that for the next three days we went together to the Army recruiting centre, situated in those days in Rushcutters Bay. It was such a lovely position for such a formidable place. She didn't exactly drag me there by the ear, but it felt like it! Indomitable resolve and strength of purpose are mighty powerful weapons.

The initial requirement for entry into the army was to pass a general knowledge and IQ test of silly questions like, "If a paw is to a cat what is a hoof to?" Despite my mother's assurances, I still wasn't convinced that joining the Army would suddenly make my life meaningful and happy. Free from her constant presence for half an hour while I sat the exam, I spontaneously ticked the box for platypus instead of horse. After that there was no stopping me and I made all sorts of mistakes; that I might be going a smidgeon over the top didn't enter my head. In the maths section five nines became eighty-four, and to the conundrum, "If a man walks twenty-eight miles in seven days, on average how many miles does he walk each day?" I put "eleven." As for the question: "Name three state capital cities of Australia," I put down: "Sydney, Maroochydore and Julia Creek." That should do it — surely they wouldn't take anybody as stupid as me!

There were four other boys in attendance that day, two of whom, I was relieved to see, were also escorted by their mothers. After handing in our papers, we were told to go and have some lunch and come back to hear the results. When we got back, a warrant officer emerged holding a clipboard. "You'll be pleased to know you all passed the written test," he smiled, addressing us as one. My gaping mouth must have given it away, and he looked at me briefly. "Yes! You too. Being able to spell Maroochydore clinched it. Right!" He stuck his clipboard smartly under his arm. "Be back here at nine o'clock tomorrow for your medicals," and he left the room.

Shit!

The medical consisted mainly of the doctor holding my balls while I coughed — other than finding out you've got balls and can cough, why did they do that? But it was signing on the dotted line a day later that was the hardest bit, and even as we sat outside the captain's office waiting to be called in, my mother sitting resolutely beside me as she was obliged to sign me away, I was desperately trying to think of a way out. But the opportunity to escape never came. Besides, I am sure my mother would have rugby tackled me if I'd tried to run for it.

Three days later, myself and half a dozen other boys of a similar age found ourselves on Central Station, ready to board the train for the recruit training centre near Wagga Wagga. Three of the boys were those that had been at the Rushcutters Bay centre with me;

the fourth had not been accepted, they told me, because he had flat feet. Some people have all the luck! As we settled back onto the hard benches of the recruit class compartment I was suddenly struck by a vision of Mr Archer, hollering at me from across the playground. "Ah! So you've joined the Army, have you, Pommie boy! Good! That should sharpen your ideas up!" He was right!

The very first thing you learn in the Army is how to mop a floor. Not using much water was the secret, although the Corporal didn't tell me that until after I'd sloshed it everywhere. Oh, very funny! Arsehole! The second thing you learn is that there is a rule, law and regulation for absolutely every conceivable situation. On my second day I discovered that even pulling a face was a chargeable offence; 'dumb insolence', it was called. I was fined ten shillings and banned from the wet canteen for a week, no matter that I was still too young to enter it! Just before I was marched in to confront the officer who would pronounce my punishment, I was told to stand up straight, not to move and never to look at the officer. "Pick something on the wall behind him and just stare at it," the Bombardier escorting me advised. I did exactly as he said, and I can still vividly remember what was on that wall. It was a map of a strange-looking country I'd never heard of before, and I had to turn my head slightly at an angle to read it. Vietnam, it said.

"Are you listening to me, Recruit Thomas!"

"Yes."

"Yes, Sir!"

Ohhh shit!

THE BEGINNING